Interpreting Arnauld

Interpreting Arnauld

Edited by

ELMAR J. KREMER

B
1824
$.A864$
$I57x$
1996
$WEST$

UNIVERSITY OF TORONTO PRESS
Toronto Buffalo London

© University of Toronto Press Incorporated 1996
Toronto Buffalo London
Printed in Canada

ISBN 0-8020-0841-0

Printed on acid-free paper

Toronto Studies in Philosophy
Editors: James R. Brown and Calvin Normore

Canadian Cataloguing in Publication Data

Main entry under title:

Interpreting Arnauld

(Toronto studies in philosophy)
All the essays but one were presented at a colloquium held at St. Michael's College,
University of Toronto, Sept. 9–11, 1994.
ISBN 0-8020-0841-0

1. Arnauld, Antoine, 1612–1694 – Congresses. I. Kremer, Elmar J. II. Series.

B1824.A864I57 1996   194   C95-933240-5

University of Toronto Press acknowledges the financial assistance to its publishing
program of the Canada Council and the Ontario Arts Council.

Contents

Contents vi

Preface

The essays in this volume, with one exception, were originally presented as papers at a colloquium held at St Michael's College, University of Toronto, on 9–11 September 1994, commemorating the three-hundredth anniversary of the death of Antoine Arnauld (1612–1694).[1]

Arnauld was an enormously prolific theologian and philosopher who exercised considerable influence in both fields during his lifetime. He was the most important theologian of the Jansenist movement, as well as a talented philosopher whose pursuits in that field, in a broadly Cartesian framework, continued for over half a century and had considerable influence on Malebranche and Leibniz, as well as on Descartes.

Arnauld was a member of a very prominent French family. He was born on 8 February 1612, the twentieth and last child of Antoine Arnauld, after whom he was named, and Catherine (née Marion). His father and his paternal grandfather were prominent lawyers; both held the post of *procureur général* to Catherine de Medici. His father died on 29 December 1619, before the younger Antoine's eighth birthday.

The life of the Arnauld family was intertwined with the monastery of Port-Royal. Arnauld's sister Angelique became abbess of Port-Royal in 1602 and eventually carried out a thoroughgoing reform of the monastery, which became a centre of intense religious life. Of the ten children in the family who survived to adulthood, six became nuns at Port-Royal, where they were joined by Arnauld's widowed mother; his older brother, Robert Arnauld d'Andilly, retired to the life of a 'solitary' in the neighbourhood of the monastery.

As a young man, Arnauld decided to study law, but was soon convinced by his mother and her confessor, Jean Duvergier, the Abbé de Saint-Cyran, to devote himself to theology and the service of the church. He was ordained a priest in September 1641 and received his doctorate in theology from the Sorbonne in December of that year. His public career began auspiciously in 1641 with the *Fourth Objections* to Descartes's *Meditations*. But the beginning of his career was also marked by his undertaking, at the request of Duvergier, to defend Jansen, who had been accused by various Church officials of heresy. Jansen was the bishop of Ypres in Belgium, and an old friend of Duvergier's, with whom he had discussed the question of how to interpret St Augustine's position on original sin, grace, and predestination. Jansen died in 1638, and his book, *Augustinus*, was published posthumously in 1640. It proved at once to be controversial, and Habert, the *théologal* of Paris, attacked it in a series of sermons at the cathedral. Arnauld responded with the first of his *Apologies pour Jansénius*, published in 1644. His continued defence of Jansen eventually led to his dismissal from the faculty of theology at the Sorbonne, after a famous trial that lasted from 1 December 1655 to 30 January 1656. Pascal's *Provincial Letters* were written in defence of Arnauld, the first being published on 23 January 1656, as the trial was coming to an end. During the following twenty-three years, Arnauld was embroiled, off and on, in a controversy arising from the demand that all priests and religious in France sign a formulary condemning five propositions found in Jansen's book. In 1679, Arnauld left France for Belgium, where, except for a sojourn of two years in Holland, he lived until his death on 7 August 1694. His years in self-imposed exile were his most productive, and included both his controversy with Malebranche and his correspondence with Leibniz.

Arnauld took seriously his calling as a theologian and, as A.-R. Ndiaye points out, thought he was justified in taking time off for philosophy only because it made a contribution to theology. Voltaire said of Arnauld that, although 'no one was ever born with a more philosophical mind,' he wasted his time on theological disputes and never realized his potential.[2] More recently, Robert McRae remarked that Arnauld's dedication to theology was a loss to philosophy because he would otherwise surely have been one of the greatest philosophers of his century. Yet Arnauld made no small contribution to philosophy and, paradoxically, has had a more enduring influence there than in the field of his chosen profession. Modern theologians tend to view him as a figure in the (happily) defunct Jansenist movement. But his work continues to draw fresh responses from philosophers.

The essays in this volume are presented, for the most part, in the order in which they were given at the colloquium. They are not connected in any simple, linear order, but rather in several different, overlapping ways, both historical and systematic. Most of the essays discuss Arnauld's role both in the development of Cartesianism and in the continuation of medieval disputes in the seventeenth century. Also, most of essays deal either with the relation between philosophy and theology in Arnauld's thought or with theological topics that are of special interest to philosophers.

Arnauld thought it important to keep the distinction between philosophy and theology clear, as can be seen in this comment at the beginning of his *Fourth Objections*:

> Although philosophy can claim this entire work [Descartes's *Meditations*] as its own, nevertheless, because the author has respectfully and willingly submitted himself to the tribunal of the theologians, I shall here act in two capacities: I will first put forward what it seems to me could be objected to by philosophers regarding the important questions of the nature of our mind and of God; and then I shall set forth what could be offensive to theologians in the entire work.[3]

What emerges in the essays in the volume, however, is the unity of Arnauld's thought. Arnauld's skill in logical analysis is discussed in all of the essays, especially in the opening essays, by Buroker and Nelson, and the final essay, by Sleigh – although he may not always have put this skill to good use.[4] All of the remaining essays deal with topics that are part of both philosophy and theology. In particular, Arnauld's attitude towards the Cartesian doctrine of the creation of the eternal truths is discussed in the essays by Ndiaye, Kremer, Carraud, and Solère. The topics discussed by Hunter (miracles), Nadler (theodicy), and Sleigh (the compatibility of grace and free choice) also straddle the two disciplines.

Arnauld emerges in these essays as a figure who wanted to continue the medieval theological tradition and, at the same time, to embrace the new philosophy. He is, thus, a Cartesian who emphasizes the continuity of Descartes with the Middle Ages and who understands, and fears, in his contemporaries what Sleigh has characterized as a certain 'boldness of reason which would, in time, spark the Enlightenment.'[5] His attempt to defend this position is marked by skilful logical analysis of many propositions and arguments central to seventeenth-century philosophy and theology.

Notes

1 The exception is the paper by Jean-Luc Solère, which was presented at the Department of Philosophy, University of Toronto, in December 1994. The colloquium was funded mainly by a grant from the Social Science and Humanities Research Council, with assistance from the Department of Philosophy, University of Toronto, and St Michael's College. The editor would like to thank the *Journal of the History of Ideas* for permission to publish the paper by Steven Nadler,

an earlier version of which appeared in that journal.

2 Voltaire, *Siècle de Louis XIV* (Paris: Librairie Hachette 1890), 728.

3 *OA* 38, 8; AT 7, 197; CSM 2, 138.

4 See the essay by Lennon, in particular, for a negative assessment of one important logical manoeuvre used by Arnauld in his response to the church's condemnation of Jansen.

5 Robert C. Sleigh, Jr, *Leibniz and Arnauld: A Commentary on Their Correspondence* (New Haven, CT: Yale University Press 1990), 47.

Abbreviations

The following abbreviations are used throughout this volume.

OA   *Oeuvres de Messire Antoine Arnauld*, edited by G. Du Pac de Bellegarde and J. Hautefauge, with *Vie de Messire Antoine Arnauld* by N. De Larrière, 43 vols (Paris-Lausanne: Sigismond D'Arnay et Cie 1775–83).

AT   *Oeuvres de Descartes*, 12 vols, edited by Charles Adam and Paul Tannery (Paris: Leopold Cerf 1897–1913).

Alquié   *Oeuvres philosophiques de Descartes*, edited by Ferdinand Alquié, 3 vols (Paris: Garnier 1963, 1967, 1973).

CSMK   *The Philosophical Writings of Descartes*, vols 1 and 2 edited and translated by J. Cottingham, R. Stoothoff, and D. Murdoch; vol 3 edited and translated by J. Cottingham, R. Stoothoff, D. Murdoch, and A. Kenny (Cambridge: Cambridge University Press 1984–91).

OC   *Oeuvres complètes de Malebranche*, under the direction of André Robinet, 20 vols (Paris: J. Vrin 1958–67).

G   *G.W. Leibniz: Die philosophischen Schriften*, edited by C. I. Gerhardt, 7 vols (Berlin 1875–90).

Interpreting Arnauld

1

Arnauld on Judging and the Will

JILL VANCE BUROKER

The Cartesians of the seventeenth century had very little to say about language. They were primarily concerned about the nature of mental functions, especially conceiving and judging. Despite their focus on the mental, their theory of judgment incorporates a semantic theory, which invites comparison with current views in speech-act theory. In this essay I discuss Antoine Arnauld's account of judgment in the Port-Royal *Logic* from two perspectives. The first is Descartes's theory of judgment; the second is that of contemporary philosophy of language. The first comparison shows how Arnauld and Descartes divide up the functions of understanding and willing somewhat differently. The contemporary perspective provides a good basis for appreciating the strengths, and ultimately the weaknesses, of both seventeenth-century theories. I shall reverse chronological order and start with the contemporary treatment of judgment.

Judgment and Illocutionary Force

Frege was the first philosopher clearly to distinguish the sense expressed by a sentence, which he calls the *thought*, from the way a sentence is used in a given context. This latter aspect of meaning he calls the *force* of the utterance. So he recognizes the difference between merely expressing a thought, for example, 'five is greater than four,' and the act of asserting that five is greater than four.[1] In his 1918 essay 'The Thought,' Frege distinguishes thinking from both judging and asserting. On his view, when one thinks, one merely apprehends a thought; judging occurs when one mentally acknowledges the truth of a thought; and, finally, assertion is the linguistic or external expression of a judgment. Frege was motivated to separate the sense of an utterance from its force through recognizing the possibility of using declarative sentences without assertoric force, for example, in making suppositions and in fictional contexts. Most important, this is the only way to understand the use of embedded clauses in complex sentences, such as conditionals and disjunctives. When I assert the conditional 'If you go to Paris, you ought to see the Rodin museum,' I cannot be taken to be asserting that you are in fact going to Paris. Frege was concerned about the roles such sentences play in inference, though ironically his own treatment of valid inferences does not allow for unasserted suppositions. In any case, his primary focus on scientific and mathematical contexts prevented him from giving an adequate general account of force.[2] Despite the incompleteness of his account, however, the distinction is clearly a step in the right direction.

Since the 1950s, developments in the philosophy of language have altered the conception of judgment in at least two major respects. First, the trend has been towards *externalism* in philosophy of mind, according to which mental acts are analysed in terms of linguistic or other behavioural activities. From this perspective, the unit of cognitive significance is the speech act, and mental acts such as judging are seen as derivative of speech acts such as asserting. The second change concerns the increased prominence of force in this theory. Speech acts are utterances performed in a social context against a background of conventional rules, including linguistic rules. The most general significance of the utterance is called its *illocutionary force*. This is the immediate effect the speaker intends to produce in the hearer by getting the hearer to recognize the speaker's intention. For example, your promise to me to visit the Rodin museum on your next trip to Paris succeeds as an illocutionary act when I recognize it as that promise. In addition to assertions and promises, other common illocutionary acts are questions, commands, requests, and so on. What Frege called the *sense* of the sentence is here viewed as the propositional content of the act, and speech acts with different illocutionary force may contain the same propositional content. So my assertion that the window is open contains the same proposition as the question 'Is the window open?' and the command 'Open the window' (assuming I am referring to the same window in all three cases). Despite the wide variety of speech acts, assertion is taken to be primary, since it is essential to propositions that they be suitable for being asserted. But, contrary to Frege's tendency to reify the thought as an eternal object, recent thinkers consider the thought to be one ingredient of the act, one that is really an abstraction from the entire act.

For my purpose, the key feature is the relation between merely apprehending a thought (in some utterance) and asserting the sentence. In this theory, whenever one *says* anything meaningful, the act has some illocutionary force. But it is possible merely to express a thought without committing oneself to its truth or to its falsity. This happens if I say 'Suppose you travel to Paris next year ...' as opposed to predicting that you will in fact travel to Paris next year. Of course, there is no point to merely entertaining a proposition except in preparation for some other activity. Making assumptions or hypotheses, for example, is usually significant only in the context of inferring consequences from them. In any case, in terms of illocutionary force, acts of apprehension are on a par with judgments or assertions. Rather than being a necessary condition of assertion, considering a proposition is just one of many different kinds of illocutionary acts.

Now a word about the relation between assertion and negation. As Frege saw clearly, the difference between affirming a proposition *P* and denying it is not in the nature of the act, but in the proposition. Denying *P* is equivalent to asserting *not-P*. In other words, assertion has no logical poles – there is only one form of assertion, and negation generally belongs to the content of the proposition. Of course, it is possible to refuse to assert a proposition, but this is not the same as denying the proposition. From the modern point of view, then, affirmations and denials do not differ as assertive acts.

Finally a brief comment about the treatment of truth. While there is some disagreement among externalists, the most externalist position (favoured by Dummett, for example) takes truth-values to be properties of assertions rather than of the propositions asserted. When we speak of the truth or falsity of the thought, we really mean that its assertion would be correct or incorrect, given the circumstances. (Recall that Frege had to 'decontextualize' the thought by getting rid of token-reflexives such as pronouns and demonstratives to ensure that it had an eternal truth-value.) There are items, such as 'eternal truths' of mathematics, for which conditions of utterance are irrelevant. But it does not follow from this that propositions are the genuine bearers of truth-values. Dummett prefers to say that the truth-value of the utterance depends jointly on the sense of the sentence and the conditions of utterance; in limiting cases, such as eternal truths, the conditions of utterance play no role at all.[3]

Descartes on Judgment

Descartes embraces the more familiar theory of *internalism*. From this intuitively appealing standpoint, speech is merely the external expression of mental states, and, so, judging is a prerequisite of assertion. For Descartes, mental states are produced by the understanding or the will. Whereas the understanding merely conceives ideas, the will acts or operates in some way on those conceptions. Judging is an act of willing since it consists in taking a proposition to be true or false. Now, although Descartes thinks of propositions as composed of ideas, he does not draw a sharp line between conceiving a non-propositional idea and thinking a proposition. For him the content of an idea can be very complex, and this complexity can be expressed propositionally. One famous example is Descartes's statement in the *Fifth Meditation* that understanding the idea of a right triangle entails recognizing that it has 'the properties which license the inference that its three angles equal no more than two right angles.'[4] Similarly, his version of the ontological argument depends on the view that an adequate apprehension of the attributes contained in the idea of God logically entails the proposition that God necessarily exists. Although to my knowledge Descartes never refers to simple or unanalysable ideas, he does take understanding to be simpler than willing. He also characterizes acts of understanding as passive, in contrast with the actions of the will.

For Descartes, willing is more complex than understanding precisely because acts of will incorporate perceptions of the understanding. In Part I, article 32, of the *Principles,* Descartes lists the modes of willing as 'desire, aversion, assertion, denial and doubt.'[5] In the *Meditations* he adds emotions to the list. What these mental states have in common is spelled out in the *Third Meditation*: In contrast to ideas, which he says are 'as it were the images of things,' volitions include 'something more than the likeness of that thing.'[6] In general the extra element is an attitude the subject takes towards the object of thought, such as a desire for the object, or fear or love of the object, or a judgment concerning the object.

Descartes's most explicit statement about judgment occurs when he reponds to Regius in *Comments on a Certain Broadsheet.* Noting that Regius assigns both perception and judgment to the intellect, Descartes makes this correction:

> For I saw that over and above perception, which is a prerequisite of judgement, we need affirmation and negation to determine the form of the judgement, and also that we are often free to withhold our assent, even if we perceive the matter in question. Hence I assigned the act of judging itself, which consists simply in assenting (i.e. in affirmation or denial) to the determination of the will rather than to the perception of the intellect.[7]

In short, the view is this: Like other volitions, judgments contain conceptions of an object or possible state of affairs. In the case of judgment, the conception takes propositional form, and the volitional attitude is one's commitment to a truth-value of the proposition. When one affirms, one commits oneself to the truth of the proposition; when one denies, one commits oneself to its falsity. Refraining from judging is no less an act of the will: so doubting is among the modes of willing.

In this model, the conception of the understanding is a necessary ingredient of the judgment: it represents the object of the judgmental attitude. But since one can apprehend a thought without judging it, conceiving is separable from judging. When we add to this Descartes's view that intellectual intuition is passive, what emerges is a *transitive model* of judgment. First, the understanding supplies the propositional content; then, the will acts on it. In this framework, merely apprehending or entertaining a thought is not only possible, but necessary. As opposed to doubting or refraining from judging, however, mere apprehension is not an act of will.

Although Descartes sometimes describes judging as giving assent, he just as frequently treats affirmation and denial as different acts of the will. In the passage previously cited from the *Principles*, for example, he compares affirmation and denial to desire and aversion. Whether this makes sense for desire and aversion, it clearly does not work for judgment. As Frege argued in his essay 'Negation,' this model requires two types of negation: one characterizing the act of denial, another belonging to the propositional content.[8] On this model, to affirm 'The Earth is round' and to deny 'The Earth is not round' would be two different types of acts, operating on different propositions, in spite of their logical equivalence. But propositional negation is also necessary, since it is surely possible to apprehend a negative proposition. This leads to cases where it is not clear whether the negation belongs to the proposition or to the act. Is asserting a previously apprehended negative proposition an affirmation or a denial? These are some of the reasons Frege abandoned the view that affirmation and denial are polar forms of judgment, as well as the traditional classification of propositions into affirmative and negative.

Finally, a word about Descartes's conception of truth. In the *Third Meditation*, Descartes officially states that 'formal' truth and falsity reside in judgment. But in fact it seems that the propositions being grasped are the bearers of truth-values, since clear and distinct perception is tantamount to perceiving the truth of the proposition. This is understandable, given Descartes's preoccupation with eternal truths, such as mathematics, the laws of physics, and those concerning God's nature. This fits nicely with the transitive model, according to which one grasps a proposition which is true or false independently of its being thought, and then commits oneself to a truth-value. The problem here is the notion of the commitment to a truth-value, since it is not clear whether the apprehension of the thought '*P* is true' would be a mere conception or a judgment.

Judgment in the Port-Royal *Logic*

Arnauld's conception of judgment in the Port-Royal *Logic* differs from Descartes's in some interesting respects. Arnauld agrees with Descartes that thought is prior to language, and so judging can take place independently of its linguistic expression. But, whereas Descartes says very little about language, Arnauld gives it a central focus in the Port-Royal *Logic*'s semantics. What results is a 'constructivist' model of judgment, as contrasted with Descartes's 'transitive' model. This shift exposes two different ways of dividing up the functions of the understanding and the will.

In general, Arnauld holds the traditional view of the order of mental operations. As he explains in the introduction, the Port-Royal *Logic* is organized according to the four operations of the mind: conceiving, judging, reasoning, and ordering. Part I concerns ideas, which are the products of conceiving, defined as 'the simple view we have of things that present themselves to the mind.'[9] The things represented by ideas are substances and their properties, which Arnauld generally calls 'attributes.' Arnauld says expressly that the act of conception is simple in the sense that it does not include an explicit judgment. By contrast, judging is an action in which the mind, 'joining together different ideas, affirms of one that it is the other, or denies of one that it is the other' (p. 37). For example, both the affirmation 'The Earth is round' and the denial 'The Earth is not round' contain the same ideas, 'earth' and 'round'; the difference is in the action the mind takes towards them.

Up to this point, the theory looks Cartesian, but it turns out that, for Arnauld, joining ideas to form a proposition is an act of the will rather than of the understanding. This is clear from Chapter 3 of Part II, which begins:

> After conceiving things by our ideas, we compare these ideas and, finding that some belong together and others do not, we unite or separate them, which is called *affirming* or *denying*, and in general *judging*.
>
> This judgment is also called a *proposition*, and it is easy to see that it must have two terms. One term, of which one affirms or denies something, is called the *subject*; the other term, which is affirmed or denied, is called the *attribute* or *Praedicatum*. (p. 113)

Here Arnauld equates forming the proposition with judging it.[10] In the act of connecting the subject and the predicate, one necessarily commits oneself to a truth-value. This reading is reinforced by his treatment of the verb. In Chapter 2 of Part II, Arnauld explains that what distinguishes a complex idea, for example, of Peter living, from the affirmation 'Peter is living' is the presence of the verb. And he defines a verb as

> *a word whose principal function is to signify an affirmation*, that is, to indicate that the discourse where this word is employed is the discourse of a person who not only conceives things, but who judges and makes affirmations about them. This is what distinguishes the verb from several nouns that also signify affirmation, such as *affirmans, affirmatio* [affirming, affirmation], because they signify

affirmation only in so far as it has become an object of thought by mental reflection. Hence they do not indicate that the people who use these words are making an affirmation, but only that they conceive of an affirmation ... Accordingly, we can say that the verb in itself ought to have no other use than to indicate the connection the mind makes between the two terms of a proposition. (p. 109)

So, in the Port-Royal *Logic*, the verb simultaneously performs two functions: it connects the subject and predicate to form a proposition, and it indicates the affirmation or denial one makes. When a negative particle such as 'not' is attached to the verb, the judgment is (apparently) a denial; otherwise one is affirming the proposition.[11]

Like Descartes, Arnauld treats affirmation and denial as two polar forms of judgment. But since he cannot separate the proposition from the judgment, the question of whether the negation affects illocutionary force or the propositional content cannot even arise. But this is not the worst problem: in explaining how affirming differs from denying, Arnauld makes it impossible for one to deny a proposition, since he thinks of denying as an action opposite to affirming. In affirming, one connects the subject and predicate to form a propositional unity (while assenting to the truth of the proposition so formed); thus, in denying, one must separate the subject from the predicate. Here is what he says in Chapter 3 of Part II:

As we have already said, this action of the mind [judging] is indicated in discourse by the verb *is*, either by itself when we make an affirmation, or with a negative particle in a denial. Thus when I say, *God is just*, ... the word *is* indicates the action of the mind that affirms, that is, that connects the two ideas *God* and *just* as belonging together. If I say, *God is not unjust*, the word *is*, when joined to the particle *not*, signifies the action contrary to affirming, namely, denying, in which I view these ideas as repugnant to one another, because the idea *unjust* contains something contrary to what is contain in the idea *God*. (p. 113)

In his essay 'Negation,' Frege points out the implication of this view: If, in denying, the mind separates the subject and predicate ideas, then there is no propositional unity to be judged. And if there is no proposition, then clearly there is nothing to take a truth-value. Hence Arnauld undercuts the entire idea of denying as taking a proposition to be false. In one of his brilliant metaphors, Frege adds that this view of denial makes of double negation a magical sword 'that could heal on again the limbs it had cut off.'[12]

Independently of the problem of denial, Arnauld's model of judging differs from Descartes's transitive model in some important ways. I call Arnauld's theory a 'constructivist' model because for him the act of judging creates the propositional content being judged at the same time. Here the proposition cannot be passively apprehended by the understanding. So Arnauld's view of conceiving must also differ from Descartes's. For one thing, such acts of the understanding as forming complex ideas and analysing them into parts cannot be equivalent to propositional acts for Arnauld. Whereas Descartes attempts to draw a sharp line between forming a proposition and judging it, Arnauld attempts to draw the line between conceiving an idea and connecting it with others to form (and judge) a proposition. I say 'attempts' because neither succeeds. Descartes had difficulty classifying the state in which one apprehends the truth of a proposition. And Arnauld, in his treatment of relative clauses, maintains that some complex ideas do contain judgments and others do not.[13] In short, neither version is coherent. Here is how Arnauld and Descartes go wrong.

It seems fair to equate the Cartesian notion of acts of the will to the illocutionary force of speech acts, since both involve taking an attitude to some propositional content. Recall that, in speech-act theory, merely considering a proposition is also an illocutionary act, typically preceding some other act. Descartes allows that one can apprehend a proposition without judging it, which seems right. But he sees mere apprehension as an act of understanding rather than of will, and that is where he goes wrong. By contrast, Arnauld recognizes that merely apprehending a proposition involves some mental activity, which is right, but he errs in not separating mere apprehension from judging as different types of acts.

The underlying problem for both Descartes and Arnauld is the relation between the will and the understanding. Although they divide up the functions of the understanding differently, each one sees it as a prerequisite to willing, rather than as a feature of some attitudinal activity. This point is not clarified until 1781, with Kant's full-blown constructivist theory of judgment in *Critique of Pure Reason*.[14] Whether the synthetic activity involved in judging should be called an act of will is another question. Kant never refers to it that way in the first *Critique*; since ordinary sense perception involves judging, most of the time we are not even conscious of judging. But we should also recall that part of Kant's revolutionary treatment is to reject Descartes's notion that human understanding is capable of a passive, instantaneous, intellectual intuition of the truth. Although Arnauld apparently agrees with this view, he does not see its far-reaching consequences for his theory of judgment.

Notes

1 A clear explanation of this aspect of Frege's theory is available in Michael Dummett's *Frege: Philosophy of Language*, 2d ed. (Cambridge, MA: Harvard

University Press 1981). See especially ch. 10, 'Assertion,' 295–363.

2 In fact, in 'On Sense and Reference,' he claims that what distinguishes assertions from interrogatives, imperatives, and optatives is the sense rather than the force. And in the *Begriffschrift*, he introduces only two signs for force: the judgment-stroke indicating assertion ('|-'), and the sign for definition, indicating stipulation ('||-').

3 See Dummett, *Frege*, 418–20.

4 AT 7, 68.

5 AT 8, 17.

6 AT 7, 37.

7 AT 8B, 363.

8 Reprinted in *Translations from the Philosophical Writings of Gottlob Frege*, Peter Geach and Max Black, eds (Oxford: Basil Blackwell 1966), 117–35.

9 Antoine Arnauld and Pierre Nicole, *La Logique ou l'art de penser*, critical edition by Pierre Clair and François Girbal (Paris: J. Vrin 1981), 37. All references to the *Logic* are to this volume. All translations are my own.

10 It is noteworthy that in the first (1662) edition of the *Logic*, Arnauld apparently wavers between this and Descartes's conception of judgment, that is, as to whether the act of judging also constitutes the proposition. Here is what he says at what later becomes Chapter 17 of Part II: 'It is not easy to make clear nor even to understand what takes place in the mind whenever we affirm something, and to decide whether this is done by the simple view of the mind accompanied by consent, by which it represents something as containing a certain attribute by a single idea, or whether there really are two ideas, one for the subject and the other for the attribute, with a certain act of the mind which connects one with the other' (168). Here he expresses uncertainty about whether affirming consists in assenting to a single propositional idea, or in forming a complex idea by connecting the subject and attribute.

11 On this conception, verbs signify quite differently from the way the subject-term and the predicate-term signify. The latter words, typically nouns and adjectives, express ideas of substances and attributes. In medieval parlance, such words are called 'categorematic' expressions. The verb, by contrast, signifies neither a substance nor an attribute, but the action of the mind in forming and judging the proposition. Other examples of syncategorematic expressions are quantifiers such as 'all' and 'some.' In this same discussion, Arnauld recognizes illocutionary acts other than assertion, since he points out that verbs can also signify 'other actions of the soul, such as desiring, requesting, commanding, etc. But this happens only by changing the inflection and the mood' (109).

12 *Translations from the Philosophical Writings of Gottlob Frege*, 124.

13 I discuss this in 'Judgment and Predication in the *Port-Royal Logic*,' in *The Great*

Arnauld and Some of His Philosophical Correspondents, Elmar J. Kremer, ed. (Toronto: University of Toronto Press 1994), 3–27.

14 Ironically, in so far as Frege treats thoughts as objects that are passively grasped, he backslides towards a more Cartesian view.

2

The Falsity in Sensory Ideas: Descartes and Arnauld

ALAN NELSON

Do Ideas Deceive?

Since Arnauld's set of *Objections* to the *Meditations*, many commentators have found parts of Descartes's theory of sensory ideas particularly difficult.[1] Some are inclined to attribute changes of position, confusion, and worse to the texts dealing with material falsity.[2] This essay develops an interpretation of Descartes's doctrines of materially false ideas and of sensory error that strives to be wholly Cartesian in spirit. It also makes aspects of Arnauld's own positive theory relevant to understanding Descartes. Finally, there is a new theory of 'obscurity and confusion' (and hence of clarity and distinctness) as it applies to sensory ideas. The drawback of this interpretive strategy is that Descartes's interests and goals do not turn out to be as continuous with contemporary philosophical concerns as some have hoped. In particular, Descartes does not have (or need) an impressive theory of what is now called 'intentionality'; worse still, his frequent, and in some ways seminal, talk of *representation* turns out to be driven by concerns in natural science and not in semantics.

This essay's interpretation relies on a picture of the relation between false ideas and false judgments that departs from a widely accepted one. The widely accepted picture begins with Descartes's distinguishing a class of ideas as 'materially false.' Descartes plainly thought that many people have an inclination to make judgments on the basis of these materially false ideas, particularly sensory ideas, that turn out to be false judgments. It is important to ask what Descartes thought explained this inclination to make false judgments. The widely accepted picture goes wrong in answering this question. Its answer is that materially false ideas 'present themselves,' in a phenomenological sense, as representing or exhibiting objects as having properties that those objects don't really have. So, for example, when I see an apple, I have a sensation of redness – the sensory idea of red is occasioned in my mind. This sensory idea of red presents itself to me as though its content, the redness, is really in the apple. If I am not on guard, or if I am a young child, and naïvely judge that 'what the idea tells me' is true, I will mistakenly judge that the redness is a property of the apple, that it is 'in' the apple. My inclination to judge falsely in this case is explained by my uncritically acceding to 'what the idea presents to me' or 'seems to tell me.' In general, the widely accepted picture explains this class of false judgment by appealing to an intrinsic deceptiveness in the phenomenological contents of false ideas.

The picture advanced in this essay offers a different interpretation of what Descartes thought explained false judgments. I argue that the inclination to judge falsely is not explained by the faculty of judgment (or will) gullibly going for what is held up to it by deceptive ideas. The inclinations are instead explained as habits of judgment. They are, from the perspective of philosophy, bad habits fostered partly by poor techniques of reasoning that serve us well in childhood, and even in everyday life, but not when doing philosophy. In scholarly circles, however, the bad habits are reinforced by the practice of bad science. According to Descartes, bad science includes the sort of 'folk physics,' or 'folk physiology of perception' that insufficiently thoughtful people engage in from time to time, and also organized, institutional, bad science of the kind that he was concerned to overthrow. One upshot of this picture is the shifting of much of the blame for the mistakes in question from the intrinsic deficiency of our ideas (which turn out not to be so bad after all) to correctable habits of judgment. Moreover, any intrinsic deficiency in our ideas turns out to be traceable to prior bad judgments.

Preliminaries: Material Falsity and Objective Reality

Let us begin with the difficult *Third Meditation* treatment of sensory ideas that drew a sharp response from Arnauld. Arnauld focused on Descartes's characterization of some ideas as 'materially false.' In the *Fourth Replies*, Descartes elaborates on this terminology:

> As I interpret this claim, it means that the ideas are such as to provide subject matter for error. (AT 7, 231; CSMK 2, 162)[3]

> It is this idea [of cold] which, I claim, can provide subject-matter for error if it is in fact true that cold is an absence and does not have as much reality as heat; for if I

consider the ideas of cold and heat just as I received them from my senses, *I am unable to tell* that one idea represents more reality to me than the other. (AT 7, 232–3; CSMK 2, 163; emphasis added)

So an idea is materially false if it provides 'subject-matter' for error, for false judgment. This plain fact about Descartes's use of the term 'materially false' has some straightforward, but interesting consequences.[4]

First, it is not only ideas occasioned by motions in the sensory organs and brain that can be materially false; any idea that provides subject-matter for false judgment is materially false. Since we very easily make false judgments, what ideas could fall outside the range of the materially false? They would have to be ideas that are true, and whose truth is invariably accompanied by a judgment that they are true. Descartes consistently calls these 'clearly and distinctly perceived ideas.' Clear and distinct perceptions are *invariably* accompanied by assent to the truth of the perceived ideas:

I could not but judge that something which I understood so clearly was true; but this was not because I was compelled so to judge by any external force, but because a great light in the intellect was followed by a great inclination in the will ... (AT 7, 58–9; CSMK 2, 41)

Admittedly my nature is such that so long as I perceive something very clearly and distinctly I cannot but believe it to be true. (AT 7, 69)

The will of a thinking thing is drawn voluntarily and freely (for that is the essence of will), but nevertheless *inevitably*, towards a clearly known good. (AT 7, 166; CSMK 2, 117; emphasis added)

These texts plainly say that clear and distinct perceptions are invariably accompanied by assent.[5] The only way to avoid the 'compulsion' of a clear and distinct idea is to distract the attention so that the idea is no longer clearly present to the intellect. If we allow the attention to wander in this way, then we no longer 'continue in the same thought' so *that* particular thought no longer compels assent.

The second consequence of Descartes's notion of material falsity to consider here is that it is a matter of degree. All ideas that are not clear and distinct are materially false to the degree that one is likely to make false judgments when considering them.

Yet ideas which give the judgment little or no scope for error do not seem as much entitled to be called materially false as those which give great scope for error. It is easy to show by means of examples that some ideas provide much greater scope for error than others. (AT 7, 233; CSMK 2, 163).

The ideas with the least amount of material falsity (setting aside the clear and distinct ideas that give no material whatsoever for false judgment) are the factitious ideas. Since they are made up at will, we typically have some recognition of their origin, and that can suggest that the composites produced need not correspond closely to things outside me. Those labouring under the prejudices of childhood or bad science, however, will often go wrong in these cases. The greatest scope for false judgments is provided by those ideas concerning which our composite nature inclines us to judge falsely: sensations, and especially appetites.[6] In the *Sixth Meditation*, Descartes says that God has endowed us with the faculty of sensation to provide for the preservation of lives as embodied humans. When we follow our natural inclinations to act on the basis of these ideas, the ordinary result will be something beneficial to the union. The situation is completely different when our immediate goal is, not to preserve the union, but to discover and contemplate the truth. In this case, we should employ our faculty of *understanding* (the literal translation of *intellectio*, 'intellection,' might be preferable) and assent to only those ideas which it clearly and distinctly perceives.

> For the proper purpose of the sensory perceptions given me by nature is simply to inform the mind of what is beneficial or harmful for the composite of which the mind is a part ... But I misuse them by treating them as reliable touchstones for immediate judgments about the essential nature of the bodies located outside us ... (AT 7, 83; CSMK 2, 57–8; see also *Principles* II, 3)

If we misuse our faculties by uncritically attempting to gain the truth about the extramental world through our senses, we almost always fail.

It is tempting to characterize material falsity differently. The *Third Meditation* seems to suggest that some materially false ideas 'represent non-things as things' (AT 7, 43; CSMK 2, 30), and this seems to lead to a famous puzzle about these ideas' objective reality. Objective reality is characterized in the *Third Meditation* in terms of representation: 'Undoubtedly, the ideas which represent substances to me amount to something more and, so to speak, contain within themselves more objective reality than ideas which represent merely modes or accidents' (AT 7, 40; CSMK 2, 28). Now, if the idea of cold represents a non-thing to me, then, since the objective reality of an idea has as its efficient and total cause the formal reality of what is represented, ideas of this kind appear to have no objective reality. That would be a bad result because all ideas are like images in so far as they have objects – in so far as they are 'as if of things' (AT 7, 44; CSMK 2, 30). We should, however, strive to find an interpretation in which there can be no special difficulty about the degree of objective reality of any materially false ideas, including the sensory ideas. Let us consider some further texts concerned with what Descartes calls 'objective reality.' It is important first to mark that Descartes conceives objective reality as quantifiable into exactly three discrete degrees or levels. In Axiom VII, from the 'Geometrical Exposition' in *Second Replies*, he wrote:

> There are various degrees of reality or being: a substance has more reality than an accident or a mode; an infinite substance has more reality than a finite substance. Hence, there is more objective reality in the idea of an infinite substance than in the idea of a finite substance. (AT 7, 165–6; CSMK 2, 117).

When Hobbes explicitly challenges him to 'consider afresh what "more reality" means,' Descartes replies in exactly the same terms.[7] Both these passages simply echo what he originally wrote in the *Third Meditation*, which now appears in a different light:

> Undoubtedly, the ideas which represent substances to me amount to something more and, so to speak, contain within themselves more objective reality than the ideas which merely represent modes or accidents. Again, the idea that gives me my understanding of a supreme God, ... certainly has in it more objective reality than the ideas that represent finite substances. (AT 7, 40; CSMK 2, 28)

This should be read as saying that some ideas represent to me modes of substances and contain the *modal level* of objective reality; some represent substances and contain the (finite) *substantial* level of objective reality. Both kinds of ideas contain finite objective reality; the idea of God contains the *infinite level* of objective reality.[8] This interpretation carries with it a reading of 'represent' (or 'exhibit') that is applicable in the current context. In this sense of 'represent,' ideas represent either God or created substances or modes, without further differentiation. In other words, in this sense of 'represent,' ideas do not specifically represent such particular objects as the sun, dogs, heat, etc. They simply represent, in virtue of their objective reality, the amount of formal reality their causes have.[9] The general point is familiar from the *Third Meditation*'s 'causal proof' of God's existence. We might say that ideas *present* this reality, but let us instead coin the term *reality-representation*.[10] Reality-representation is intrinsic to the idea and does not depend on any judgment. We might err in judging how much reality an idea represents if the idea is not clear and distinct, but that does not affect how much reality it actually, intrinsically represents. Of course, I shall have to explain in what follows Descartes's other use of 'represent,' the sense in which the sun, a dog, heat, etc., could be individually represented. It also remains to be explained how 'representing a non-thing as a thing' is connected with material falsity.

Let us summarize what the texts reviewed in this section establish: (1) the materially false ideas are, by definition, exactly those that are not clear and distinct – these are two complementary sets of ideas; (2) material falsity is analysed in terms of the philosophically prior notions of clarity and distinctness – ideas are materially false to the degree that they fall short of clarity and distinctness; and (3) objective reality falls into three discrete levels: infinite, substantial, and modal. What ideas reality-represent (or present, or exhibit) in virtue of their objective reality is some degree of (formal) reality. If, however, an idea is not clear and distinct, I might 'not be able to tell' how much reality is represented to me.

'Representation' and the Idea of Cold

Why has this natural interpretation of the texts been overlooked? Since the quoted texts are mostly from Descartes's responses to objections to the *Third Meditation*, the obvious answer is that Descartes does not make his intentions clear in that particular text. Arnauld (and some recent commentators) are misled especially by Descartes's treatment of the idea of cold, which is regarded as a kind of test-case in the *Third Meditation*. Let us review it. As an example, Descartes considers this possibility: 'if it is true that cold is nothing but the absence of heat, the idea which represents it to me as something real and positive deserves to be called false; and the same goes for other ideas of this kind' (AT 7, 44; CSMK 2, 30). It is important to remember that, in the context of the *Third Meditation*, the meditator, who might start as a Scholastic, has achieved hardly any Cartesian knowledge concerning corporeal nature – he does not even know for certain whether it exists. He might go so far as to wonder at this point whether heat and cold are themselves substances instead of modes. Might they be substances (or perhaps 'real qualities') emitted by ordinary bodies or associated with them in some other way? Another alternative is that both heat and cold are positive modes of bodies. Yet another alternative is that heat is such a positive thing, but that cold is 'nothing but the absence of heat.' Supposing this last alternative, an apposite example of a false judgment would be to judge that coldness is a substance associated with a cold body when, as a matter of (hypothetical) fact, coldness is the absence of heat, a privation.[11] In this case, we could be judging that 'a non-thing was a thing.'

> For although, as I have noted before, falsity in the strict sense, or formal falsity, can occur only in judgements, there is another kind of falsity, material falsity, which occurs in ideas, when they represent non-things as things. For example, the ideas which I have of heat and cold contain so little clarity and distinctness that they do not enable me to tell whether cold is merely the absence of heat or vice versa, or whether both of them are real qualities, or neither is. And since there can be no ideas which are not as it were of things, if it is true that cold is nothing but the absence of heat, the idea which represents it to me as something real and positive deserves to be called false ... (AT 7, 43–4; CSMK 2, 30)

The example is doubly hypothetical. For all we know at this point in the *Meditations*, cold might be a positive mode of bodies, and therefore a 'thing' (*res*), even if it is not a substance in its own right. Furthermore, for all the meditator knows, the idea of cold might even resemble such a positive mode. The point is that the idea, being obscure and confused, is materially false and does not compel us to assent to *anything*. To remove the obscurity and confusion from the idea, we need to direct our attention to it, and somehow manage to perceive simply that we have the idea. This is expressed in *Principles* I, 68:

> In order to distinguish what is clear in this connection from what is obscure, we must be very careful to note that pain and colour and so on *are clearly and distinctly perceived* when they are regarded merely as sensations or thoughts. But when they are judged to be real things existing outside our mind, there is no way of understanding what sort of things they are. (AT 8A, 33; CSMK 1, 217; emphasis added)

We shall likely fall into error if we use a sensory idea as the basis for any judgment about what is outside our minds. If we did go ahead and *judge* that the idea of cold was caused or occasioned by an extramental thing, then (given the hypothesis that cold is a privation) we would falsely judge that the idea '*represents*' a thing to me.

This is the second way Descartes uses 'represent' (*repraesentare*). In the first sense explained above, ideas represent some amount of reality. In the second sense, ideas represent what we 'refer' them to as causing them.[12] Let us call this *sign-representing*. Sensory ideas' actual occasioning causes are generally very complex because they are always proximately occasioned by characteristic brain states, but only remotely and partially caused by such things as the sun, a dog, heat, etc. There are, therefore, many candidates to choose among when someone 'refers' a sensory idea to a cause or, in our new terminology, assigns a sign-representation to it. Sign-representation is always a result of an active judging and assigning. No idea comes with an intrinsic sign-representation.[13] This is an important difference between reality-representation and sign-representation.

One might incidentally get the impression from the way Descartes handles the example of the idea of cold that sign-representing a non-thing as a thing is the *sine qua non* of material falsity. But this is only an *example* of the way that materially false ideas fit the correct criterion – providing the material for error. After completing the *Meditations* and studying the *Principles*, Descartes's readers should know that, in fact, the ideas of both heat and cold are occasioned by motions in the brain that are themselves caused by motions in the sensed object and the intervening medium.[14] Anyone who does not know this might make some very bad judgments when assigning sign-representations.

There is a further matter to consider regarding Descartes's use of 'represent.' It is necessary to distinguish the notion of objective reality already discussed from another notion for which I shall use the term *objective being*. Descartes himself sometimes seems to use these terms interchangeably, but there are indeed two notions at work. In the *First Replies*, Descartes writes:

> 'Objective being in the intellect' ... will signify the object's being in the intellect in the way in which its objects are normally there. By this I mean that the idea of the sun is the sun itself existing in the intellect – not of course formally existing, as it does in the heavens, but objectively existing, i.e., in the way in which object normally are in the intellect. (AT 7, 102; CSMK 2, 75)

This might be taken to suggest that the idea of the sun reality-represents the sun as it exists formally; instead, we should understand this as saying that, when we use an idea to sign-represent the sun, we can say that the sun has objective being in the intellect. We might even say that the objective being of this idea is the sun. This is, however, just a way of talking about how ideas represent the things that they sign-represent. This text and others like it have no bearing on what we are calling 'reality-representation.'[15]

Let us return to the problematic passages from the *Third Meditation*. Arnauld's objections bring the troubles to the fore. He brings out two problems with the idea of cold. The first concerns what the idea is an idea of, its intentionality. The second problem concerns the formal source of the idea's objective reality. Since objective reality is a kind of reality, it cannot derive from nothing; there ultimately must be a causal source of the objective reality which itself has sufficient formal reality to account for that objective reality. Suppose that we conflate the cause of the idea's objective reality with what the idea is 'of.' Since the idea of cold should have objective reality (as all ideas do), if cold is (hypothetically) a privation, a non-thing, it seems strange that this idea could, after all, be the idea *of* cold. We shall see that Descartes has ready replies, given the interpretation being developed.

Here is Arnauld's formulation of the trouble:

> But if cold is merely an absence, then there cannot be an idea of cold which represents it to me as a positive thing, and so our author is here confusing a judgement with an idea.
>
> What is the idea of cold? It is coldness itself in so far as it exists objectively in the intellect. But if cold is an absence, it cannot exist objectively in the intellect by means of an idea whose objective existence is a positive entity. Therefore, if cold is merely an absence, there cannot ever be a positive idea of it, and hence there cannot be an idea which is materially false. (AT 7, 206; CSMK 2, 145)
>
> Lastly, what does the idea of cold, which you say is materially false, represent to your mind? An absence? But in that case it is true. A positive entity? But in that case it is not the idea of cold. (AT 7, 207; CSMK 2, 146)

Descartes's response is going to be that the idea we call 'the idea of cold,' assuming that cold is a privation, is a sensory idea that reality-represents the modal level because it is a mode of mind. In what sense does it 'represent' a non-thing as a thing? The answer is that the victim of all this confusion will be falsely judging that the idea in question is occasioned by a privation. The victim then attempts to refer the idea to what is not there; he uses it to sign-represent a privation. So something that reality-represents a thing (the sensory idea) is used to sign-represent a hypothetical non-thing (the privation). Let us see how Descartes arrives at this response to Arnauld's problem.

Bad Science and the Idea of Cold

Commentators have taken it for granted that there is no question about exactly which ideas Descartes is talking about in the *Third Meditation* when he mentions the ideas of heat and cold. This leaves an important gap in our story because the answers to Arnauld's questions depend on how 'the idea of cold' is understood. I think it important to bring out three ways to understand 'the idea of cold' because Arnauld and Descartes seem to understand it differently. This will also illustrate how bad science can lead to habits of judgment that confuse our sensory ideas. Descartes's preferred way of taking 'the idea of cold' as the particular, conscious, sensory experience is saved for last. Suppose, first, that a particular cold thing affects one's sensory organs; for example, one touches a piece of ice. It would be natural to say that, in normal conditions, one then has an idea of that piece of ice, but suppose that attention is concentrated on the *ice's* coldness. In other words, one forms an idea of whatever it is in the ice or about the ice that causes or occasions one's conscious experience of coldness. Whatever that turns out to be (a scientific matter), there can be no problem about the objective reality of this idea. It would reality-represent to me either modal or substantial reality, depending on which scientific account of the ice's coldness is adopted. But this much reality could derive from the ice itself, or the internal motions of the ice, or the intervening media, or the brain, etc. Does this mean that, if science tells us the ice's coldness is a privation, there is a problem about the idea's intentionality? If there is no *thing* answering to the description 'the ice's coldness,' then the idea must actually be occasioned by something else: a rash judgment, the desire to think about that idea, or even the ice, or internal motions of the ice, etc. That might lead us to judge that the idea sign-represents one of those things. That, in turn, should lead us to reconsider our verbally *describing* this idea as 'the idea of the ice's coldness.' A scientific discovery that what we call 'the ice's coldness' is not a thing would make evident the fatuity of the idea we had thought up for ourselves. The verbal description 'the ice's coldness' would be misleading in the extreme, and an invitation to a host of bad judgments – judging a non-thing to be a thing, for instance. Descartes warns against just this kind of error in *Principles* I, 74, whose title reads: 'The fourth cause of error is that we attach our concepts to words which do not precisely correspond to real things.'

In short, the highly obscure and confused idea of the ice's coldness need not be occasioned by any particular thing, though there are facts of the matter about its actual occasioning cause and about its reality-representation. There is, therefore, no salient candidate for its sign-representation, and there are various assignments one might make. And, to repeat, its failure to intrinsically sign-represent does not mean that it fails to reality-represent, although this idea might be too obscure and confused to enable us to tell whether it reality-represents the modal or the substantial level. Part of Arnauld's difficulty seems to come from his thinking that, given the hypothesis that cold is a privation, the idea of 'the ice's coldness' must nevertheless (a) be 'of' a privation, and consequently, (b) fail to reality-represent. Descartes, however, is committed to neither (a) nor (b).

Let us begin in a second way. If we now begin instead with an idea of coldness that has been *abstracted* from ideas of a particular piece of ice, or from ideas of various cold things, then we would again be judging a non-thing to be a thing if we supposed that this abstraction had an extramental existence. This possibility might seem to reinstate Arnauld's worries, if it was not indeed part of what was worrying him. Descartes has a theory of abstraction; is it adequate for handling the problem at hand? For Descartes, all abstractions are abstract *ideas* – mental entities. Many of them are materially false since we are liable to judge incorrectly (as Platonists do) that the abstraction has extramental being. When we judge correctly, Descartes thinks we realize that abstractions simply *are* modes of thought.[16] So the abstraction would still reality-represent. The objective reality would correspond to the formal reality of the mode of thought, namely, the modal level of objective reality. What is the abstract idea of cold an idea *of*? One correct judgment to make would be to judge it a mode of our mind. If we have made this correct judgment, then the idea can sign-represent the appropriate mode of mind. If one has erroneously reified the abstraction with a bad judgment, then there is no telling what sign-representation the deluded one will assign to the resulting obscure and confused idea. We now turn to the question of how sensory ideas become obscure and confused and in what their obscurity and confusion consists.

Obscure and Confused Ideas

There is yet another interpretation of 'the idea of cold'; it is the one most natural to twentieth-century readers and, I think, to Descartes himself. Suppose that we neither derive the idea in question from a scientific hypothesis about a particular object nor produce it by a process of abstraction. Suppose we are experiencing the sensory idea itself, the brute 'quale' of cold. We are simply feeling cold very vividly. In this case we cannot pin the intentionality on anything in a body that resembles the idea because bodies do not actually have sensory qualities. Does that mean trouble for reality-representation? No; if I perceive clearly and distinctly regarding this quale (as described in the above quotation from *Principles* I, 68), then I will realize that it is a mode of my mind. Therefore, it reality-represents the modal level. If the idea is obscured and confused as a result of bad judgments, then I might be unable to tell how much reality it represents, but that does not mean that it fails intrinsically to represent reality.

It might be objected here that it is pointless to insist that ideas intrinsically reality-represent, even if we cannot tell how much. Why not say instead that, if we cannot tell how much reality is represented, as we typically cannot when dealing with obscure and confused ideas, the idea altogether fails to reality-represent? In more conventional terminology, why not say that sensations or sensory ideas have no objective reality? This question is easily answered if one is prepared to take *Principles* I, 68, and similar texts seriously.[17] A sensory idea properly attended to will be clearly and distinctly perceived, provided that no false judgments are made concerning it. It is, therefore, a metaphysical fact that these ideas reality-represent the modal level. A troubling question remains: If sensory ideas can be clear and distinct in this way, how do they become the Cartesian paradigm of obscure and confused ideas?

The answer is that the potentially clear and distinct sensory idea is typically obscured by, and confused with, judgments that are made in connection with it. The underlying clear and distinct sensory idea remains there, as it were, but it is overlain by other ideas – usually the results of bad judgments concerning the underlying sensory idea. The contents of these bad judgments, which are themselves ideas, augment the bare sensory idea, thereby creating obscurity and confusion. In other words, a confused idea is quite literally the result of the confusion of more than one idea. And one (or more) of the components of a confused idea might be a sensory idea. The following important text says as much:

> For example, when someone feels an intense pain, the perception he has of it is indeed very clear, but is not always distinct. For people commonly confuse this perception with an obscure judgment they make concerning the nature of something which they think exists in the painful spot and which they suppose to resemble the sensation of pain; but in fact it is the sensation alone which they perceive clearly. (*Principles* I, 46; AT 8A, 22; CSMK 1, 208)

To understand how this works, consider first that the terms 'obscure' and 'confused' are always to be understood in their technical senses as the complements of 'clear' and 'distinct.' Descartes makes use of a visual metaphor to explain that clear perceptions are 'present and accessible to the attentive mind.'[18] Similarly, we see clearly when our eyes are strongly stimulated, even if we can't tell what is stimulating them. Very clear ideas are attention-grabbers. A clear idea is obscured if it has to compete with other elements for the attention of the mind's eye. The visual metaphor is extended to say that a distinct perception is 'so sharply separated from all other perceptions that it contains within itself only what is clear' (*Principles* I, 45). A confused idea, therefore, is a complex of simples which can be mistakenly regarded as itself simple.

The quotation from *Principles* I, 46 confirms that sensations can be clear and distinct, it says they are 'not *always* distinct,' not that they *cannot* be distinct. This brings us to the principal point I want to make about this text. The explanation of confusion given here is that the sensory idea itself is somehow juxtaposed with, or overlain by, or augmented with, a bad, 'obscure' judgment. We might say that the judgment about the sensation's resembling something outside the mind is an *obscuring* judgment. It diverts our attention from the sensory idea itself so that it is no longer clear, and hence no longer distinct, in the technical senses of those terms. This obscuring judgment is separate from, and additional to, any further false judgments we make on the basis of the now confused, materially false idea. For example, once a clear and distinct sensory idea is obscured, one is liable to make bad scientific judgments about its occasioning cause.

We have seen that a sensory idea might be perceived distinctly in Descartes's technical sense: 'it is so sharply separated from all [others] that it contains within itself only what is clear' (*Principles* I, 45). If this idea is then made the basis of a bad judgment, and the bad judgment augments the original, distinct sensory idea, then the original idea is now obscured by, and confused with, the results of the judgment. What kind of obscuring and confusing judgment might augment otherwise clearly and distinctly perceived sensory ideas? Descartes is very explicit about this at almost every opportunity.

In the example of pain quoted above from *Principles* I, 46, the judgment is 'concerning the nature of something which they think exists in the painful spot and which they suppose to resemble the sensation of pain.' The general problem is that 'we easily fall into the error of judging [e.g.,] that what is called colour in objects is something exactly like the colour of which we have sensory awareness. (*Principles* I, 70; AT 8A, 35–6; CSMK 1, 218).[19] Descartes says that we 'easily fall' into this kind of error. We indeed fall into it so easily that almost every sensory idea we happen to attend to in our thinking will have been obscured and confused by having annexed to it this kind of erroneous judgment.

A reader of Descartes might want to object that she does not remember making a raft of false judgments of this kind. Descartes's response to this reaction follows immediately in various texts; the judgments that obscure and confuse our sensory ideas are a residue from a time when we rarely or never exercised our pure intellects.

> In our childhood the mind was so immersed in the body that although there was much that it perceived clearly, it never perceived anything distinctly. But in spite of this the mind made judgements about many things, and this is the origin of the many preconceived opinions which most of us never subsequently abandon. (*Principles* I, 47; AT 8A, 22; CSMK 1, 208)

Children make these obscuring and confusing judgments, not because they are particularly gullible, but because they are exclusively concerned (if young enough) with pursuing pleasure and avoiding pain.[20] They become cognizant of how bodily effects (e.g., damage) are correlated with sensations, emotions, and appetites (e.g., pain, sadness, and avoidance). Useful judgments of correlation eventually slip into the paradigmatic mistaken judgments that pleasures and pains are in the affected parts of the body, and that colours, light, etc., are in the external bodies that occasion the sensations.[21] These mistaken judgments, in turn, become so frequent that they are performed very swiftly and can become so habitual that they cannot be remembered and go unnoticed. Or instead of performing a new judgment of this kind, we swiftly remember an old one and reaffirm it.[22] The final step in this epistemically sorry (but biologically important) process is that the potentially clear and distinct sensory ideas become almost automatically obscured and confused by false judgments about the location of their occasioning causes or about their degree of resemblance to those causes.

One result of our cognitive development from infancy to potential systematic users of pure intellect is, therefore, that our sensory ideas become obscure and confused. This seldom entails dire consequences for the survival of substantially united human beings; on the contrary, judgments involving sensations are typically efficacious in preserving life. The obscurity and confusion in sensory ideas can be disastrous, however, for anyone embarking on a philosophical or scientific project. One of Descartes's principal goals was to prevent these disasters in the search for knowledge. His writings contain countless references to how his philosophical method enables one to detach from the senses and recover what can be clear and distinct. Descartes thought that most bad science of his time resulted from judgments concerning obscured and confused sensory ideas. This coheres very naturally with the *Fourth Meditation* injunction that when seeking the truth one should never make judgments when not perceiving clearly and distinctly. Those who have not repaired their cognitive habits leftover from childhood through the process of Cartesian meditation have materially false, obscured and confused, sensory ideas. By definition, materially false ideas provide scope for error – for what sorts of error do these particular materially false ideas provide scope? We have already seen two examples. One might reify a sensory idea: 'Heat is a substance in the fire that burns me.' One might also reify an abstraction: 'There is some positive quality, heat, which all hot things have.'

In this section we have seen wherein the source of obscurity and confusion in sensory ideas lies. It is our failure to separate the sensory idea as a mode of mind from ill-informed hypotheses about the occasioning cause of that mode. It is not something intrinsic to the offending ideas. Our underlying, potentially clear and distinct, sensory ideas are obscured and confused by the results of overlying bad judgments. Armed with this theory of how sensory ideas are corrupted, we can resume our analysis of the exchange between Descartes and Arnauld.

The Idea of Cold Again

An important test of any interpretation of these matters must make good sense of the *Third Meditation* and Descartes's notorious reply to the problems posed by Arnauld. More can now be said, for example, about the characterization of materially false ideas as representing non-things as things. Let us consider again the passage already quoted which begins one line earlier by characterizing sensory ideas as confused and obscure:

> But as for all the rest, including light and colours, sounds, smells, tastes, heat and cold and the other tactile qualities, I think of these only in a very confused and obscure way, to the extent that I do not even know whether the ideas I have of them are ideas of real things or of non-things. For although, as I have noted before, falsity in the strict sense, or formal falsity, can occur only in judgements, there is another kind of falsity, material falsity, which occurs in ideas, when they represent non-things as things. (AT 7, 43; CSMK 2, 30)

Descartes calls these ideas obscure and confused; we now know this means that they have been obscured and confused by bad judgments. The bad judgments concern the occasioning causes, and therefore the sign-representations one assigns to these ideas. We can now also see how to interpret the rest of this passage:

> For example, the ideas which I have of heat and cold contain so little clarity and distinctness that they do not enable me to tell whether cold is merely the absence of heat or vice versa, or whether both of them are real qualities, or neither is. And since there can be no ideas which are not as it were of things, if it is true that cold is nothing but the absence of heat, the idea which represents it to me as something real and positive deserves to be called false and the same goes for other ideas of this kind. (AT 7, 44; CSMK 2, 30)

To see how this kind of trouble arises, suppose someone under the influence of bad science entertains the palpably false hypothesis that cold is an absence of some positive thing called 'heat.' Let us also suppose this person tries to use the sensory idea of cold to sign-represent the supposed privation, and proceeds to make judgments concerning this idea and concerning what it supposedly sign-represents. He might, for example, judge that privations can have causal powers. He would be treating what he first thinks of as a non-thing as a thing. This train of thought will, of course, result in his sensory idea of cold being obscured and confused. Since the idea reality-represents a mode (although it is too confused for me to realize that at this point), it 'deserves to be called false.' It is, of course, materially false simply by virtue of its containing 'so little clarity and distinctness.'

Suppose that someone listening to a different bad scientist decides to have his sensory idea of cold sign-represent whatever it is that all cold things have in common. If he makes the further judgment that it is this abstraction that causes his sensory idea, the sensory idea will become obscured and confused. Observing this, we might describe his plight by saying that his obscured and confused idea came to sign-represent to him a non-thing as a thing.[23]

Arnauld posed another problem:

> What is the idea of cold? It is coldness itself in so far as it exists objectively in the intellect. But if cold is an absence, it cannot exist objectively in the intellect by means of an idea whose objective existence is a positive entity. Therefore, if cold is merely an absence, there cannot ever be a positive idea of it, and hence there cannot be an idea which is materially false. (AT 7, 206; CSMK 2, 145)

Descartes might well have replied that, if cold is an absence, there is really no idea of cold after all, there is only the idea that we call 'the idea of cold.' He instead goes back to basics: '[material falsity] arises solely from the obscurity of the idea – although this does have something positive as its underlying subject, namely, the sensation involved' (AT 7, 234; CSMK 2, 164). This says that an idea is materially false just in case it is obscured and confused, that is, not clear and not distinct. When a sensory idea is clear and distinct, we inevitably form a true judgment; namely, that the idea is a mode of our mind. The clear and distinct sensory idea, therefore, is what Descartes here calls the 'underlying subject.'[24] This is one sense in which materially false ideas are positive regardless of what we judge them to sign-represent. This much positivity is required, of course, since God allows us to have materially false ideas.

Descartes also writes:

> Thus if cold is simply an absence, the idea of cold is not coldness itself as it exists objectively in the intellect, but something else, which I erroneously mistake for this absence, *namely, a sensation which in fact has no existence outside the intellect.* (AT 7, 233; CSMK 2, 163; emphasis added)

This can now be interpreted as saying that on the (palpably false) hypothesis that cold is an absence, the idea that we call the idea of cold will typically be the obscured and confused sensory idea. Returning to the question of intentionality, what should we now say this idea is an idea of? The most plausible way of talking is to say that the idea is of itself. If it were a clear and distinct sensory idea – that is, if one realized it was simply a mode of one's mind – then it would be true. And the truth expressed would be simply that one had that sensory idea. It is interesting in this regard that Arnauld himself came to think that every perception involves a reflective awareness of what the perception is 'of.'[25] Since the materially false idea also contains other obscuring and confusing elements, there might be contexts in which we would choose to say the idea is 'of' one or more of those other elements. It is not easy, however, to think of many contexts for which anything other than the underlying sensory idea would be a plausible choice.

Arnauld and Descartes

Many think that Arnauld got the better of Descartes in their exchange concerning sensory ideas. This is hard to square with the fact that Arnauld himself seems to have been well satisfied with what Descartes wrote! He seems to have been satisfied, moreover, with something very close to the interpretation of Descartes developed above, as shown by the official statement on sensory ideas from the *Logic*.

> Our ideas of colors, sounds, smells, tastes, cold, heat, heaviness, and other sensible qualities, as well as our ideas of hunger, thirst, bodily pain, and so on, are confused and obscure ideas. *And the reason these ideas are confused can be explained as follows*:

> ... the mind was unsatisfied with judging merely that there was something external to it causing these sensations, although in this judgment there would have been no error. The mind went on to judge that there was something in the external object exactly like the sensations or ideas which the object occasioned ... Such a transference results in *the confused and obscure ideas we possess of sensible qualities, for the mind has added false judgments to what nature reveals to us*. (emphasis added)

The doctrine here is that[26] obscured and confused sensory ideas are 'results' of false judgments. What of sensory ideas that we do not obscure and confuse in this way? Arnauld has again accepted Descartes's account. In *On True and False Ideas*, he cites with approval the assertion in *Principles* I, 68 that sensory ideas can be clear and distinct, and concludes: 'pain, color and other similar things are known obscurely and confusedly only when we refer them to bodies as if they were there modifications.'[27] One might question whether Arnauld thought, against Descartes, that particular extramental objects like dogs literally have a kind of being in our thought,[28] but there seems little room for doubt that he came to understand Descartes, and to agree with him, concerning the falsity of sensory ideas.[29] I take it to be a virtue of the interpretation presented in this essay that it shows how this meeting of the two great minds was effected.

Notes

This essay is based on ideas presented at the 1994 conference on Arnauld at the University of Toronto. I benefited from the discussion on that occasion. I have also received valuable help from Vere Chappell, Keith DeRose, Paul Hoffman, Jeremy Hyman, Elmar Kremer, Lex Newman, Lawrence Nolan, Calvin Normore, and Kurt Smith.

1 Standardized terminology is essential here, but neither Descartes nor subsequent commentators have settled on one. I use 'sensory idea' to refer to the mode of mind present when a human being is sensing or having a sensation. I use 'sensation' to refer to what happens to a human being when a motion of the pineal gland occasions a sensory idea.

2 An excellent introduction to some of the problems can be found in M. Wilson, *Descartes* (London: Routledge 1978), 101–20.

3 English translations of Descartes are taken from the three volumes of Cottingham, Stoothoff, Murdoch, and Kenny, which give cross-references to volume and page numbers in AT.

4 Descartes's *Third Meditation* characterization of materially false ideas as representing non-things as things is discussed below.

5 There are many similar texts. See for example the *Fifth Meditation* (AT 7, 433) and the 2 May 1944 letter, probably to Mesland (AT 4, 115–16 and 117).

6 On both of these points see AT 7, 234. Judgments of this type are explained later in this essay.

7 'I have also made it quite clear how reality admits of more and less. A substance is more of a thing than a mode; if there are real qualities or incomplete substances, they are things to a greater extend than modes, but to a lesser extent than complete substances; and, finally, if there is an infinite and independent substance, it is more of a thing than a finite and dependent substance. All this is completely self-evident': AT 7, 130.

8 Objective reality is something that is intrinsic to ideas. If an idea is not clear and distinct, we can easily be mistaken about how much objective reality it has. This is important in what follows.

9 But isn't the objective reality of my idea of the sun caused by the sun itself? No; the *Third Meditation* specifies that the cause in question is the 'efficient and total' cause. The 'total' cause obviously includes much more than the sun itself. Descartes emphatically reiterates the point in the 31 December 1640 letter to Mersenne: 'It is certain that there is nothing in an effect which is not contained formally or eminently in its EFFICIENT AND TOTAL cause. I added these two words on purpose. The sun and the rain are not the total cause of the animals they generate': AT 3, 274; caps in original. We can add than the sun is not the total

cause of the objective reality belonging to the idea of the sun. The efficient causal connection between the two is exceedingly complex, even when psycho-physical connections are ignored.

10 The apt term 'present' is best eschewed here to avoid confusion with Wilson's related, but quite different, distinction between 'presentational representation' and 'referential representation,' in M. Wilson, 'Descartes on the Representationality of Sensation,' in *Central Themes in Early Modern Philosophy*, J. Cover and M. Kulstad, eds. (Indianapolis: Hackett 1990).

11 Descartes's real position, of course, is that heat is a sensation occasioned by certain motions. Although the sensation of heat tends to be occasioned by external objects with violent internal motions, and cold by less violent motions, it would be a mistake to conclude that cold is in any sense an absence of heat.

12 The Latin is *referantur*. See for example AT 7, 233.

13 In the case of clear and distinct ideas, however, the relevant judgment is always correct, and the assignment that gets made is inevitably the true one. This is the case because of the special, divinely guaranteed, connection between clear and distinct ideas and truth. One might want to use the term 'intrinsic' for this kind of sign-representation, but this question is merely terminological.

14 See for example *Principles* I, 69–71, and IV, 196–8.

15 It is possible that Descartes and Arnauld did not see eye to eye on this matter. See note 28, below.

16 See *Principles* I, 57–9 and 62, which make Descartes's view explicit.

17 See also *Principles* I, 66, which is similarly explicit. Also relevant is the famous claim from the *Notae*: 'The ideas of pain, colours, sound and the like must be all the more innate if ... our mind is to be capable of representing them to itself ...' (AT 8B, 359). In so far as these ideas are innate, they are bestowed upon us by God and subject to clear and distinct perception. And, in the *Sixth Meditation*, we find: 'And since the ideas perceived by the senses were much more lively and vivid and *even, in their own way, more distinct* than any of those which I deliberately formed ...' (AT 7, 75; emphasis added).

18 *Principles* I, 45. I am going to ignore the difference between applying the notions of clarity and distinctness to perceptions, on the one hand, and to ideas, on the other.

19 Descartes makes this point throughout his career. See also *The World*, ch. 1 and 2, and the *Regulae* (AT 10, 423).

20 Descartes held this view as early as 1641 (see AT 3, 424) and later incorporated it into his theory of the passions (see AT 4, 604–6).

21 But doesn't a toothache 'present itself' as if it is in the tooth? No; we judge that it is in the tooth, though this kind of judgment can be so habitual that we do not remember having made it a moment afterward. Part of the illusion that pains present themselves as if in the painful body part might come from such purely

mechanical reflex actions as reaching to soothe the offended part.

22 Descartes explains these psychological mechanisms in a slightly different context at AT 7, 439. Even though we might not notice that we are consciously making these judgments, they must remain conscious, Wilson, in 'Descartes on the Representationality of Sensation,' raises some good questions about the degree of consciousness of such habitual judgments.

23 It is also possible to mistakenly judge that the confused and obscure idea, which actually really reality-represents the modal level, instead reality-represents the substantial level, for example, of some imagined fluid-like, subtle body that makes cold things cold. That error could also be called judging a non-thing to be a thing since the shift from the modal level to the substantial level is analogous to the shift from nothingness to the modal level. This, however, does not seem to be Descartes's point in the *Third Meditation*.

24 'Underlying [*fondement*],' added in the French (AT 9A, 181), supports my interpretation as it suggests that an obscuring judgment 'overlays' the potentially clear and distinct sensory idea.

25 S. Nadler, in *Arnauld and the Cartesian Philosophy of Ideas* (Princeton, NJ: Princeton University Press 1989), 118–22, has textual citations and a helpful account of Arnauld's doctrine of virtual reflection.

26 *The Art of Thinking*, by Antoine Arnauld, translated and edited by J. Dickhoff and P. James (Indianapolis: Bobbs-Merrill 1964), 66–7. Arnauld has absorbed Descartes's doctrine of material falsity so thoroughly that he can even call confused and obscured sensory ideas 'false ideas.' He writes: 'These confused ideas may also be called false ideas for the reason we stated [in the passage quoted in the text]': Dickhoff and James, 22.

27 E. Kremer, trans. and ed., *On True and False Ideas, by Antoine Arnauld* (Lewiston: Edwin Mellen 1990), 139.

28 For an interpretation of Arnauld as a 'direct realist' see Nadler, *Arnauld and the Cartesian Philosophy of Ideas*. For an examination of how Arnauld thought that the objects of knowledge are 'immanent' to the knower, see Kremer, trans. and ed., *On True and False Ideas*, xxiii–xxvii. See P. Hoffman, 'Descartes on Misrepresentation,' *Journal of the History of Philosophy* (forthcoming), for an interpretation of Descartes that makes him rather like Kremer's Arnauld in this respect.

29 More evidence that Arnauld was satisfied on this score comes from an examination of the subsequent letters he wrote to Descartes (3 June 1648, AT 5, 184–91, and July 1648, AT 5, 211–15). These contain substantial and wide-ranging queries about the various issues, but nothing about the theory of ideas.

3

Arnauld and the Modern Mind (the *Fourth Objections* as Indicative of Both Arnauld's Openness to and His Distance from Descartes)

PETER A. SCHOULS

I

There are important issues underlying the questions arising from Arnauld's interaction with Descartes on the latter's *Meditations*, an interaction known as the *Fourth Objections* and *Replies*. Here are two of the seventeenth century's brightest people who respected and liked each other, one of them (Descartes) understanding the other well, the other (Arnauld) doing his very best to understand but, on crucial points, falling short. The ultimately interesting matter is that Arnauld falls short in his understanding of Descartes because he is still situated in a tradition whose very rejection forms an integral part of Descartes's position.

It is no doubt true that, in his self-conscious attempt to reject tradition, Descartes was responding to a shift in point of view already well in progress. By the time Descartes started to write, Galileo had provided firm support for the view of Copernicus, which placed human beings in a more peripheral position in the universe than that to which they had grown accustomed, thus at least relativizing an important aspect of the tradition and, in the process, attracting the wrath of its guardians, the church's Inquisition. And Thomas Hobbes had for several years been an intimate of Mersenne's intellectual circle, where, without anything like the Cartesian fanfare called *Discourse on the Method*, he had accepted something very like this method and was beginning to apply it in his work on optics as well as in civil philosophy.[1] Descartes, however, makes it very clear that, unlike his predecessors and contemporaries, he aims to reject, not this or that aspect of tradition, but all of it. Unlike his contemporaries, he universalizes method, making it apply to all objects of thought – a method which dictates initial rejection of that to which it is applied. His attempt announces modern philosophy's intention 'to rise above tradition, above the particularity of any historical location' and so, 'purified of historical contingency' by rejecting it as prejudice, to speak only the absolutely trustworthy and universally valid language of reason. Today, we tend to recognize this language for what it is: 'local custom masquerading as universal speech.'[2]

In this vacuum left by a rejected tradition, Descartes comes to his Archimedean point. It is to this Archimedean point, and to the 'rational scheme' built on it, that Mersenne asks Arnauld to respond. Arnauld does so in a language sometimes different in sound, often incommensurable in signification, from that used by Descartes. But Arnauld's is as well a language of local custom, of longer standing and wider spread than Descartes's, equally masquerading as universal speech. As he looks at Descartes's scheme, Arnauld withdraws – perhaps recoiling at the terror of the vacuum of perfect freedom? – and tries to fit the Cartesian position within the confines of the established tradition. It is on this unsuccessful attempt, thus not on the ultimate but on the penultimate matter of interest, that I focus in this essay on Arnauld and the modern mind.

II

It is no small feat to publish, at the youthful age of twenty-nine, what turns out to be a document one of whose chief statements remains the subject of vigorous debate today: Arnauld's *Objections* to Descartes's *Meditations* contains the classical formulation of the charge that the attempt to validate reason through reason fails because of circularity.[3] This, however, is hardly sufficient to warrant the judgment that Arnauld 'is one of the most important intellectual figures of the seventeenth century,' that he is 'the great Arnauld.'[4] If such an evaluation were to rest on the character of his work as revealed in these no doubt 'able,' even 'astute,'[5] *Objections*, it might well be inappropriate. Those of our contemporaries who do make this judgment have broader grounds for it, not the least of which are *La Logique ou l'art de penser* (1662) and the *Nouveaux Essays de géometrie* (1667). Primarily on the basis of works such as these and half a year's personal acquaintance, the young Leibniz wrote to the Duke of Hanover about the sixty-two-year-old Arnauld, describing him as 'the world-famous M. Arnauld.'[6] Whether Leibniz's as well as our contemporaries' judgments are warranted on these grounds is not my concern in this essay, for I restrict my attention here almost entirely to the *Objections*.

It seems reasonable to say that (possibly among other criteria) a person deserves the accolade of being a century's 'most important intellectual figure,' first, through insightfully bringing to bear traditional wisdom on the most crucial contemporary concerns or, second, through taking distance from traditional wisdom and presenting one's contemporaries with a point of view so fundamentally different from traditional wisdom that it changes the very concerns which are now thought to be of major importance. In the *Meditations*, Descartes accomplished the second of these. In his *Objections*, Arnauld attempted the first but because – in contrast, for example, to his later Port-Royal collaborator, Pascal – he did not at this time discern the profound shift in perspective and ambition which Descartes introduced, he achieved neither. The traditional wisdom he drew upon, Arnauld, no doubt ably and astutely, made relevant to matters no longer among the most crucial for his world. If the latter judgment appears excessively harsh, it has at least the virtue that it can serve as a heuristic device to bring into clear focus the young Arnauld's relationship to 'the modern mind' as expressed in the *Meditations*.

By 'the modern mind' I refer to the stance in which a thinker believes it possible and necessary to start *de novo*, in a situation where at least historical and cultural and, at specific stages, even physical contexts are ruled to be non-essential, or even hindrances, to the enterprise of developing *scientia* and the moral and political practices built thereon. It is a stance in which neither thought nor action is necessarily related to the Good (as in Plato) or to God (as in Augustine),[7] in which the validity of both thought and action is ultimately founded on immanent subjective consciousness rather than grounded in an objective order. If the pre-modern (classical or medieval) mind is characterized by relation, the modern mind is distinguished by isolation. Whereas Augustine's attitude is typically pre-modern, Descartes's is distinctively modern. It is true that the projects of both Augustine and Descartes are radically reflexive. For Augustine, however, this reflexivity is encapsulated in given relationships with God, other human beings, and the physical world. For Descartes, in contrast, reflexivity is an exercise in disengagement from all of these and is to establish the thinker's thoroughgoing autonomy.[8] When, believing that there was an intrinsic affinity between (on the one hand) Descartes's *sum res cogitans* and its immanent idea of God and (on the other) Augustine's *Deum et animam scire volo*, Port-Royal Jansenists accepted Descartes's methodology as the correct way of thinking, they made more than a single error – errors which were foreshadowed in Arnauld's *Objections* to Descartes's *Meditations*. These errors do not preclude astute observations about, for example, material falsity or the Eucharist; on matters such as these Arnauld excelled in relating traditional wisdom to contemporary concerns. But, though not without interest to Descartes, these are not the sort of items of central concern to him – and they are certainly not the items of his position which embody the thrust of the Cartesian revolutionary, modern stance. Items of the latter kind, though they do not escape scrutiny in the *Fourth Objections*, there remain beyond Arnauld's grasp.

Already in these *Objections*, Arnauld's lifelong preoccupation with issues of a moral and theological nature predominates,[9] but neither their morality nor their theology here reveals innovation, whether in statement or in application. Their statement is hallmarked by a brand of orthodox safety; their application is an attempt to assimilate Descartes to the orthodoxy of the tradition as shaped initially by Augustine – an enterprise Arnauld would hardly have embarked upon had he discerned the revolutionary drive of Descartes's work.

Arnauld's objections are of four kinds: (i) He raises points of ostensible or possible agreement with Descartes which coincide with real agreement. Among these are (a) the insistence that an act of will (in the form of an act of attentiveness) is required if one is to achieve knowledge,[10] (b) that time is discontinuous or atomic,[11] and, as a consequence of (b), (c) that in reality there is no distinction between creation and conservation.[12] (ii) There is ostensible or possible agreement which does not coincide with real agreement. Here, there are matters such as the (a) indicators of epistemic individualistic autonomy,[13] (b) insistence on separating understanding, belief, and opinion,[14] which for Arnauld is important especially because it allows for separation of epistemological error and moral wrong,[15] and (c) identification of Augustine's and Descartes's *cogito*. (iii) There is ostensible disagreement coinciding with real disagreement, as on (a) the circularity of Descartes's argument[16] and (b) the extent of Descartes's doubt.[17] (iv) Finally, there is ostensible disagreement not (at least according to Descartes) coinciding with real disagreement on issues such as (a) material falsity[18] and (b) the Eucharist.[19]

This incomplete[20] list is sufficient to indicate Arnauld's thoroughness: he had read the *Meditations* – and, as is clear from passing comments, also the *Discourse on the Method* – with extreme care. Agreements as well as disagreements, ostensible or real, can therefore tell us much about the young Arnauld's position with respect to the modern mind. As I now develop this theme, I shall restrict myself to two of the four kinds of objections raised: I shall disregard the first and last kinds and focus on the second and third, on some of the ostensible points of agreement which do not coincide with real agreement, and on some of the ostensible points of disagreement which really are disagreements.[21]

III

What ostensible agreements tell us. (a) The second paragraph of Arnauld's objections can hardly be less than a deliberate echo of the opening paragraph of the *Meditations* and, likely, of the opening paragraph of Part II of the

Discourse. In the latter, Descartes relates the circumstances under which this crucial part of the *Discourse* had come into being: not subject to clamours of war and politics, diversions of conversation, cares about personal well-being, and troubles of passion, he could say he was 'completely free to converse with myself about my own thoughts' (AT 6, 11). In the former, he set out to accomplish the task of rightly founding the sciences, once he could say that 'I have expressly rid my mind of all worries and arranged for myself a clear stretch of free time,' that he was 'quite alone' and so could devote himself to the task 'sincerely and without reservation (*libere*).' Arnauld, likewise, set himself to his task of commenting on the *Meditations* with 'a calm mind' which had to be 'free from the hurly-burly of all external things' because it needed 'the leisure to consider itself – something which ... can happen only if the mind meditates attentively and keeps its gaze fixed upon itself.' In the case of Descartes, these phrases indicate an epistemology and methodology characterized by individualistic autonomy. The *Discourse* paragraph which begins by stating the need and achievement of solitary self-centred reflection ends with an intimation of distrust of one's cultural situation and natural condition – a distrust given concrete resolution in the immediately following paragraph: 'regarding the opinions to which I had hitherto given credence, I thought that I could not do better than undertake to get rid of them, all at one go.' The task to be accomplished during the free and detached time of the *First Meditation* is (in words from its first paragraph) 'the general demolition of my opinions' which (the second paragraph adds) can be accomplished by 'undermining' 'the foundations' or 'the basic principles' 'on which all my former beliefs rested.' Arnauld's phrases, in contrast, are meant to convey anything but individualistic epistemic autonomy. Instead of distrust, there is trust: trust in the (more than eucharistic) presence of God, in the value of philosophical and theological traditions, in the genuine willingness of Descartes to submit himself to the discipline of these traditions, in the responsibilities which attend friendship ('you have done me a kindness' and, now, 'since you command, I must obey' are words from the two opening paragraphs which set their tone as much as any others). In short, it is the duties imposed by Mersenne's friendship and by scholarly responsibility which make Arnauld take Descartes's work utterly seriously, a fact which he tries to make clear from the outset by adopting some of Descartes's language, which is therefore used here to indicate that the task of responding is accepted with the kind of wholeheartedness which responsibly shuts out distracting influences. Where Descartes's stance will soon turn out to be founded on the potentially solipsistic *cogito ergo sum*, Arnauld's position – in spite of these echoes from *Discourse* and *Meditations* – is from the very beginning one that can perhaps be best captured by the necessarily other-involving *respondeo ergo sum*.[22] For Descartes, truth and goodness are to be discovered and developed by the individual on self-determined foundations; for Arnauld, they are to be given by, or discovered and developed in relation to, a Platonic–Aristotelean reality translated by Augustine and Thomas into the being of or emanations from the Christian God. For Descartes, change demands the revolutionary act of wholesale uprooting, which requires that the old – if it is to survive at all – is to stand the test of newly articulated criteria discovered within the individual's reason. For Arnauld, change is the reformer's act in which the new – if it is to stand at all – is to survive the test of traditional criteria, a test passed when the new can be seen harmoniously to fit (or even be a retelling of) long-sanctioned positions.[23]

The contrast I have drawn is that between the modern and pre-modern mind. Is it warranted by the material so far adduced? I believe it is fair to say that this material at least indicates that direction. Through cumulatively relating the other points on which I will focus, the grounds for this contrast will become stronger, hence its validity more assured.

(b) Both Arnauld and Descartes insist on separating understanding, belief, and opinion; Arnauld takes there to be no disagreement here between himself and Descartes or, more broadly, between Descartes and the tradition. To bring home the latter point, Arnauld quotes at length from Augustine and then concludes that 'Descartes, prudent man that he is, will readily judge how important it is to make the distinctions just outlined' (AT 7, 217; CSMK 2, 217). When Descartes responds, he gives no indication that he disagrees with the particulars of Arnauld's and Augustine's distinctions, and he ostensibly makes a concession as a consequence of apparent agreement with respect to what is for Arnauld a crucial distinction, that between epistemological error and moral wrong. There is, however, implicit disagreement which, as we shall see later, becomes in part explicit in their conflict about the circularity of the argument for the validation of reason.

The details of Arnauld's distinctions in Augustine's words, and Descartes's (at this juncture unstated) points of disagreement with them, are as follows.[24] First, Arnauld holds that one *understands* if one 'grasps something by means of a reliable reason [*qui certa ratione aliquid comprehendit*].' For Descartes, but apparently not for Arnauld at this stage, this is only half the story of what it is to understand. It omits the crucially important grasping of foundations: these are grasped *per se* not *per aliud*; hence, there is in their case no grasping 'by means' of 'a reliable reason,' for they are understood immediately rather than mediately.[25] Second, one *believes*, says Arnauld, if one is 'influenced by weighty authority to accept a truth even though he does not grasp it by means of a reliable reason.' For Arnauld, following Augustine, believing can be a permanent state in which legitimately to rest.[26] For Descartes, believing can be legitimate so long as it is for the time being, because authority, though it can be weighty, is at best second best; hence, to rest in belief is to abrogate the basic human responsibility for autonomy. Third, for Arnauld, one commits the 'very grave fault' 'of being *opinionated* if he thinks he knows something of which he is ignorant.' Descartes agrees, but would impute this fault to all who are content to rest in belief on the grounds of authority, for all such persons believe authorities because they think they know that these authorities know – and (unless the authority is known to be God) *that* they cannot know.

In the response (AT 7, 218; CSMK 2, 172) to this lengthy invocation of Augustine, Descartes points Arnauld to his reply to the *Second Objections*, where, he claims, the maxim 'we should assent only to what we clearly know' is 'explained quite explicitly' as 'always subject to the exception of "matters which belong to faith and the conduct of life".' In addition, he claims that he has 'also given advance warning of [this restriction] in the Synopsis.' Both claims are disingenuous. As to the first, he advances as his position in the *Second Replies* that, whether with respect to faith or life, 'we commit a sin by not using ... reason correctly' (AT 7, 148; CSMK 2, 106) and the correct use of reason with respect to obscurities of faith or unresolved complexities of life is: to accept doctrine or pursue action only on the ground of good reasons for such acceptance or pursuit. He there refers to Part III of the *Discourse*, where it is made very clear, on the one hand, that life is such that we cannot always know while yet we must act, and that, therefore, *until we know, prudence* dictates that, *for the time being*, we conform to the most moderate manifestations of the status quo in politics, morality, religion, and everyday concerns. In the meantime, on the other hand, we may never relinquish the freedom to review this conformity (AT 6, 24–27; CSMK 2, 123–4): 'For since God has given each of us a light to distinguish truth from falsehood, I should not have thought myself obliged to rest content with the opinions of others for a single moment if I had not intended in due course to examine them using my own judgment; and I could not have avoided having scruples about following these opinions, if I had not hoped to lose no opportunity to discover better ones, in case there were any.' As to the second, the advance warning in the Synopsis: 'in order to show how much I respect M. Arnauld's judgement' Descartes entered a disclaimer in the Synopsis to the effect that, in the *Fourth Meditation*, he did 'not deal at all with sin, i.e. the error which is committed in the pursuit of good and evil.' But in the *Fourth Meditation* itself he quite emphatically leaves in place the explicit references to error in extra-intellectual pursuits when he writes about the 'true and good/verum & bonum' (p. 40), 'error and sin/fallor & pecco' (p. 41), and 'falsity and wrong/falsitates & culpae' (p. 42). The *Meditations*, as Descartes insisted time and again, are themselves of instrumental value only. They are to be the foundation for the intellectual pursuits which result in the sciences, which themselves are to determine the quality of life as reason applied through mechanics (power over nature), medicine (power over the body), and morals (power over the passions). The *Meditations* are to be the foundation for activity which is to result in paradise regained: freedom from labour, pain, and evil – not by faith in and grace from God, but by trust in the efficacy of human reason and actuality of human generosity.[27] Arnauld, in sharp contrast, is at this time preoccupied with the kind of Augustinian view about the human state in which human beings unassisted by divine grace are pretty well incapable of good and prone to all evil, so much so that, if God were to bestow grace but were to leave it up to individuals to make use of it, the grace bestowed would not be efficacious – a view which underlies the first of Arnauld's controversial writings which was to be published two years after the *Objections* to the *Meditations*, the anti-Jesuit *De la frequente Communion*. On this score of human rational ability assisted only by human generosity to produce moral good and so, in principle, overcome sin and obviate culpability, Arnauld and Descartes are miles apart, as far apart as is the Augustinian mind from the modern.[28]

(c) From this perspective it is not difficult to show that the ostensible agreement on the nature of the foundation of philosophy is in fact Arnauld's misjudgment of the spirit of Descartes's project. Arnauld's very first comment on the *Meditations* is that he finds it 'remarkable' that Descartes 'has laid down as the basis for his entire philosophy exactly the same principle as that laid down by St Augustine,' namely, that 'you yourself exist' (AT 7, 197–8; CSMK 2, 139).[29] Descartes responds only by saying: 'I shall not waste time here by thanking my distinguished critic for bringing in the authority of St Augustine to support me' (AT 7, 154; CSMK 2, 219). This curtness may be indicative of Descartes's characteristic irritation when critics complement him on (or charge him with) stating what others have already said; or it may be his way to pass over a point whose greater explication will bring out his departure from tradition in colours too stark for safety let alone the comfort of respect.[30] Where, for Augustinian Arnauld, the Archimedean point of his philosophizing would be found in belief which relates the embodied thinker to the transcendent God, for Descartes this point lies in the subjectivity of the independent and isolated immanent *cogito* – a point so firm that not even God can shake it. In other words, for Arnauld, philosophy is carried out in dependence on God, while for Descartes we have in the *cogito* the unilateral declaration of philosophy's independence from God. In Gareth Matthews's words, Augustine's (and, through his identification with him, Arnauld's) 'inquiry is conducted from the standpoint of faith' so that 'even in his most rational and systematic moods, Augustine never tries to undermine all appeal to outside authority,' while Descartes 'makes himself his own authority'; and where, for Augustine, 'some things cannot even be understood unless they are first believed,' for Descartes knowledge is strictly a '"do-it-yourself" achievement' in which 'systematic doubt' serves the isolated individual's total 'reconstruction of knowledge.' In Augustine, says Matthews, there is no such 'rational reconstruction of knowledge,' let alone a *cogito* which is 'the independent foundation for reconstructing knowledge.'[31]

Now for my last two points, which will produce greater relief in the picture so far sketched.

IV

What stated disagreements tell us. The assertions concerning (d) the circularity of Descartes's argument and (e) the extent of Descartes's doubt express real disagreements.

(d) Arnauld's formulation of 'the circle' (at AT 7, 214; CSMK 2, 150) is probably the best-known part of his *Objections*:

> I have one further worry, namely how the author avoids reasoning in a circle when he says that we are sure that what we clearly and distinctly perceive is true only because God exists.
>
> But we can be sure that God exists only because we clearly and distinctly perceive this. Hence, before we can be sure that God exists, we ought to be able to be sure that whatever we perceive clearly and evidently is true.

Arnauld's objection is inevitable, coming as it does from a person who at this point considers understanding to be always a matter of 'grasping something by means of a reliable reason.' In that case, if '*whatever* we perceive clearly and evidently' is true 'only because we clearly and distinctly perceive' that a trustworthy God exists (here is the reliable reason), and if the existence of a non-trustworthy God has been posited (thus removing the reliable reason) and has thus cast doubt on the very trustworthiness of the criteria of clarity and distinctness in *all* cases of purported knowledge, then circularity is inescapable.

In his brief rebuttal (AT 7, 245–6; CSMK 2, 171) Descartes again refers Arnauld to the much longer response in his *Second Set of Replies* (AT 7, 140–6; CSMK 2, 100–5). In this response it is clear that Descartes works with a distinction which makes illegitimate Arnauld's use of 'whatever' in 'whatever we perceive clearly and evidently,' namely, the distinction between *notitia* ('awareness of first principles' – which, once one is aware of them at all, are always fully known and hence never remembered), and *scientia* (which is systematic knowledge ultimately founded on such principles, 'knowledge of those conclusions which can be recalled when we are no longer attending to the arguments *by means* of which we deduced them'). In other words, Descartes distinguishes between things known immediately through intuition and things known mediately through deduction. Once, through focusing on the immediately known *cogito*, Descartes has shown (first) that, with respect to what is immediately known, the criteria of clarity and distinctness remain intact whether or not there exists a God and whether or not this God is a deceiver, and (second) that a trustworthy God exists, he can reinstate trust in the criteria of clarity and distinctness with respect to whatever is mediately known, for it is only the hypothesis of the existence of a deceiving God which called into question the efficacy of these criteria in the context of mediation. But first showing the absolute trustworthiness of some things[32] known immediately is a necessary prerequisite for the second move.

Two decades later, Arnauld himself articulates this doctrine of the two kinds of knowledge and their corresponding human capacities in the terminology of 'intellection' and 'understanding.'[33] But if we were to import this later distinction into the debate we are now considering, I suspect Arnauld would have had a different objection to the legitimacy if not validity of Descartes's argument. The crucial foundational item intuitively known is that if I think, then I am. It is knowledge with which God cannot tinker. Thus for the foundation of philosophizing it holds that it is irrelevant whether or not God exists as good or evil. Showing this absolute trustworthiness of foundational thinking, showing that the foundation for philosophy lies in pure subjectivity and does not require authentication from anything transcending the individual thinker's act of consciousness, is an emancipation of this act from all that transcends it – an emancipation which firmly launches Western philosophy on the adventure later named 'the Enlightenment.' From all we have so far seen, it would seem safe to conclude that Arnauld would refuse to be a passenger, let alone a member of the crew, aboard a ship with this destination. This conclusion stands even when we realize that Descartes's act is one of partial rather than full emancipation.

For it is emancipation of *thinking*, not of *being*. The very existence of the person *qua* thinking and extended substance (if only because of the discontinuous nature of time) is, for both Arnauld and Descartes, dependent on the providence of God. But autonomous thought, first in metaphysics, then in the pure, and finally through the applied sciences, determines the quality of this existence. Autonomous thought holds out the promise of paradise regained in *this* world, through human, not divine activity'. Descartes's radicalism is a watershed: before him, paradise was lost in a distant past to be regained by select humans in a non-earthly context through the merit of Christ; after him, paradise lies in an earthly future, to be regained by the work of human reason coupled with human generosity. That to which in his *Objections* Arnauld was blind, his younger contemporary, and later defender and collaborator, Pascal[34] eventually saw clearly: 'I cannot forgive Descartes. In all his philosophy he would have been quite willing to dispense with God. But he could not help granting him a flick of the forefinger to start the world in motion; beyond this he has no further need of God.'[35]

Arnauld's early disregard of the distinction between knowledge *per se* and *per aliud* may have been the screen that prevented him from seeing the radicality of the Cartesian *cogito*. His use of Augustine's distinctions among understanding, belief, and opinion led him to impute circularity to Descartes's argument; this charge of circularity possibly kept him from more carefully examining the foundation of Descartes's system, thus misjudging it to the extent that he pronounced it Augustinian.

(e) There now remains the matter of doubt. It is perhaps telling that Arnauld's worry about the extent of Descartes's doubt is the first point raised under those 'which may cause difficulties to theologians' (AT 7, 214–15; CSMK 2, 151): 'I am afraid that the author's somewhat free style of philosophizing, which calls everything into doubt, may cause offence'; for example, 'where we find the clause "since I did not know the author of my being",' Arnauld suggests as a substitution 'the clause "since I was pretending that I did not know ..."' The *Meditations*, says Arnauld, are 'dangerous for those of only moderate intelligence' – a judgment which, given its locus, would seem to refer to theologians. Descartes's response? 'I completely agree' (AT 7, 247; CSMK 2, 172). The activity of pretending, which is the use of non-corporeal imagination in philosophy,[36] is absolutely crucial for Descartes. It is that which allows for the generation of hypotheses, hence is necessary if any progress is to be made in philosophy as in any systematic thinking. Descartes already shared Arnauld's language before the latter raised the point. As we read in the penultimate paragraph of the *First Meditation*, 'I think it will be a good plan to turn my will in completely the opposite direction and deceive myself, by pretending [*fingam*] for a time that these former opinions are utterly false and imaginary. I shall do this until the weight of preconceived opinion [*praejudiciorum*] is counterbalanced and the distorting influence of habit no longer prevents my judgment from perceiving things correctly.' The agreement here between Descartes and Arnauld is strictly superficial, at best covering the judgment that the average theologian is none too bright, and that therefore it is best to use the language of make-believe.

Arnauld seems oblivious of what this pretending in fact is meant to accomplish. It allows for efficacious universal doubt. And although, for both Descartes and Augustine, doubt leads to awareness of the existence of the doubter, the resemblance is again superficial. For Augustine, this doubt undermines scepticism in that it leads it into self-contradiction. For Descartes, the consequences of this doubt are intended to be both deeper and more extensive: it is to authorize the *cogito* as the immovable foundation for the autonomous construction of *scientia*;[37] it is to free the mind from all habit or custom, from the 'habitual opinions' which 'keep coming back, and, despite my wishes ... capture my belief, which is as it were bound over to them as a result of long occupation and the law of custom' (as the opening sentence of the penultimate paragraph of the *First Meditation* has it); it is to free the thinker from any influence of culture and location; it is to throw the thinker back on strictly individual resources, and as such it is the first sounding of Kant's Enlightenment call for each to be self-emancipated from self-incurred tutelage.[38] Counterbalancing a 'supremely good' God with a 'malicious demon of the utmost power and cunning (*summe potentem & callidum*)' has the effect of freeing the thinker from both.[39] Here is the typically modern mind.

V

Conclusion. In a recent essay,[40] Nicholas Jolley writes that, 'for Arnauld, Descartes' philosophy offered the best philosophical support of the Christian faith; it provided the best arguments for the existence of God and the spirituality of the mind.' This accurate statement about Arnauld indicates the point I have argued: Arnauld's is not the modern mind. To the contrary, he is so enveloped in pre-modern Augustinianism that he fails to recognize modernity's character when it faces him. He believes it sufficiently innocuous to allow its incorporation into Christian traditional thought with few adjustments in doctrine and tone. In this respect Arnauld differed from many of his contemporaries, both Protestant and Catholic.

It did not take long for Descartes to become *persona non grata* at major Protestant Dutch universities. At Utrecht, Regius was forbidden to teach Cartesianism within two years of the publication of the *Meditations* and its *Objections* and, two years after that, Utrecht's city council pronounced a formal ban on all discussion of Descartes in print. Within a few years, the University of Leiden followed suit. In both places Cartesianism was seen as anti-Christian, in part because of its assertion of the limitlessness of human freedom. In Rome, Descartes's works were placed on the *Index* in 1663, and in 1671 French universities were forbidden to teach Descartes by royal decree. Both Roman church and French king acted under the strong influence of Jesuit thought, which held that Descartes's position undermined central tenets of the Catholic faith. Throughout, Arnauld remained a steadfast champion of Descartes as defender of the faith. It would seem that Dutch Protestants as well as Italian and French Jesuits had more insight than Arnauld into Descartes the revolutionary challenger of tradition (although it would be anachronistic by a century to say that they consciously were this revolutionary's anti-revolutionary opponents).

In the subsequent century, Arnauld's enervated orthodox type of Cartesianism was alive and well in the staid confines of the French Academy. In the meantime, Cartesianism of the radical revolutionary kind – that promulgated by Descartes when he did not feel constrained to say less than he would through fear for loss of personal safety or respect – returned to French soil, in part through the influence of the writings of Locke as these were embraced by the equally revolutionary *philosophes* such as d'Alembert, Voltaire, Diderot, and Condoret.[41]

Notes

I am indebted to my colleagues Vivien Bosley and Martin Tweedale for helpful discussions of various aspects of this essay.

1 This is not to say that Hobbes consistently and exclusively applied a single scientific method to political and physical science. The former was at least in part structured by his negative reaction to the rhetorical tradition of classical and Renaissance humanism. On this point see Quentin Skinner's '"*Scientia civilis*' in Classical Rhetoric and in the Early Hobbes,' in *Political Discourse in Early Modern Britain*, Nicholas Phillipson and Quentin Skinner, eds (Cambridge: Cambridge University Press 1993), 67–93.
2 The phrases in quotation marks in this paragraph are from Jeffrey Stout, *Ethics after Babel: The Languages of Morals and Their Discontents* (Boston: Beacon Press 1988), 74.
3 Arnauld's was not the first charge of circularity to which Descartes replied. His first reply came in the *Second Set of Replies*, in response to objections Mersenne supposedly collected from various philosophers and theologians but which were most likely largely Mersenne's own. As we shall see, in his response to Arnauld, Descartes refers to the *Second Set* as containing grounds to counter Arnauld's charge. Neither of these replies have been convincing to all philosophers. Beginning with Gassendi in 1644 (see *The Selected Works of Pierre Gassendi*, Craig Brush, ed. and trans. [New York: 1972], 204), the debate has remained continuous until our day – as evidenced, for example, by Willis Doney's selection of articles on the topic published in *Eternal Truths and the Cartesian Circle* (New York: Garland 1987). The most recent interesting discussion of 'the circle' is that of Georges Dicker in his *Descartes: An Analytical and Historical Introduction*

(New York and Oxford: Oxford University Press 1993), ch. 3.

4 The first of the quoted phrase is from the opening sentence of Steven Nadler's review of A.-R. Ndiaye's *La Philosophie d'Antoine Arnauld* (Paris: Vrin 1991) in the *British Journal for the History of Philosophy* 1/1 (1993), 138–41; the second is from Genevieve Rodis-Lewis's 'Descartes Life and the Development of His Philosophy,' in *The Cambridge Companion to Descartes*, John Cottingham, ed. (Cambridge: Cambridge University Press 1992), 21–57, 47.

5 John Cottingham writes of Arnauld as 'Descartes' astute critic' who 'ingeniously proceeds to show ...': *Descartes* (Oxford: Blackwell 1986), 112. His comments echo those of Bernard Williams, who speaks of Descartes's 'able critic Arnauld': *Descartes: The Project of Pure Enquiry*, (Sussex: Hassocks 1978), 160. Cottingham praises Arnauld for showing the difficulty with Descartes's argument as it moves from (i) I can doubt that I have a body, through (ii) I cannot doubt that I exist, to (iii) therefore I who doubt am not a body. (Williams has said that Arnauld's formulation reveals this argument's 'embarrassing resemblance to the masked man fallacy' – (p. 112). Williams's accolade comes in the context of Arnauld's objection to Descartes' proposal that God can be the efficient cause of his own existence.

6 *Gottfried Wilhelm Leibniz: Samtliche Schriften und Briefe* (Darmstadt and Berlin, 1923–), ii. 1, 230.

7 I contrast the (neo-)Platonic/Augustinian rather than the Aristotelian/Thomistic mind with the modern mind because Arnauld approached Descartes from an Augustinian rather than a Thomistic position. The contrast between Augustine and Descartes is different from that between Thomas and Descartes – which is not to imply that the Thomistic stance is an expression of the modern mind. By the late thirteenth century, (neo-)Platonic Augustinianism had been supplanted by the Aristotelian epistemology as the main bulwark of scholasticism. As in Descartes's position, and as distinct from that of Augustine (e.g., *Confessions*, VI.5 and *City of God*, X.2), Aristotelian/Thomism treats human reason as essentially independent of divine grace. But, unlike Descartes, it emphasizes the need for intimate familiarity with traditional authorities, the chief of these being Aristotle himself. Thus the difference between the latter two traditions does not lie primarily in the emancipation of human reason from God, but from the tradition of rational inquiry. Hence an oversimplified statement of these various relationships is that the modern mind has affinities with the Augustinian mind in its view of the (for Augustine, relative) unimportance of traditional thought but sharply differs from it on the necessity of a relationship between human reason and divine grace, and has affinities with the Thomistic mind on the (for Thomas, partial) irrelevance of a relationship between human reason and divine grace, but sharply differs from it on the importance of traditional authority.

8 For a similar contrast drawn in recent literature between Augustine and Descartes, see Charles Taylor, *The Sources of the Self: The Making of the Modern Identity* (Cambridge, MA: Harvard University Press 1989), 115–49.

9 This predominance is stressed in Ndiaye's *La Philosophie d'Antoine Arnauld*. For example, p. 11: Arnauld's writings are essentially polemical, but 'toujours en rapport avec ses preoccupations morales et theologiques.'

10 For Arnauld's use, see AT 7, 197, 214, 218; for Descartes's, see AT 7, 229, 246. For an account of the relation between attention and will in Descartes's *Meditations* see Peter A. Schouls, *Descartes and the Enlightenment* (Edinburgh: Edinburgh University Press; Kingston and Montreal: McGill-Queen's University Press 1989), 90–5. That Arnauld retained this position in later life is clear from *The Art of Thinking*, e.g., Part IV, ch. 1, the opening paragraphs.

11 For Arnauld, see AT 7, 209; for Descartes, AT 7, 49.

12 For Arnauld, see AT 7, 210, 212; for Descartes, AT 7, 49.

13 See Arnauld's second paragraph, which echoes both the opening paragraph of the *Meditations* and the opening paragraph of Part II of the *Discourse on the Method*.

14 AT 7, 216–17.

15 AT 7, 215.

16 AT 7, 214.

17 AT 7, 215, related to 216.

18 AT 7, 206–7.

19 AT 7, 217–18.

20 There are other matters, two of which I indicated in note 5, above.

21 Whether the items mentioned under (4) are disagreements not coinciding with real disagreement is an aspect of two other essays in this volume: Alan Nelson's 'The Falsity in Sensory Ideas: Descartes and Arnauld,' and Elmar Kremer's 'Arnauld's Interpretation of Descartes as a Christian Philosopher.'

22 Even when, two decades later, in *The Art of Thinking*, there are *cogito*-like statements, these function quite differently from Descartes's *cogito*. In Part I, ch. 9, it occurs only as an example of a clear idea: 'The ideas that each has of himself as a thinking being is very clear ... We cannot claim that there is no such thing as thinking substance, since to do so we must in fact think.' And, in Part IV, ch. 2, it functions as part of an illustration of the process of analysis, where the illustration is in terms of the question 'Is the soul of man immortal?': 'In the first place we note that thinking is the essential characteristic of the soul and that, since doubt itself is a thought, the soul can doubt everything else without being able to doubt whether it thinks.'

23 Arnauld's defence of Cornelius Jansen is the best illustration of this point: he found the defensibility of Jansen's position primarily in its comporting with that of Augustine.

24 All quotations in this paragraph are from Arnauld's reproduction of Augustine at
AT 7, 216–17.

25 In *The Art of Thinking*, Arnauld's position is much closer to Descartes's on this
point. See again the first chapter of Part IV, which begins with two sentences
characterizing the *first* aspect of knowledge: 'When we know any maxim to be true
in itself – that is, when the evidence offered by the maxim suffices to convince us
of its truth – then we know by intellection. First principles are known in such a
fashion.' He had, by that time, read Clerselier's copy of the manuscript of
Descartes's *Rules for the Direction of the Mind*, in which the notion of knowledge
per se, of items grasped intuitively rather than discursively, occupies a prominent
position. Arnauld – although he does not adopt Descartes's word 'intuition' but
instead uses 'intellection' – here explicitly accepts this notion of non-discursive
knowledge which, for him, as for Descartes, is knowledge of items foundational to
the sciences. In the sentence immediately following those quoted above, Arnauld
introduces as a *second* item that which, in the *Objections*, he had (in Augustine's
formulation) stated as the first and only item sufficient by itself to characterize
knowledge and belief: 'If the maxim alone does not convince us of its truth, *we
require some further basis for accepting the maxim as true; and this basis is to be
found either in authority or in reason.*' Since the 'further basis' can under certain
circumstances be 'authority,' Arnauld's pre-modern stance is still intact on this
point at this later stage of his career. He is still closer to Augustine than he is to
Descartes, for it is only the former of these for whom 'understanding' can be 'the
reward of faith' so that one does 'not seek to understand in order to believe, but
believe that you may understand' (*Homilies on the Gospel of John, 29.6*. John
Gibb and James Innes, trans., in *A Select Library of the Nicene and Post-Nicene
Fathers*, Vol. 7, Philip Schaff, ed. (New York, 1888), 7–452.

26 See the last few sentences of the preceding note.

27 On 'generosity' see *The Passions of the Soul*, Art. 153: 'true generosity ... has
only two components. The first consists in his knowing that nothing truly belongs
to him but this freedom to dispose his volitions, and that he ought to be praised or
blamed for no other reason than using this freedom well or badly. The second
consists in his feeling within himself a firm and constant resolution to use it well
– that is, never to lack the will to undertake and carry out whatever he judges to be
best. To do that is to pursue virtue in a perfect manner.' (AT 11, 445–6; CSMK 1,
384)

28 In the Preface to the *Principles*, Descartes reiterates his position on the nature of
the moral rules of the *Discourse* and, by implication, the need for him to be
concerned with moral good and evil in addition to epistemic truth and falsity. He
there writes that, in the *Discourse*, 'I summarized the principal rules of logic and
of an imperfect moral code which we may follow provisionally while we do not yet
know a better one.' (AT 9B, 15; CSMK 1, 186)

29 Arnauld's quotation is from Augustine's *On Free Will*, II, ch. 3. There are other passages in Augustine's works which contain a *cogito*-like statement. There is *On the Trinity*, X, 10; e.g., in *Philosophy in the Middle Ages: The Christian, Islamic, and Jewish Traditions*, 2d. ed, Arthur Hyman and James Walsh, eds. (Indianapolis: Hackett, 1973), 71. And there is the *City of God*, XI, 26; e.g., in *The Essential Augustine*, Vernon J. Bourke, ed.; (Indianapolis: Hackett, 1964), 33. Moreover, Arnauld was not the only one to draw Descartes's attention to this similarity; it was pointed out by both Mersenne and Colvius, not with respect to the *Meditations* but with respect to the *Discourse*, where the *cogito* appears in the form *I am thinking, therefore I exist*. Mersenne's reference concerns (say Adam and Tannery) 'sans dout le fameux passage *Civit. Dei*, lib. XI, cap. 26'; Descartes gives it short shrift: 'il ne me semble pas s'en servir a mesme usage que ie fais' (25 May 1637; AT 1, 376). Colvius's reference, as well, is the *City of God*. Disingenuously (given his correspondence with Mersenne) Descartes intimates ignorance of the passage and again distances himself from its import: 'I am obliged to you for drawing my attention to the passage of St Augustine relevant to my *I am thinking, therefore I exist*. I went today to the library of this town to read it, and I do indeed find that he does use it to prove the certainty of our existence. He goes on to show that there is a certain likeness of the Trinity in us, in that we exist, we know that we exist, and we love the existence and knowledge we have. I, on the other hand, use the argument to show that this *I* which is thinking is *an immaterial substance* with no bodily element. These are two very different things' (14 November 1640; AT 3, 247; CSMK 3, 159).

30 Perhaps it is both of these. This is, after all, the third time that a critic confronts him on this matter; and it is certainly the case that Descartes distances himself from this identification. On both points, see the preceding note.

31 These statements are from pp. 36, 133–4, 142–3, and 145 of Gareth B. Matthews's admirable *Thought's Ego in Augustine and Descartes*, (Ithaca and London: Cornell University Press 1992). See as well what Matthews has to say (on pp. 150 and 190) about the appearance of a *cogito*-like statement in Augustine's *Soliloquies*.

32 I use the plural ('some things') because, both in the *Meditations* and in the restated argument of the First Book of the *Principles of Philosophy*, there are two ways in which the *cogito* is established as first item of certain knowledge: first, in terms of volition, and, second, in terms of intellection. See my 'Human Nature, Reason, and Will in the Argument of Descartes's *Meditations*,' in *Reason, Will, and Sensation: Studies in Cartesian Metaphysics*, John Cottingham, ed. (Oxford: Clarendon Press 1994), 159–76.

33 See note 25, above.

34 Pascal's *Lettres provinciales* (1656–7), written in defence of Arnauld's Jansenist views, are probably the result of colaborative work at Port-Royal among Pascal, Arnauld, and Pierre Nicole (Arnauld's co-author of the *Art of Thinking*).

35 Blaise Pascal, *Pensées*. H.S. Thayer, ed. (New York: Washington Square Press 1965), Section 2, 77, p. 26.
36 The role of non-corporeal imagination in Descartes is a fascinating though largely ignored topic. I am in the process of completing a monograph – provisionally called *Descartes on human nature and progress in science* – in which this role is the central focus of attention.
37 See Matthews's *Thought's Ego*, 171–4.
38 The opening paragraph of Kant's *What Is Enlightenment?* reads: 'Enlightenment is man's release from his self-incurred tutelage. Tutelage is man's inability to make use of his understanding without direction from another. Self-incurred is this tutelage when its cause lies not in lack of reason but in lack of resolution and courage to use it without direction from another. *Sapere aude!* "Have courage to use your own reason!" – that is the motto of enlightenment.' The translation quoted is that of Lewis White Beck, appended to his translation of the *Foundations of the Metaphysics of Morals* (New York: Macmillan 1985), 83.
39 Apparently as unaware as Arnauld of Descartes's contribution on this score, Peter Gay has called this balancing act the new intellectual style of the eighteenth-century Enlightenment. See Peter Gay, *The Enlightenment: An Interpretation*, Vol.2: *The Science of Freedom* (London: Weidenfeld and Nicolson 1970), xiii, 160.
40 Nicholas Jolley, 'The Reception of Descartes' Philosophy,' in *The Cambridge Companion to Descartes*, John Cottingham, ed., 393–423, 401. Jolley's essay contains a broader statement of several of the points of my conclusion.
41 This sentence expresses the central theme of my *Descartes and the Enlightenment*.

4

Arnauld and Scepticism:
Questions de fait and
Questions de droit

THOMAS M. LENNON

Arnauld was viewed in his time as an extraordinary genius of great learning and insight. This was a view shared by Pierre Bayle, who expressed it in so many words.[1] Arnauld's initial celebrity has not been fully retained by the historical sieve, however. Although Bayle's assessment of him might be justified just by Arnauld's long polemic with Malebranche, for example, there is only one argument nowadays connected with his name: the argument concerning the circularity of Descartes's reasoning about clear and distinct ideas and the existence of God in the *Meditations*. Otherwise, there is no concept, no innovation or rupture that history has come to associate with him. There is no equivalent for him of Descartes's *cogito*, for example, or Pascal's wager. If there is an exception to this untagged intelligence, to this failure of history to find a niche for the name of Arnauld, it would perhaps be the distinction between *questions de fait* and *questions de droit*. In the period, at least, this distinction would have been the likeliest conditioned response to the name of Arnauld.[2]

I first explored the *fait–droit* distinction fifteen years ago in an article on Jansenist scepticism.[3] My thesis there is that a sceptical outlook was logically, temperamentally, and strategically characteristic of Jansenism: logically, in that it followed from their views on grace; temperamentally, in that it sat well with their rejection of speculative theology; and strategically, in that it obscured their unorthodox views. As a Cartesian, even as a Cartesian fellow-traveller, Arnauld ought to have been the arch-opponent of scepticism; but especially with respect to Arnauld's strategy, the article draws attention to a distinction of sorts between the *question de fait* of what Arnauld asserted and the *question de droit* of what he was committed to. The thesis is that Arnauld's use of the *fait–droit* distinction itself committed him to scepticism.

Here I expand that thesis, both historically and structurally, especially with respect to Arnauld's use of the distinction in response to criticism from Bayle and from Pascal. My thesis is that the distinction implies that the church's infallibility is, at best, hypothetical in the sense that it is infallible with respect to a proposition *P* if, but only if, in asserting its infallibility it means *P*, but that we can never be sure that it means *P*. The result is an open-ended challenge to church authority. None of the church's pronouncements need be binding because of open questions about what any of them might mean. For anyone relying on church infallibility to overcome doubt, scepticism in matters of religion is the result. This result is very important in the larger, philosophical context. To take a notable example from the seventeenth century, Gassendi's objection to Descartes was that, even if clarity and distinctness were reliable criteria of the truth of propositions, we would still need a means of determining which propositions are clear and distinct. To put it more generally, a standard does not guarantee its own application. The issue raised by Arnauld, then, is scepticism in a sense wider than the religious context. But first, some background.

I

In 1653, the bull *Cum occasione* of Innocent X condemned the famous Five Propositions that everyone took to be definitive of the Jansenist position on grace – everyone, that is, but a group from among the Jansenists headed by Arnauld. Faced with the inconsistent triad of (1) papal infallibility, (2) papal condemnation of the propositions, and (3) the Augustinian, hence orthodox, character of the propositions, this group chose to deny that the Pope had condemned the propositions *in the sense in which they accepted them*. Following the suggestion of Nicole, apparently, Arnauld distinguished between questions *de fait*, about which the church is fallible, in this case the question whether certain propositions are to be found in a certain book, or are held by certain people, and questions *de droit*, about which the church is infallible, in this case whether certain propositions are heretical. Arnauld claimed to cede on the *question de droit*, but maintained a respectful silence on what he took to be the *question de fait*. The Pope had no doubt condemned something, and correctly, but he had not condemned Jansenism – at least not as Arnauld understood it, which, of course, is what (he thought) it really was. What the Pope thought was Jansenism is not Jansenism, according to Arnauld.[4]

On 12 December 1661, the Jesuits published and defended a thesis, *Assertiones Catholicae*, in which they argue that the Pope has the 'same infallibility' that Christ had, that the Pope is 'an infallible judge of controversies of faith, ... as well in questions *de fait* as *de droit*. Therefore, since the Constitutions of

Innocent X and Alexander VII, we may believe with a divine faith that the book entitled the Augustinus of Jansenius is heretical, and the Five Propositions drawn from it, are Jansenius's and in the sense of Jansenius condemned.'⁵ Ferrier, for instance, argued that, if indeed the Pope had not understood Jansenius in condemning him, he might not have understood Augustine, for example, in approving him.

In reply, Arnauld argued, *ad verecundiam*, citing even people like Bellarmine, that the Pope is not infallible with regard to matters *de fait*, and, *ad absurdum*, that the Jesuits might as well have argued that the Pope is unable to sin as that he is unable to err with respect to matters *de fait* – history shows the one to be about as likely as the other. The Jesuit position amounts to idolatry; it deifies the Pope, endowing him with omniscience. According to Arnauld, the role of the Pope is to *interpret* what has *already* been revealed by God. Nicole replied to Ferrier that the questions he raises must be handled on a case-by-case basis, relying on reason; history shows the church sometimes to have been right, sometimes in error concerning these *questions de fait*. 'One cannot therefore know in general whether it be lawful or not to affirm that an author has been ill understood by the Church, since it depends on the particular reasons that induce one to say it.'⁶

Not irrelevantly, Bayle indirectly accepted the Jesuits' premise and supported the thesis I defend in my article, at least with respect to religious knowledge. He argued that there is no church infallibility. For him there is no infallibility *de fait* (as he thought most Catholics other than the Jesuits admitted), and therefore no infallibility at all. However certain we may be about some matter *de fait*, we might always be mistaken.

We shall return to Bayle's position below. Meanwhile, the upshot of Arnauld's use of the distinction would seem to be, not just fallibility, but religious scepticism: we must suspend belief with regard to matters of faith because we literally do not know what to believe. Before we can determine whether a believed proposition is true or false, we must determine what it means, but this is always problematic. No appeal to an external criterion of religious knowledge such as the Pope or church councils could be certain, even if the criterion were certain, because no use of the criterion could guarantee its own relevance to an individual belief. (That every criterion is crippled in this way is the case that sceptics had traditionally argued against the dogmatists – for example, as noted above, Gassendi against Descartes.) Given Arnauld's distinction, the applicability of the criterion must always be infected with matters *de fait*: interpretation, vagueness, ambiguity, etc. But since Arnauld did accept this external criterion, the effect of his distinction and the extreme uses to which it was put was really to question the possibility of any kind of religious knowledge, and perhaps of any knowledge at all. One observer remarked that 'the [Jansenists] are come now generally to disavow, not only the *Popes*, but all *human Infallibititie*. This is one of the last refuges they have made use of against their adversaries.'[7] The extreme use of this argument, however, was made by others. Popkin points to three works of 1688, 1700, and 1757 where the following argument was employed. 'The Pope and no one else is infallible. But who can tell who is the Pope? The member of the Church has only his fallible lights to judge by. So only the Pope can be sure who is the Pope; the rest of the members have no way of being sure.'[8] Yet even the knowledge by the Pope that he is the Pope is a matter *de fait*. This is no artificial question. The more general version of the argument concerns the characteristics of the true church, how they are to be determined and applied, etc. In this dispute, of course, Arnauld and Bayle were as prominent as anyone addressing the issue.

II

Soon after its appearance in 1685, Arnauld's *Réflexions philosophiques et théologiques* was reviewed by Bayle in the *Nouvelles de la République des Lettres*.[9] As seems to have been typical of all his reviews, Bayle's account of Arnauld's book is complete, fair, and accurate, but also generally sympathetic. Alas, on one point, and on one point only, among many others, Bayle's fairness led him to defend Malebranche. He went so far as to accuse Arnauld of quibbling in an effort to taint Malebranche's religious orthodoxy.

Bayle found eminently defensible Malebranche's view that pleasure makes those who enjoy it happy while they enjoy it. The various kinds of pleasure, and their moral status, are distinguished on the basis of their efficient cause, but not their formal cause. There may be no difference in the pleasure itself caused by the sovereign good and by some passion. In addition, the intrinsic distinction Arnauld tries to draw between spiritual and bodily pleasures is not going to be very effective in converting voluptuaries, who are ensconced in their pleasures.[10] Nadler has shown that the difference between Arnauld, on the one hand, and Bayle and Malebranche, on the other, is with respect to the intentionality of sensations, particularly pleasure and pain.[11] For Bayle and Malebranche, pleasure and pain are non-intentional – at least considered in themselves. For Arnauld, all conscious states are intentional, so he is in a position to claim that there is an intrinsic difference between physical and spiritual pleasures based on the intentional relation that each bears to its object. (Without this distinction, he thinks, concupiscence would be justified, and one of the main proofs of original sin would be upset.)

Arnauld was not long in responding. He produced an anonymous twenty-three-page pamphlet dated 10 October of the same year.[12] It is no quibble, he says, to point out that the term 'happy' in Malebranche's position can be taken in two senses – one popular, according to which those are happy who think themselves happy, the other philosophical, according to which the only happiness is enjoyment of the sovereign good – which is the only sense in which he took the term.[13] He goes on to insist that, for the proper evaluation of his arguments, two questions must not be confused: 'One, whether he has understood [*bien pris*] his opponent's sense. The other, whether in the sense he has understood his opponent, he has refuted him.'[14] The first is a *question de fait*, but of the Five Propositions to which Arnauld conveniently reduced Malebranche's view on sensory pleasure, three are 'independent of this *question de fait*; that is, concerning them one can not claim that he has not attacked the true position of Malebranche.' Arnauld continues, confusingly, as follows: 'thus, in order for what [Bayle] says about his [Arnauld's] attack to be true, viz. that what the attack says about sensory pleasure is neither evident nor reasonable, his [Bayle's] criticism must extend also to these three propositions.'[15]

Bayle's reply to Arnauld's invocation of the *fait–droit* distinction makes a perhaps obvious but important point. On the *question de fait* whether Arnauld properly understood Malebranche, Bayle thinks that Malebranche did not mean by happiness what Arnauld means, and thus that what Arnauld says proves nothing against him. Arnauld fails to prove anything against Malebranche because he fails to understand him. Bayle does not develop the point here, but the drift is towards saying that the *question de fait* must be presupposed if there is to be refutation, or even disputes, at all, or perhaps for there to be communication of any sort. (The point becomes even more obvious when put in terms of confirmation and agreement.) However obvious or not, the point comports with Bayle's position that restricting the church's authority to *questions de droit* eliminates its authority altogether.

On the other hand, Arnauld did not claim scepticism on the *question de fait* concerning the more important set of Five Propositions, although he was respectfully silent on the matter. On the contrary, he must have believed, or have been committed to believing, that the Five Propositions condemned by the Pope are *not* to be found in Jansenius – otherwise he would have accepted the condemnations without any *fait–droit* distinction. This is on the assumption, of course, that Arnauld was sincere in his acceptance of church infallibility – an assumption open to question. In any case, the point of relevance with respect to scepticism is that the denial of church infallibility concerning a question does not mean that it cannot be answered at all. The upshot may be that infallibility takes on a hypothetical character: if the church says 'P' and means P by 'P,' then P. That the questions whether the church says 'P,' and whether it means P by 'P,' are *questions de fait* does not upset the infallibility of its pronouncement that P. Still, this concession may mean only that, when the church speaks, what it says is true, not that we thereby are ever in a position to know what is true. That is, the church's infallibility is by itself not sufficient to overcome doubt. Arnauld's own responses to the church's pronouncements on questions of grace show that an answer to the *question de fait* making them sufficient would never be forthcoming.

III

Arnauld's response to the church's attempted condemnation of Jansenius's doctrine is, apart from his respectful silence, essentially the following: 'I agree that what you say is true, indeed must be true; but I don't agree with what you say you mean.' However much they may question Arnauld's motivation, commentators have been remarkably uncritical in taking his statement at face value as embodying a transparently valid distinction. Yet, if it is not to be dismmissed as a mere anticipation of Lewis Carroll's Humpty Dumpty who made words mean whatever he wanted them to, the statement ought at least to be examined on its own terms for its philosophical significance.

To begin, then, Arnauld's response to Bayle is confusing, for the *fait–droit* distinction ought to apply to all five propositions that Arnauld attributes to Malebranche, and not to just three of them. (Refer again to note 15 for these five propositions, although what the propositions were is not crucial to the argument here.) That is, of *each* of the propositions we should be able to ask whether it is to be found in Malebranche, i.e., whether Arnauld and Malebranche meant the same thing by the same words – in short, whether Arnauld has understood Malebranche (*question de fait*); and second, we should be able to ask of *each* of the propositions whether in the sense intended by Arnauld it is true (*question de droit*). The only way to separate three of the propositions (the second, fourth, and fifth propositions) as independent of the *question de fait* would be to make their attribution to Malebranche irrelevant. But this would be paradoxical, since Bayle did not undertake to defend *whatever* Malebranche said; that is, he was not in a position like the Catholic's position vis-à-vis the church, for the Catholic had to defend propositions simply because they were uttered by the church. Rather, he was defending a proposition that was *incidentally* held by Malebranche. So perhaps Arnauld's point, the most charitable interpretation of his remark, is that in three of the propositions he was making points independently of what Malebranche may have held. A charitable interpretation of what he thought he was doing with respect to the other two then becomes problematic, however. For it seems that he was refuting *whatever* Malebranche said, an impression not without support from elsewhere in his exchange with the Oratorian.[16]

To call the question whether a certain proposition is to be found in a given book a *question de fait* is, moreover, highly misleading. Consider Charles Dillon 'Casey' Stengle, who used to entertain sportswriters with stories involving unusual and often preposterous facts from baseball history. To quell the dismay greeting his stories, his stock response was: 'Ya could look it up!' The *question de fait* concerning Jansenism is not a Casey Stengle question, since the *Augustinus* of Jansenius was obviously available to everyone for quotation. The real question that Arnauld tried to separate from the faith is what any quoted proposition might *mean*. By contrast, the *question de droit* concerned its truth, to which the church had infallible access in so far as it concerned faith or morals. Although this was not the settled significance of the distinction, which tended to be used in a bewildering variety of ways too numerous to be investigated here, Arnauld's argument focused on the distinction in just these terms, i.e., *fait* – meaning; *droit* – truth.

IV

Recall the church's condemnation of the famous Five Propositions, which assert, very roughly, that the grace merited by Christ is necessary and sufficient for salvation. Arnauld claimed repeatedly, in so many words or in effect, that he 'sincerely condemned the five condemned propositions, in whatever book they may be found, without exception.'[17] If what Arnauld said was true, did he condemn Jansenius's book or any part of it? He did so if the Five Propositions are in Jansenius's book; but he did not condemn Jansenius's book or any part of it under that description, because he restricted his condemnation to a *question de droit*, and he took it to be a *question de fait* whether the Five Propositions were in Jansenius's book. Did Arnauld think that as a matter of fact the Five Propositions were in Jansenius's book? This is the question on which Arnauld professed a respectful silence, but, for the reason given above, it is hard to believe that he did not, although the question was a matter of dispute at Port-Royal. Certainly, the church must have thought that Arnauld, by abstaining on the *question de fait*, agreed that the propositions were in Jansenius, but did not take them to be heretical the way the church did. For Arnauld failed to explain what he condemned as a Catholic, and what by contrast was in Jansenius. Nor could he, in practical terms, have done so. For assuming that Jansenius is clear, at least to smart theologians, and that Arnauld is a smart theologian, anything relevance to the disputed questions of grace that he found in Jansenius is the same as what the smart Catholic theologians would have found and would have been condemned by the church. More mischievously, or perhaps more realistically, even if Jansenius is not clear, any proposition on grace in Jansenius as interpreted by Arnauld would have been condemned. Arnauld's refusal to recognize this while insisting on remaining in the church raises a question repeatedly raised in the period, *viz.* the question of the sincerity of Arnauld's intentions with respect to Catholic orthodoxy.

If it is hard to believe that Arnauld did not think that the Five Propositions were in Jansenius, it is also hard to believe that the church condemned a view that it erroneously thought was in Jansenius. If the church erred by indirectly condemning Augustine when it condemned the *Augustinus* of Jansenius, at least the church knew it was directly condemning Jansenius. Such was the view of at least some members of the Jansenist camp, who, in abandoning Arnauld's distinction, not only raised questions about Arnauld's sincerity, but also precipitated deep philosophical questions. For in response, Arnauld brought in a host of issues from the philosophy of language and of mind.

The most important member of Port-Royal to throw in the towel on the *fait–droit* distinction was Pascal, who finally decided that it was of no use in justifying the signing the famous formulary whereby one accepted condemnation of the Five Propositions. He made his case in the *Ecrit sur la signature*, published for the first time by Brunschvig in 1914. Even if Pascal did as much as anyone to propagate the *fait–droit* distinction by introducing it right at the outset of his first *Provincial Letter*, his own, unyielding position on the issue of grace is clear at the outset of this *Ecrit*: 'the truth of the matter is that there is no difference between condemning the doctrine of Jansenius on the Five Propositions and condemning efficacious grace, St. Augustine, [and] St. Paul.'[18] He is also clear that *even given* the *fait–droit* distinction, the Pope and bishops have condemned that common position. For 'they claim that it is a point of *droit* and of faith to say that the Five Propositions are heretical in the sense of Jansenius; and Alexander VII has declared in his constitution that to be in the the faith, one must say that the words "in the sense of Jansenius" express only the heretical sense of the propositions, and that it is a fact that conveys a *droit* [*un fait qui emporte un droit*] and comprises an important part of the profession of faith, as would be the case in saying that the sense of Calvin on the Eucharist is heretical, which is certainly a point of faith.'[19] For Pascal, the intention of the Pope and bishops is clearly to promulgate as a matter of faith the condemnation of what was in Jansenius, and not just propositions described as being in Jansenius, so that the ambiguity introduced at this point by reservations in signing the formulary is mischievous (*méchant*). Those who sign in this way take a path that is 'abominable before God and contemptible before men.'[20]

Arnauld responded to Pascal with a work called *The true meaning of the words 'the sense of Jansenius' in the Constitution of Pope Alexander VII*. This work was to respond to the fundamental issue, for even Innocent X had earlier made clear that by condemning the Five Propositions he was condemning, or intending to condemn, the doctrine of Jansenius.[21] Arnauld begins his response in typically engaging fashion, accusing Pascal of 'pure sophisms' and claiming that only inattention will prevent 'reasonable readers' from being persuaded of his case to this effect. The case is strung out over eleven 'maxims,' some of which are premises and others conclusions that become further premises. The putative logical structure is inverted since only at the end are the two maxims revealed that are said to serve as a foundation for all the rest, and the argument is generally obscure. Fortunately, help in understanding it is to be had from the Port-Royal *Logic*, which was published the year following the problematic signings.[22]

According to Arnauld, '*the sense of Jansenius*, in the natural and proper sense of those words [*sic*],' is too general and must be *determined*, because everyone agrees that not everything meant by Jansenius is heretical, and only, at most, the Five Propositions' (Maxims 1–3). *Determination* is one of the two kinds of predication, or what the *Logic* calls addition, whereby complex terms are produced. Addition is expressed by a subordinate clause introduced by a relative pronoun. Determination is the restrictive sense and sometimes makes a general word individual; for example, 'the man who is now Pope' specified Alexander VII in 1622. This determination can be either expressed, as in this example, or only understood, as when 'the king' is assumed to refer to the current king of France, *viz*. Louis XIV. An expression of this sort can pick out an individual and yet be equivocal because of disagreement about which individual it is – for example, 'the greatest geometer in Paris,' or 'the doctrine of an author on a given subject.' (The other kind of addition, expressed by the unrestrictive sense of the relative pronoun, is called *explication*, which 'only unfolds what is contained in the comprehension of the idea of the first term, or at least what belongs to it as one of its accidents provided that it belongs to it generally and in its full extension'; for example, 'man, who is rational' or 'man, who is bi-ped.')[23] The distinction between determination and explication is important, as Jill Buroker has shown, for distinguishing in the *Logic* between judgments and merely complex ideas.[24] Here its significance is that, for Arnauld, the expression 'the sense of Jansenius' does not pick out an individual sense, at least not the sense of Jansenius. Even if it did pick out exactly one sense, the expression might still be equivocal and open to debate because there might yet be debate as to what that sense is.

The same point can be made another way. A conclusion drawn by Arnauld's response to Pascal is that the Pope's pronouncement supposedly condemning Jansenius contains an 'incidental proposition,' which is that the condemned doctrine is in Jansenius, and which is a *question de fait*. The subject of the condemnation is the doctrine, and this is a *question de droit*. The *Logic* also discusses incidental propositions, and divides them according to the species of addition.[25] In an obviously significant example, one of each kind is to be found in the following proposition: the doctrine that places the sovereign good in bodily pleasure, which was taught by Lucretius, is unworthy of a philosopher. 'Placing the sovereign good in bodily pleasure' determines the doctrine, but being taught by Lucretius does not. The test is substitution for the relative pronoun. We cannot say, 'the doctrine that was taught by Lucretius places the sovereign good in bodily pleasure,' for Lucretius taught other doctrines as well. On the other hand, we can say, 'the doctrine which places the sovereign good in bodily pleasure was taught by Lucretius,' for Lucretius taught that whole doctrine. (The *Logic* also notes that to decide which sense is being employed, we often need to take into account the speaker's sense or intention as judged from circumstances, e.g., in using 'the king' to refer to Louis XIV. This requirement, of course, introduces another element *de fait*.) The conclusion, again of obvious significance, is that the assertion 'the doctrine of Lucretius concerning the good is false' contains an incidental proposition, which determines what that doctrine is.[26]

Perhaps the simplest way to put the problem is in terms of a dilemma. An incidental proposition is required in the statement of condemnation; but either (more plausibly) the incidental proposition is determinative, in which case the truth of the condemnation depends on a matter of fact, or (less plausibly) the incidental proposition is explicative, in which case the condemnation applies to *whatever* was said. Thus, Jansenius stands condemned either only factually, i.e., fallibly, or by definition, i.e., vacuously. Moreover, the problem is one that, given the *fait–droit* distinction, emerges with respect to the overthrow of Jansenius's proposition on the basis of papal infallibility, but more generally with respect to the overthrow of any proposition by appeal to a cognitive norm, e.g. Lucretius's propositions on the basis of, say, clarity and distinctness.

V

In the reply to Pascal, Arnauld says that the statement *de fait* implicitly expressed in certain statements *de droit* is easily overlooked, as in the assertion that the doctrine of Arius is heretical. But this oversight is attributable to general agreement as a matter of fact on what that doctrine was (the kind of agreement that Pascal thought there was on Jansenius's doctrine). Arnauld does not quite say so explicitly, but it appears that no statement *de droit* can ever be expressed alone and, as such, without any statement *de fait*. In principle, the determinateness of a stated doctrine can always be questioned by asking, what does it mean? And this question can always be repeated, however many incidental propositions are supplied in answer to it. The effect of Arnauld's distinction is, if not to silence authority, at least to make it inaudible as such. The dilemma that Arnauld precipitates is clear: *droit* is, although distinguishable from *fait*, inseparable from *fait*; thus, either papal pronouncements are infallible with respect to at least some matters *de fait* or not at all. This predicament, of course, is what led the Jesuits to argue in 1661 that the Pope is infallible on *questions de fait*. For Bayle, of course, this is not a predicament at all. He rejects papal infallibility of any sort, and, moreover, famously accepts the wider scepticism to which a general version of Arnauld's distinction might lead.[27]

Notes

I am grateful, once again, to R.A. Watson for many useful comments on an earlier version of this essay.

1 *Réponse aux questions d'un provinciale*, in *Oeuvres diverses* (The Hague, 1737), I, 446.
2 *Question de fait* might be unproblematically translated as 'question of fact'; but the translation of *question de droit* depends on philosophical issues it is the purpose here to explore. Both expressions will therefore be left untranslated.
3 'Jansensism and the *Crise Pyrrhonienne*,' *Journal of the History of Ideas* 38 (1977), 297–306.
4 The papal bull itself might have suggested the distinction to Port-Royal, for it comdemns the first four propositions as heretical, the last merely as false. For the argument here, precisely what the Five Propositions were does not matter; suffice it to say that they amount to the claim that the grace merited by Christ is necessary and sufficient for salvation.
5 *Assertiones Catholicae de Incarnatione contra saeculorum omnium ab incarnato Verbo praecipuas haereses.* Quoted by Arnauld, *La Nouvelle hérésie des Jésuites, ...* (1662), *OA* 21, 515.
6 *Les Imaginaires, ou Lettres sur l'hérésie imaginaire* (s.l.n.d.) 2nd letter (March 1664) written under the pseudonym 'Le Sieur de Damvilliers.' The letter was important enough to be translated into English along with two others by Nicole, Arnauld's *Nouvelle hérésie*, and other documents, by John Evelyn: *Mysterion ... that is, another part of the mystery of Jesuitism, ...* (London, 1664), 108.
7 Theophilus Gale, *The True Idea of Jansenism, Both Historic and Dogmatic* (London, 1669), 161.
8 *The History of Scepticism from Erasmus to Descartes* (New York: Harper Torchbooks 1968; 1st ed. 1964), 13.
9 August 1685, Art. iii; *OA* 1, 346–9.

10 *OA* 1, 348. Here, rarely, Bayle confuses the truth of a view with its usefulness.
11 Steven Nadler, *Arnauld and the Cartesian Philosophy of Ideas* (Princeton, NJ: Princeton University Press 1989), 176–8.
12 *Avis à l'auteur des Nouvelles de la République des Lettres* (Delf [*sic*], 1685); in *OA* 40, 1–9.
13 Ibid., 3.
14 Ibid., 4.
15 Ibid., 5. Recall that Jansenism was thought to be condemned when the famous Five Propositions were condemned. (See note 4, above.) That there should have been exactly five propositions in Malebranche cannot have been anything but sarcasm on Arnauld's part. In any case, these five propositions are as follows: (1) Those who enjoy pleasures of the senses are happy in so far as, and to the extent that, they enjoy them. (2) They none the less do not make us permanently happy. (3) Although they make us happy, they must be avoided for several reasons. (4) They must not lead us to love bodies, because bodies are not their real, but only occasional cause, God being their real cause. (5) Pleasure is imprinted in the soul in order that it love the cause making it happy, i.e., God. *Réflexions sur le système de la nature et de la grace* (Cologne 1685), in *OA* 39, 362. Arnauld says that he finds great difficulties in all these propositions; the second, fourth, and fifth are the questions that are independent of the *question de fait*.
16 Quite apart from Arnauld's general belligerence and readiness to attack Malebranche, which is a moral or at least psychological issue, there is surely a logical, or epistemological issue here. If the tacit assumption is that a proposition is false in so far as it is held by Malebranche, if a Malebranchean proposition is in this sense false by definition, argument against (or for) it is vacuous. See below.
17 *Seconde lettre*, in *OA* 19, 455.
18 Pascal, *Oeuvres*, L. Brunschvig, P. Boutroux, and F. Gazier, eds. (Paris: Hachette 1914), 171.
19 Ibid., 172.
20 Ibid., 173, 175.
21 For an *entrée* to this issue, see Louis Cognet, *Le Jansènisme* (Paris: Presses Universitaires de France 1968), 65.
22 *Privilège*, 1 April 1662; publication, 6 July 1662. Attention is drawn to the connection by the editors of Pascal, *Oeuvres*; see vol. 10, 221–28.
23 *Logic*, Part I, ch. 7.
24 Jill Vance Buroker, 'Judgment and Predication in the *Port-Royal Logic*,' in *The Great Arnauld and Some of His Philosophical Correspondents*, E.J. Kremer, ed. (Toronto: University of Toronto Press 1994).

25 *Logic*, Part II, ch. 4. Thus calling them incidental is perhaps misleading because the kind is anything but incidental.

26 Roughly, the unrestrictive incidental proposition is a strict proposition involving judgment; it asserts the containment of the subject's extension by the predicate's extension. The restrictive incidental proposition expresses a complex idea and involves only conception; it asserts that the predicate's comprehension, or intention, is compatible with that of the subject. I am grateful to Jill Vance Buroker for discussion on this topic.

27 This is not to say, however, that Bayle has no way of going beyond this stultifying scepticism.

5

The Status of the Eternal Truths in the Philosophy of Antoine Arnauld

ALOYSE-RAYMOND NDIAYE

The philosophy of Antoine Arnauld has been described as 'Cartesianism without the creation of the eternal truths.'[1] In Robinet's words, 'Arnauld presents a tranquil Cartesianism that is not troubled about the eternal truths.'[2] In the abundant, essentially polemical work of the Augustinian doctor, written in a troubled period and unfavourable circumstances, we find no text sufficiently explicit, clear, and precise to determine his position on the Cartesian doctrine of the creation of the eternal truths. But it is hard to believe that he was indifferent and without reaction to this important metaphysical question, while his fellow theologians declared themselves for or against the Cartesian position. The fact that the philosophers of Port-Royal, even the Cartesians among them, were not of one mind on all questions, does not explain Arnauld's silence on this point. The rule of the Port-Royalists was to take an interest in philosophy only to the extent that it has implications for theology. Arnauld himself took part in a long polemic against Malebranche only because he was persuaded that the Oratorian's theological errors regarding grace were owing to his philosophy of ideas and his position that we see the ideas in God. The theological implications of the Cartesian doctrine of the creation of the eternal truths were too obvious not to draw a reaction from Arnauld.

I

We will approach Arnauld's position by considering whether he was aware of the objections that his contemporaries, especially Malebranche and Leibniz, raised against Descartes. But first we should review the Cartesian doctrine. In reply to a question posed by Mersenne, Descartes claims that the truths of mathematics are created: 'The truths of mathematics that you call eternal, like all the rest of God's creatures, have been established by Him and depend entirely on Him.'[3] Thus the eternal truths are assigned the status of creatures. They are not independent. They are created. Later, in his correspondence with Mersenne, Descartes returns to the question. In a letter of 6 May 1630, he replies to a theological difficulty raised by Mersenne: 'What you say about the production of the Word is not, it seems to me, contrary to what I say; but I do not want to meddle in theology. I am indeed afraid that you will judge my philosophy too impoverished to include an opinion on such lofty matters.'[4] To appreciate the difficulty, one must know that the creation of the eternal truths contradicts the doctrine of the 'production' of the Word. For the theologians, the eternal truths have their identity in the Word. Given this theological position, anyone who said that the eternal truths had the same status as creatures would risk reducing the Word to the status of a creature. Descartes's doctrine suggests that God could produce the Word in the same way as any other creatures. To avoid contradicting the traditional theological teaching in this way, Descartes would need to distinguish, to separate the created eternal truths from the eternal, uncreated Word. Otherwise, to assume that the eternal truths are created would be to assume that the Word who contains them is himself created, and that is unacceptable. The Word is consubstantial and co-eternal with God. Hence, to say that God creates the eternal truths would be to say that God gives being to his own essence – hence, that God is possible – and that is absurd. To the question of his illustrious correspondent, in *quo genere causae Deus disposuit aeternal veritates*, Descartes replies in his letter of 27 May 1630: 'As the same sort of cause whereby he created all things, that is to say as an efficient and total cause.'[5] We will return to this reply later.

Was Arnauld aware of the content of these letters when Mersenne sent him the manuscript of the *Meditations*, not yet published, and engaged him to give his opinion of the work in writing? We know that he took pleasure in reading the *Meditations*, and yet produced the critical comments which constitute the *Fourth Objections*, to be published at the same time as the *Meditations* themselves. In the letter that accompanied the *Objections*, Arnauld gave this testimony to Mersenne about his relations with Descartes: 'You know in what esteem I have long held his person and the importance I attach to his mind and his views.' It is obvious that the relations between the two famous philosophers did not begin with the *Meditations* and the *Fourth Objections*. In 1637, Descartes's first essays had been published and Arnauld had read them. But what captures Arnauld's attention in 1640 is the Augustinian tone of the *Meditations*: 'The first thing I find worth noting is that Descartes establishes as the foundation and first principle of his entire philosophy the same thing that was taken as the basis and support of philosophy by St. Augustine, a person of great intellect and noteworthy doctrine not only in theology but also in human philosophy.'[6] Arnauld immediately saw the likeness of Descartes's *cogito* to certain texts of St Augustine. In the *Fourth Objections*, he cites the text of *On Free Will*. But later he will cite the texts of the *De Trinitate* more often and at greater length. Indeed, he is persuaded that the two authors have something in common. Descartes's purpose agrees with that of St Augustine. Both want to prove the existence of God and the immortality of the soul. Indeed, it seems that Arnauld was attracted to Descartes's philosophy at least in part because of the Augustinian spirituality that was very clearly affirmed in the *Meditations*.

But to return to our problem, in 1630 Mersenne drew Descartes out on the question of whether the eternal truths are created or independent, and in 1640 Arnauld proclaimed publicly in his *Objections* that Descartes's philosophy deserved the attention of a theologian. Was he at that time ignorant of the discussion between Mersenne and Descartes and about what was at stake in the debate between them? It should be mentioned that Mersenne's letters were published by Clerselier in 1657 and 1659. Some years later, Leibniz, in his correspondence with Arnauld, tried in vain to elicit his opinion on the question. As for Malebranche, he did not hesitate to give a public and forceful critique of the Cartesian doctrine on the origin of the eternal truths, a doctrine that he thought ruined science, morality, and religion. But the two adversaries of the Cartesian doctrine, Leibniz and Malebranche, did not get Arnauld to take a public position.

II

It was especially Leibniz, more than Malebranche, who tried to draw Arnauld out. Let us consider the matter more closely. Leibniz distinguishes two sorts of necessary truths: First there are those that can be called eternal, such as the truths of geometry, arithmetic, and logic. Their necessity is absolute and their negations imply a contradiction and hence are logically impossible. On the other hand, there are contingent truths, whose negations do not imply a contradiction, and hence are possible. These are the truths of fact, the truths of experience, the laws of nature, and the truths of history. Their necessity, in contrast with the necessity of the eternal truths, is hypothetical, because they depend on the free decrees of God. They are founded on God's will, whereas the eternal truths are based on God's understanding. Two important Leibnizian principles are connected with this distinction, the principle of reason and the principle of contradiction. The principle of contradiction determines only the possibilities.

It does not provide a sufficient reason for the existence of anything. The reason for existence is not provided by logical necessity. It goes back to what regulates the divine choice. The principle of contradiction is the law of essences or of possibilities, that is, of the eternal truths contained in the divine understanding: 'The understanding of God is the region of the eternal truths.'[7]

Malebranche adopts the same classification of necessary truths. In the *Recherche de la vérité*, he distinguishes two sorts of truths, necessary truths and contingent truths: 'There are two sorts of truths; one sort is necessary and the other contingent. I call necessary those truths that are immutable by their nature, or that have been fixed by the will of God, which is not subject to change. All other truths are contingent.'[8] Thus, for Malebranche, there are two sorts of necessary truths, just as for Leibniz, truths necessary by their nature, which are called eternal, and truths necessary because they have been established by God. The first are uncreated; the second are created and depend on God's immutable will. The eternal truths are in the Word, and it is there that we see them. They include truths of mathematics and truths of morality, the former constituted by relations of quantity, the latter by relations of perfection. But when we consider the status of the necessary truths that depend on divine decrees, we see that they have a certain relation to reason. For Malebranche the divine decrees are necessary because they are the work of the Eternal Reason. God's volitions and actions are guided by Wisdom. God's choice of general laws is a function of the end God seeks in his creation. When he chooses the general laws, he knows that he will never want to revoke them. Consequently, from God's point of view, the general laws are just as eternal and necessary as the truths of mathematics. The laws are not the result of chance, but rather rest on the very Wisdom of God, which ensures their intelligibility, their immutability, and their *a priority*. So the relations that the physicist discovers among things are the same as exist among their ideas and are contemplated by God before the creation of the world. His knowledge of them is *a priori*, that is to say, mathematical. From the point of view of God, the laws of physics are like the truths of mathematics. In both cases, necessity and immutability are guaranteed by the Wisdom on which the truths are founded.

Leibniz's position is the same. Contingent truths depend on the principle of sufficient reason. They express existence and reality. Although contingent, they do not lack a reason. Thus there is a reason for the choice by which God preferred this world and its laws to an infinity of other possible worlds. But that there is a reason means that the predicate is contained in the subject. To give a reason for the existence of our universe and its laws is to show that the contingent truths can be known *a priori*. Does this not reduce the principle of sufficient reason to the principle of identity? Since every reason can be reduced to identity, that is, to the inherence of the predicate in the subject, we can no longer oppose the principle of sufficient reason to the principle of contradiction, of identity, the foundation of contingent existence to that of essences. So, just as for Malebranche, the truths of physics are like the truths of mathematics. But it remains the case that contingent truths are known by us only *a posteriori*, that is, by experience. Under what conditions could they be known *a priori*? They could be known in that way by one who knew the reasons for which God preferred our universe to all other possible universes. Our universe is that which is 'the most prefect, that is, which is at once simplest in hypotheses and richest in phenomena.'[9] But the determination of this maximum, defined by a divine mathematics, constitutes the notion or essence of the most perfect universe, the one actualized by the will of God, and everything that happens in it is contained in its notion as a predicate in a subject. Anyone to whom this notion is distinctly present can have *a priori* knowledge of all these events; hence, for such a person the corresponding propositions would be demonstrable, reducible to identities. But Leibniz recognizes that this notion can be distinctly grasped only by God, for its determination requires an infinite calculus not available to human understanding.

It is clear that the approaches of Malebranche and Leibniz converge: the truths created by God are based on reason and in this way they are assured a sort of mathematical necessity. But this transformation of the truths of physics into truths of mathematics, knowable *a priori*, presupposes that God's understanding is distinct from his will, and that his will is subordinate to his understanding. Both authors establish a hierarchy among the diving attributes, although Malebranche introduces an almost real distinction among the divine perfections, while Leibniz holds only for a distinction of reason. On all these points Malebranche and Leibniz are opposed to Descartes. Their critique of the Cartesian doctrine of the eternal truths was a logical consequence of the principles of their own philosophies. But Leibniz, unlike Malebranche, wanted to have Arnauld on his side. He does not despair of converting Arnauld to his own view. On the occasion of their correspondence *à propos* Article 13 of the summary of the *Discours de métaphysique*, which deals with the consequences of Leibniz's conception of substance for freedom, Leibniz tries to draw Arnauld out: 'I will say a word about the reason for the difference between the notions of species and those of individual substances, in relation to the divine will rather than in relation to simple understanding. The notions of species do not depend on divine decrees (despite what the Cartesians say, which does not seem to be of concern even to you on this point).'[10] Leibniz reaffirms his own conception of the distinction between kinds of necessary truth, but he also points out that his correspondent, in the preceding letter, was not concerned about the Cartesian view that makes all necessary truths depend on a single act of God's will. In a first draft of his letter, Leibniz is more explicit: 'I notice that Arnauld has forgotten, or at least is not concerned about, the opinion of the Cartesians, who hold that God, by his will, establishes the eternal truths, like those regarding the properties of a sphere; but since I do not share their opinion any more than Arnauld ...'[11] If Leibniz is claiming that his illustrious correspondent is on his side against the Cartesians, Arnauld, for his part, refuses to confirm that he is at one with Leibniz against the Cartesians. Why this reserve? In his reply of 28 September 1686, Arnauld avoids the question. He begins by expressing his satisfaction with Leibniz's explanations: 'I am satisfied with the way in which you explain the point that shocked me about the notion of an individual nature.' Next he approaches the problem under discussion and asserts that the difficulty remains:

> There remains for me only the difficulty about the possibility of things and about that way of conceiving God as having chosen the universe he created rather than any of an infinity of other possible universes that he saw at the same time and that he did not will to create. But since that does not bear properly on the notion of an individual nature and since I would have to wander too far in order to explain what I think about it, or rather to explain what I must reject in the thoughts of others as being unworthy of God, it is just as well, Sir, that I say nothing about it.[12]

The disagreement with Leibniz remains. Arnauld does not share his conception of the possible. He refuses to say why, for fear of having to 'wander' too far and to expose publicly what he 'must reject in the thoughts of others.' He says that the question does not leave him indifferent. He has an opinion on the matter. As we have seen, Leibniz does not succeed in separating Arnauld from Descartes. But neither does he obtain from Arnauld a statement of agreement with the Cartesian position.

The results are no different in the case of Malebranche. Even in the heat of the polemic, Arnauld does not abandon his attitude of reserve. The violence of Malebranche's criticisms of the Cartesian doctrine do not deflect Arnauld from his objective, which is to show that the Oratorian is mistaken when he claims that his philosophy is in agreement with the Augustinian doctrine. From Malebranche's point of view, the free creation of the eternal truths compromises science, religion, and morals. All truths are infected by the contingency and the arbitrariness of God's free choice. The doctrine has the deeper implication that the truth of our science does not participate in the truth, because our reason is not identical with the Reason of God. 'Thus everything is overturned,' writes Malebranche,

> no longer any science, any morality, any undeniable proof of religion. This consequence is clear to anyone who follows out the false principle that God produces all

order and truth by an extremely free will. And this is what made Descartes conclude that God could have brought it about that 2 times 4 not make 8 and that the three angles of a triangle not be equal to two right angles, namely his claim that there is no order, no law, no reason of goodness or truth that does not depend on God, and that from all eternity God, as the sovereign legislator, ordained and established the eternal truths.[13]

According to Malebranche, the notion of truth loses all sense. For what our understanding perceives as true depends essentially on its own structure, constituted by its innate ideas, which could have been different if God had so willed. In other words, our science could have been different if God had created us with different ideas or essences. Thus our science might not be true science, because it might not coincide with God's science. Hence, Malebranche's violent reaction against the doctrine of the creation of eternal truths, which he does not separate from the doctrine of innate ideas. Creationism and innatism are intimately connected. They lead to scepticism. Malebranche turns for inspiration to Augustine, and finds the doctrine of the Vision in God. Ideas and truths are no longer effects of God's will. They have their source and their foundation in God's Wisdom, the eternal Word.

In his controversy with Malebranche, Arnauld avoids a direct confrontation with Descartes. He does not take a position on the thesis that Malebranche attacks. Rather he goes directly after the Oratorian's thesis. His aim is not to support the thesis of Descartes, about which he says not a word, but rather to show that Malebranche is opposed to Augustine. His tries to show his adversary that his concept of the Vision in God is not at the same as Augustine's. He avoids the confrontation between Malebranche and Descartes, into which the Oratorian tries to draw him, and substitutes a different debate, one in which he opposes Malebranche to St Augustine. According to St Augustine, the truths that we see in God are 'certain truths of morals the knowledge of which God impressed in the first man, and which original sin did not entirely efface from the souls of his children. These are the truths that St. Augustine often says we see in God.'[14] The truths we see in God are moral truths. Hence, St Augustine excludes mathematical truths. He distinguishes between the eternal truths, those which are properly divine and which reside in the essence of God, that is to say, the truths of morality, and the truths of mathematics. His disagreement with Malebranche is fundamental. Yet Arnauld will regret the fact that Augustine did not explain his position on the way in which we see truths in God.

Thus we see that neither Leibniz nor Malebranche succeeded in drawing Arnauld into a public debate about the Cartesian doctrine of the creation of the eternal truths. This silence on the part of one who had elsewhere forcefully defended Cartesian orthodoxy may cause surprise, in view of the fact that the partisans and adversaries of Descartes took clear positions on the value of the doctrine.[15] Nor was Arnauld unaware of these positions. He was perfectly well informed about the objections made to Descartes during his lifetime, and about the reservations of some of his own friends from Port-Royal about the free creation of the eternal truths. How, then, to explain the fact that the Augustinian doctor did not seem concerned about this debate? We need to go back to 1640, to the *Meditations*, and especially to the *Fourth Objections*.

III

In his *Objections*, Arnauld refers to the remarks directed against Descartes by Caterus, author of the *First Objections*, about Descartes's application of the principle of causality to God. In the *Third Meditation*, Descartes demonstrated the existence of God from the idea of God, considered with respect to its objective reality. This proof introduces a relation of causality between the idea of God in me and God existing outside of my thought as the origin of the idea. Following out this line of argument, Descartes attempts a second approach to God as the cause of me who has that idea. We must, he says, consider 'whether I myself, who has that idea of God, could exist if there were no God. And I ask, whence would I have my existence? Perhaps from myself, or from my parents or from some other causes ... But if I were independent of everything else and were myself the author of my being ... I would not lack any perfection.' The question barely formulated, Descartes responds by recognizing that I am obviously not the cause of myself. Hence, I depend on another cause about which we must inquire whether it 'derives its origin and its existence from itself, or from some other thing. For if it derives it from itself, it follows that it must be God.'[16]

In his *Objections*, Arnauld notes that the author of the *First Objections* had made the subtle remark that 'to be from itself' should not be taken 'positively' but 'negatively,' so that it means not to be from another. As a good Thomist, Caterus does not think that one can apply causality to God. According to St Thomas, God is self-subsistent being, *ens per se subsistens*, being without a cause. Descartes, in his reply to Arnauld, which I here summarize, maintains that to be from itself should not be taken 'negatively' but 'positively,' even with regard to the existence of God, in such a way that God does with respect to himself what an efficient cause does with respect to its effect. This notion of Descartes's seems to Arnauld to be 'a bit foolhardy and not to be correct.'[17] What he fears is that by applying the same principle of causality to God as to other things, we would end up lowering God to the level of a creature. To say that God is from himself positively is to admit that he gives himself a being he did not formerly have, in the same way as he gives being to other things. He concludes by noting that 'we can conceive that God exists from himself positively only because of the imperfection of our mind, which conceives God in the manner of created things.'

In support of his argument Arnauld uses an example from mathematics: 'We seek the efficient cause of a thing only on account of its existence and not its essence. For example when we look for the efficient cause of a triangle, we want to know what has brought it about that there is a triangle in the world, but it would be absurd to seek the efficient cause of the fact that a triangle has three angles equal to two right ones; and to one who seeks that, we would not respond well by giving an efficient cause. Rather we ought to reply only that such is the nature of a triangle.' Arnauld's position here is quite clear. The only cause required for the eternal truths, the truths of mathematics, is the efficient cause. But it is required in order to give a reason for their existence in the world. In other words, God is the only efficient cause of the presence in our mind of the truths of mathematics. He has placed them in us. They constitute the natural light. While he is the cause of their existence in our mind, he is not the efficient cause of what they are in themselves. 'To one who asks why the three angles of a triangle are equal to two right angles, we ought not reply by giving an efficient cause, but by saying, because such is the immutable and eternal nature of a triangle.'

This assertion is clearly contrary to what Descartes would have said. For Descartes, God is the efficient and total cause of the truths of mathematics, since he has created the eternal truths and has decided that the sum of the angles of a triangle equals two right angles. Arnauld, on the contrary, in the above text from the *Fourth Objections*, does not make the nature of the immutable and eternal truths of mathematics depend on the arbitrary will of God. He does not apply efficient causality to them considered with respect to their nature or essence. Arnauld's statement stands in contrast to Descartes's statement to Mersenne that God 'created all things as efficient and total cause, for it is certain that he is the author of the essence as well as the existence of creatures; but that essence is nothing other than the eternal truths.'[18] Clearly, Arnauld and Descartes do not agree on this point. Arnauld does not make the nature of the eternal truths depend on the efficient causality of God. He says the same thing about God as about the mathematical truths. 'If anyone ask why God exists, or why he does not cease to be, we must not seek, in God or outside God, an efficient cause or a quasi-efficient one (for I do not dispute here about the word, but about the thing). Rather we must say, with all reason, that God exists because such is the nature of the supremely perfect being.'[19] Thus the eternal and immutable truths of mathematics function like the divine essence. They are to be treated like God. With respect to their nature, they do not require an efficient cause. And with respect to their existence? They do not require an efficient cause in this respect either, except for their presence in our mind. And even in this case, we cannot say that they are created. We must rather say that they have been placed in us by God. This conclusion, inspired by Augustine, is not expounded by Arnauld in the *Fourth Objections*. There he is content to show that they do not require an efficient cause, hence that they are not created. They are not lowered to the level of creatures.

Nothing in the text of the *Fourth Objections* tells us that Arnauld knew about the discussion between Mersenne and Descartes regarding the creation of the eternal truths. But even if we cannot take his remarks about the application of efficient causality to God as a direct intervention in the debate, we can at least recognize the striking similarity of his arguments to those used by Mersenne against the production of the Word. Arnauld's fear that God will be lowered to the level of creatures if we apply the same principle of causality to him and to other things, is like Mersenne's fear with regard to the creation of eternal truths, assuming that these truths, as traditionally taught in theology, are one with the substance of the Word. Neither is it a mere coincidence that the example Arnauld chooses in order to argue against the Cartesian conception of *causa sui* is drawn from mathematics. The truths of mathematics do not function like created things. These truths do not exist; that is to say, they are not created outside of God. They are present in us, innately. But for Arnauld their being innate is not the same as their being created. He takes his inspiration from Augustinian illuminationism. Even if Arnauld has not directly confronted Descartes's doctrine on the creation of the eternal truths, the fact remains that he has a settled position on the question. He does not share Descartes's doctrine. Neither does he find it dangerous, once Descartes has given his guarantees to Mersenne, and a satisfactory response to Arnauld himself on the occasion of the *Fourth Objections*.

It may be asked how far Arnauld accepts the doctrine of his correspondent when he says that he is satisfied with Descartes's explanation of the void, given during their correspondence in 1648. Must we say that Arnauld also accepts the creation of the eternal truths, the keystone of the Cartesian position? The answer is not certain.

In conclusion, we have seen that Arnauld often gives the impression that he is ready to accept the confident explanations provided by his correspondents, as if he did not have his own personal philosophical position to defend. We have seen this in the case of both Descartes and Leibniz. But if we look more closely, it is Arnauld who sets the question and fixes the rules for these discussions, not his correspondents. They are put in the position of owing him explanations and clarifications. In his controversy with Malebranche, he concedes nothing, and he is the one who chooses the terrain for the discussion. On the question about the eternal truths, Arnauld does not follow Malebranche. Neither does he follow Leibniz or Descartes. If he does not side with Descartes, or, later on, with Leibniz, he does not for all that renounce his own convictions. He sticks to his own positions, while remaining open to discussion. If the failure of understanding between Arnauld and Malebranche was total, and their controversy aggressive, something that Arnauld found painful, we must recognize that it was the Oratorian who first lost his sense of moderation. Arnauld needs, indeed, to be reassured. He wants to be sure that the theses of his correspondents will not have consequences 'dangerous for weak minds.'[20] In his theological undertakings and his works on spirituality, Arnauld shows that was concerned about the salvation of souls. His preoccupation was pastoral. He thinks of the Christians whose conscience has been shaken by the crisis that is crossing the church and by the arguments that have been directed from all quarters against the faith. If he has devoted so much time to philosophy, and in particular to Cartesian philosophy, despite the resistance of his friends at Port-Royal, it is because he is persuaded that philosophy is useful to religion. What he always liked in Descartes was his submission to the church and his constant care not to meddle in theology, that is, in the theology that arises from Revelation. Because he recognized his incompetence in the area of theology, Descartes was assured of an ally of great authority in Antoine Arnauld.

Notes

1 Henri Gouhier, *Cartésianisme et augustinisme au XVII* siècle (Paris: Vrin 1978), 156.
2 André Robinet, in the preface to A.-R. Ndiaye, *La Philosophie d'Antoine Arnauld* (Paris: Vrin 1991), 8.
3 Descartes to Mersenne, 15 April 1630, in Alquie, 1, 259. Note that Descartes does not say that the eternal truths are created. Mersenne fears that such a position might follow from the formulae used by Descartes. Hence the difficulty he raises regarding the production of the Word. Regarding *Principles* I, no. 22, which Madame Rodis-Lewis takes to show that Descartes sets forth 'explicitly' the doctrine of the creation of eternal truths, Arnauld retains nothing of this passage except its Augustinian tone (see Ndiaye, *La Philosophie d'Antoine Arnauld*, 342).
4 Descartes to Mersenne, 6 May 1630, Alquié, 1, 265.
5 Descartes to Mersenne, 27 May 1630, Alquié, 1, 267.
6 Arnauld, *Fourth Objections*, Alquié, 2, 633.

7 Leibniz, *Monadology*, Article 43; to Arnauld, 4/14 July 1686.

8 Malebranche, *Recherche*, L I no. 2, *OC* 1, 63.

9 Leibniz, *Discours de métaphysique et correspondance avec Arnauld*, edited by Georges Le Roy (Paris: Vrin 1970), 115. Hereinafter 'Le Roy.'

10 Leibniz to Arnauld, 4/14 July 1686, Le Roy, 105.

11 Leibniz, Remark about Arnauld's letter, Le Roy, 133.

12 Arnauld to Leibniz, 28 September 1686, Le Roy, 133.

13 Malebranche, *Recherche*, ecl. 8, *OC* 3, 84.

14 Arnauld, *On True and False Ideas*, Ch. XIX, *OA* 38, 282.

15 Jean-Luc Marion presents all the texts on the creation of the eternal truths in *Sur la Théologie blanche de Descartes*, (Paris: PUF 1981), 270.

16 *Meditations*, III, Alquié, 2, 449.

17 Arnauld, *Fourth Objections*, Alquié, 2, 449.

18 Descartes to Mersenne, 27 May 1630, Alquié, 1, 267.

19 Arnauld, *Fourth Objections*, Alquié, 2, 651.

20 Ibid., Alquié, 2, 653.

6

Arnauld's Interpretation of Descartes as a Christian Philosopher

ELMAR J. KREMER

It is well known that Arnauld was an admirer and defender of Descartes's philosophy. Indeed, as Steven Nadler has said, 'Arnauld, of all the Port-Royalists of his generation, appears to be alone in his lifelong enthusiasm for Descartes.'[1] Nadler is here correcting a widely shared view that the Port-Royalists were, as a group, Cartesians. Indeed, Arnauld was criticized by others in the Port-Royal group on account of his willingness to defend Descartes. His nephew De Saci, together with whom Arnauld produced a translation of the Bible, was especially vigorous in his criticism.

But although Arnauld admired Descartes's philosophy and was prepared to defend it against the charge that it was heretical, he did not accept some of its most important principles, and cannot properly be said to be a disciple of Descartes. He considered himself a professional theologian rather than a philosopher, and his primary allegiance was to the Catholic theological tradition as he understood it. Hence, he was prepared to depart from Descartes whenever he thought it necessary to do so in order to maintain theological orthodoxy. For example, from the *Fourth Objections* on, he rejected the method of doubt, at least in part for theological reasons.[2] Again, although he shared much of Descartes's scorn for Aristotelian philosophy, his own late philosophy and theology are heavily influenced by St Thomas, and he did not hesitate to reject important Cartesian doctrines, including the doctrine on free will and on judgment as an act of will, in favour of Thomistic ones.[3]

My concern here is with Arnauld's defence of Descartes as a 'Christian philosopher.'[4] When Arnauld applies this phrase to Descartes, he means, not only that Descartes was a philosopher and a Christian, but that his philosophy was intended to be useful, and was indeed useful, to Christian theologians in their task of defending the faith. Arnauld thought that Descartes deserved to be called a Christian philosopher in part because of the way he supported the doctrine of human immortality by his argument for mind–body dualism. But he especially commended Descartes as a Christian philosopher because Descartes recognized it as a philosophical principle that 'whatever God has been pleased to reveal to us about himself or about the extraordinary effects of his omnipotence ought to take first place in our belief even though we cannot conceive [*concevoir*] it, for it is not strange that our mind, being finite, cannot comprehend [*comprendre*] what an infinite power is capable of.'[5] Arnauld was pleased that what he considered staples of the Christian tradition were upheld by the most brilliant thinker of his time. However, even while rejoicing in Descartes's support for these doctrines, he found it necessary to modify the Cartesian philosophy. I shall try to show, in particular, that Arnauld's interpretation of Descartes as a Christian philosopher led him to depart from Descartes's position on the nature of matter, on the relation of mind and body, and on divine omnipotence.

A Modification of Descartes's Position on the Nature of Matter

Descartes helped defend the doctrine of immortality, says Arnauld, by showing that the soul and the body are two totally distinct substances, in such a way that it is impossible that extension be a modification of the substance that thinks or that thought be a modification of extended substance.[6] Repeating a line of thought found in Descartes's Synopsis of the *Meditations*, Arnauld says from the Cartesian conclusion, together with a premise which any materialist will surely grant – that nothing that exists goes out of existence *in nihilo* – implies that it is unreasonable to claim that the soul dies with the body.

But the Cartesian distinction between mind and body presupposes the doctrine that the essence of matter is extension, and when the distinction is viewed as part of Christian philosophy, the problem arises that the Cartesian doctrine on the essence of matter contradicts authoritative church teaching on the Eucharist. The first of Arnauld's modifications of Descartes's philosophy mentioned above is a response to this problem. It emerges in his attempt to solve a difficulty he raised in his two letters to Descartes in 1648. But the letters of 1648 are the second occasion on which Arnauld expressed misgivings about the compatibility of the Cartesian view of matter with the doctrine of transubstantiation, and, before considering the precise objection he raised there, it will be helpful to summarize briefly the outcome of the first criticism, which was raised in the *Fourth Objections* of 1641.

In the concluding section of the *Fourth Objections* (AT 7, 214–18), Arnauld briefly indicates four 'points which may cause difficulty to theologians.' The fourth and last of these is, he says, 'likely to give the greatest offence ...' It is 'that according to the author's doctrines it seems that the church's teaching concerning the sacred mysteries of the Eucharist cannot remain completely intact.' He formulates the sacred doctrine as follows: 'We believe on faith that the substance of the bread is taken away from the bread of the Eucharist and only the accidents remain. These are extension, shape, colour, smell, taste and other qualities perceived by the senses.' He takes this to mean that such qualities, understood as qualities present in the bread, remain after the bread is consecrated, without inhering in any substance. The difficulty is that, according to Descartes, all these qualities are reduced to 'shape, extension and mobility,' and 'yet the author denies that these powers are intelligible apart from some substance for them to inhere in, and hence he holds that they cannot exist without such a substance.' In reply, Descartes says the 'accidents' of the bread which remain after the bread ceases to exist can be nothing other than 'the surface that is common to the individual particles of the bread and the bodies which surround them' (AT 7, 251). Arnauld, as we shall see, eventually accepted Descartes's reply, and indeed considered it a theological advance over the explanations previously available.

But this was not the end of Arnauld's worries about the compatibility of Descartes's philosophy with the doctrine of transubstantiation. He returns to the problem in the first of the letters of 1648, and raises a new difficulty: 'You assert that a quantified thing [*rem quantam*] is not distinct in any way from local extension [*locali extensione*]. Therefore I would like to know whether you have thought of some way to reconcile that doctrine with the catholic faith, which requires us to believe that the body of Christ is present on the altar without local extension, just as you succeeded in showing how the absence of a distinction between accident and substance could agree with the same mystery. Otherwise you easily see to what great danger you expose the most sacred of all things.'[7] This difficulty differs from that raised in the *Fourth Objections* in two ways. In the earlier text, the focus is on the continued presence of the 'accidents' of the bread and wine when the bread and wine no longer exist, while in the present text the focus is on the presence of the body of Christ. Second, the present text for the first time refers to the Cartesian doctrine that the essence of matter is *local* extension, which brings Descartes into conflict with the traditional teaching of the church that Christ is not present in the sacrament locally. Descartes had recognized this church doctrine in his *Replies to the Fourth Objections*,[8] but this is the first time Arnauld questioned its consistency with the Cartesian theory of matter. The doctrine does not mean that the body of Christ is not present *where*, or even, *in the place where*, the bread had previously been. Rather, it means that the body of Christ does not take on the *dimensions* of the place in which it is present; it does not fill or occupy the place where it is.

It is not surprising that this doctrine seemed to Arnauld incompatible with Descartes's position, for it implies that the body of Christ does not take on the dimensions of the bread when it comes to exist where the bread was. But Descartes holds that the essence of a body is an extension whereby it occupies a place. Thus, in a letter of 1641, he says that a body, unlike a mind, has a 'true extension, that is, an extension "whereby it occupies a place and excludes any other thing from it"' (AT 3, 435). It is hard to avoid the consequence that, according to Descartes, the body of Christ, as really present in the Eucharist, has the dimensions previously possessed by the bread. So it seems that Descartes's position is inconsistent with the teaching of the church.

Descartes declined to answer Arnauld's question, citing the Council of Trent, which 'did not wish to explain in what precise way the body of Christ is in the eucharist, and wrote *that it is there in a way of existing which we can scarcely express in words*' (AT 7, 251).[9] Now, in fact, Arnauld himself thought that inquiry into the precise way in which the body and blood of Jesus are present in the sacrament was ill advised, and cited the Council of Trent in support of this policy.[10] But he had not asked Descartes to explain precisely how the body of Christ is in the Eucharist. He had asked a different question, namely, how the church's doctrine that Christ's body is not present there locally is consistent with the Cartesian doctrine that a quantified thing is not distinct from local extension. He had reason, then, not to be satisfied with Descartes's response, and, as we shall see, in his second letter he presses Descartes for an answer.

Immediately after raising the above difficulty about the Eucharist in the first letter, Arnauld raises an objection to Descartes's doctrine that there cannot be a vacuum. It is clearly within God's power, he asserts, to cause a vacuum. For example, God could 'annihilate the wine in a wine jar without producing another body in its place ...' (*OA* 38, 73). He goes on to rebut the objection he expects from Descartes, namely, that if there were a vacuum, there would be properties such as length, breadth, depth, and divisibility in the vacuum, and hence the vacuum would be something and indeed would be a body.[11] Against this, Arnauld says that, after the wine was annihilated, no properties would be present in the vacuum. The distance between the sides of the jar, and other spatial features of the cavity (*concavitati*) in the jar, would remain, but these would be present in the jar, not in the vacuum.

Arnauld does not explicitly link this new objection with his difficulty about local extension and the Eucharist, but the two difficulties were almost certainly connected in his mind. There is some reason to think that in 1648 Arnauld held some version of the Scotist theory of transubstantiation, according to which the substance of the bread and wine are annihilated at the time of consecration, for this theory was influential in the seventeenth century. As Armogathe says, 'in the seventeenth century the accepted scholastic doctrine was of the Scotist type and thus includes the annihilation of the substance of the bread and wine.'[12] If Arnauld did hold the Scotist theory, then his example, that God can annihilate the wine in a container without producing another body in its place, would be exactly what he thought occurred in the Eucharist. For according to church doctrine, the wine and the bread are not replaced by a newly created body. The bread and wine are replaced, in a sense, by the body and blood of Christ. But according to the doctrine that Christ's body and blood are not present locally on the altar, they do not fill or occupy the place where the bread and wine had been.

In his first reply, Descartes does little more than refer Arnauld to the *Principles of Philosophy* regarding the impossibility of a vacuum. But Arnauld was not satisfied. In his second letter, he returns to the point: 'About the vacuum, I confess that I still cannot swallow the proposition that corporeal things are connected in such a way that God could not have created a world unless it was infinite, or annihilate a body without by that very fact being bound to create another of equal quantity, indeed without the space occupied by the annihilated body being understood to be a real and true body in the absence of any new creation' (*OA* 38, 83). He then adds that he would be very happy if Descartes would provide an answer to the question he had raised in the first letter about the Eucharist. But his repeated question was met by silence on Descartes's part.

Arnauld returned to the topic once again in 1680 in a document quoted above, in which he defends Descartes against the charge of heresy.[13] I shall interpret this text in the light of Descartes's refusal to respond to Arnauld's request in 1648. In 1680, Arnauld puts much emphasis on the proposition, taken from the Council of Trent, that the body and blood of Christ are present in the Eucharist in a way that we can scarcely understand, and takes this to indicate that it is unwise for theologians to attempt to explain the manner of this presence. But this should not encourage us to think that Arnauld was content with the reply he received from Descartes in 1648, about the way in which Christ is present in the sacrament. On the contrary, as I have pointed out, the fact that he raised the question again in his second letter suggests that he was dissatisfied with Descartes's response.

The charge of heresy against which Arnauld defended Descartes in 1680 was levelled by LeMoine, the dean of Vitré. LeMoine, as reported by Arnauld, took the position that, according to the teaching of the church, the body of Christ is present in the Eucharist in an indivisible point, without extension, and then pointed out that this teaching is inconsistent with the Cartesian position that the essence of body is extension. Arnauld begins his rebuttal by setting forth the Cartesian position on the nature of matter, not as given by Descartes, but rather by Malebranche, in Book III, Chapter 8, Section 2, of *The Search after Truth*.[14] Malebranche defines the essence of a thing as that property of the thing which we recognize to be primary in the thing, which is inseparable from it, and on which depend all its other properties. So, in order to find the essence of matter, we should consider all the properties found in matter and ask which of them satisfies all three criteria. He begins with inseparability from matter. Some properties of matter, such as hardness, softness, and motion, he says are known to be separable from matter because matter is sometimes found without them. There remain four properties, he says, which 'we conceive as inseparable from matter.' These are divisibility, shape, impenetrability, and extension. To discover which of these inseparable properties constitutes the essence of matter, he says, we should ask which are primary in matter and are such that all the other properties of matter depend on them. He asserts that only extension satisfies these further criteria.

After quoting Malebranche at length, Arnauld returns to LeMoine's position that, according to the teaching of the church, a body can exist without any extension in a mathematical point. He says that LeMoine arrives at his position by confusing extension with impenetrability. He agrees that, according to the teaching of the church, a body can exist without being impenetrable. But, in a surprising text, he says that this does not mean a body can exist without being extended, for 'as we have just seen in the passage I have reported [from Malebranche], only extension is the essence of matter, and impenetrability is merely one of its properties. But only the essence is inseparable from it; regarding the properties, nothing prevents our saying that they can be separated from it by the power of God, even if they naturally include the idea of shape and local motion [*lors même que naturellement elles renferment l'idée de figure & de mouvement local*] ... And consequently what the Fathers may have said about penetrability of bodies by the power of God does not imply that they should have said the same about their inextension, so to speak, that is to say, that they should have said that God could reduce them to an indivisible point' (*OA* 38, 105). Malebranche had said that all four of the properties – divisibility, shape, impenetrability, and extension – are inseparable from matter, but that only extension constitutes its essence. Arnauld accepts the latter point, that only extension is the essence of matter, but then introduces a distinction not found in Malebranche (or Descartes), between properties of matter that constitute its essence, and hence cannot be separated from it even by the power of God, and properties that, though they are inseparable from matter in the order of nature and can be said to be part of the nature of matter,[15] can be separated from matter miraculously by God's power. Consequently, on Arnauld's view, even if the body of Christ is present in the Eucharist without certain properties that are inseparable from extension in the order of nature, this does not imply that the body of Christ is present on the altar in a mathematical point without extension. Furthermore, Arnauld seems to say in the above text, the body of Christ, as really present on the altar, does have the property of extension, since extension cannot be separated from body, even by the power of God.

The reason why extension cannot be separated from body seems to be that a thing and its essence are identical. Arnauld puts the point explicitly in his late *Lettres au Père Malebranche*: 'Anyone who has accepted it as a principle that extension is the essence of matter, ought to say that extension and matter are the same thing.'[16] Thus the notion that the body of Christ is really present on the altar in an indivisible point, without being extended, contains a contradiction, and anything in whose concept there is a contradiction, according to Arnauld, is 'absolutely impossible.'[17] But there is no contradiction in saying that matter is really present on the altar without impenetrability, or without any other property distinct from its essence, and for this reason matter can be made to be present without any such a property by the power of God.

Arnauld mentions two miracles, cited by Augustine, in which impenetrability is removed from bodies: the birth of Jesus, which occurred 'without damage to the virginity of his mother,' and Jesus' entry into a room where his disciples were gathered despite the fact that the doors were closed. He also claims that the body of Christ, as present in the Eucharist, lacks the property of impenetrability. Thus he says that, when 'explaining the mystery philosophically,' we cannot avoid the consequences 'that God can bring it about that the same body exists in different places and that the parts of a body penetrate one another [*les parties du corps se pénetrent*]' (*OA* 38, 109). So, once again, the doctrine of the Eucharist seems to conflict with Descartes, who says, 'impenetrability belongs to the essence of extension ...'[18] The apparent conflict is removed by the distinction between extension itself, which, as the essence of matter, is absolutely inseparable from it, and the properties of matter, like impenetrability, which can be miraculously separated from it.

As the passage just quoted makes clear, impenetrability is not the only natural property of bodies that Arnauld thinks is separated from the body of Christ as it is present in the Eucharist. In other passages, he mentions the property of being enclosed in a place (*renfermé dans un lieu*) and the property of having a closed surface (*une surface bornée*).[19] So it looks as if Arnauld is concerned not only with LeMoine's attack, but with the difficulty he himself had raised some thirty-two years earlier, about the compatibility of the Cartesian theory with the doctrine that the body of Christ is present in the Eucharist without local extension. For if the body of Christ is present on the altar without having a closed surface, then Christ's body is not present there locally. The Cartesian theory of matter is brought into consistency with this revealed truth if the presence of matter without its properties, as opposed to its presence without its essence, does not involve a contradiction. The notion of a material thing present in a particular place without having any particular dimensions there is not easy to grapple with. Even within Descartes's theory, there is one example of a material thing which does not have any particular dimensions, namely, the material world, which, according to Descartes, is indefinitely large.[20] But this could not be true of any part of the material world in Descartes's account. Arnauld's position is closer to that of Aquinas, who says, 'The place in which the body of Christ exists [in the Eucharist] is not empty [*vacuus*]. But neither is it filled by the substance of the body of Christ, which is not there locally ...'[21]

A Modification of Descartes's Position on the Relation of Mind and Body

It is easy to see how this first modification of Descartes's philosophy arose when Arnauld took seriously Descartes's claim to be a Christian philosopher. After all, a philosophical position will not be of use to a theologian in defending the truths of the faith if it is inconsistent with one or more of those truths. The second modification, to which I now turn, is not so obviously related to the idea of a Christian philosophy. In this case, Arnauld modifies Descartes so as to bring him into line with the *philosophical* views of his two great predecessors in the Christian tradition, Augustine and Aquinas. The problem arises as follows: Despite his claim that all conscious activity, including sense perception, occurs in the body, Descartes thought he could say that sense perception is caused by material things.[22] But it was a deeply embedded principle in the philosophy of both Augustine and Aquinas that a material thing cannot produce an immaterial effect. Since the point at issue is largely, if not entirely, philosophical, Arnauld does not try to settle it by citing authorities. Rather, he produces the following argument: 'Since the motion of a body cannot have any other real effect but to move another body, it is clear that it cannot have any real effect on a spiritual soul, which is by its nature incapable of being pushed or moved about' (*OA* 38, 146).[23]

This departure from Descartes had two important consequences for Arnauld. First, like Malebranche, he had to deal with the question of how we could have cognition of material things despite the fact that our cognitions are not caused by material things. Second, when he tries to refute Malebranche's claim that we cannot have demonstrative knowledge of the existence of material things, he cannot rely on the sort of argument Descartes used in the *Sixth Meditation*, which depends on the possibility that the active faculty corresponding to our passive faculty of sense perceptions exists in material things. In the last chapter of *On True and False Ideas*, Arnauld provides eight arguments for the existence of an external world, but none of them relies on the notion that sense perception is *passive*. So it is clear that this was an important modification of Descartes's view. But does it tell us anything about Arnauld's idea of a Christian philosophy?

I think it does. As I mentioned above, Arnauld settles the question not by citing authorities, but by argument. None the less, he does cite authorities in favour of his position, in particular, Augustine.[24] This may at first glance seem to contradict the Augustinian *dictum* which Arnauld repeats on a number of occasions, that questions of faith are to be decided by authority, but those of philosophy by reason. However, he does not interpret this principle rigidly. Thus he says: 'Be very careful about the nature of the question you are debating, whether it is philosophical or theological. For if it is theological, it should be decided principally by authority; whereas, if it is philosophical, it should be decided principally by reason. I say, *principally*, because there is nothing to prevent one from citing authorities also in philosophical questions, but this should be done to throw light on them, not to decide them.'[25] The philosophical authorities he cites by far the most frequently, in addition to Descartes, are Augustine and Aquinas. In fact, throughout Arnauld's discussion of Cartesian philosophy, he shows himself eager to establish as much continuity as possible between Descartes and the preceding Christian philosophical and theological tradition. It would not be going too far to say that Arnauld questioned with special care the points on which Descartes departed from that tradition. Once he realized that Descartes had contradicted the view held by both Augustine and Aquinas, that a material thing cannot produce an immaterial effect, he considered the novel doctrine carefully, and found it wanting.

The first modification of Descartes's position showed that Arnauld could not accept as part of a Christian philosophy a doctrine which was inconsistent with authoritative church teaching. The second modification shows that, in his view, a Christian philosophy is more useful to theologians to the extent that it remains in continuity with the most important Christian philosophers of the past. Arnauld's reading of Descartes as a Christian philosopher is a reading of Descartes as someone in continuity with the medieval theological tradition.

Faith, Reason, and God's Omnipotence

I turn now to the second philosophical doctrine that Arnauld thought marked Descartes as a Christian philosopher. I shall refer to it as the principle of divine incomprehensibility (PDI): (a) We ought to believe everything that is revealed by God; and (b) the fact that we cannot understand how something revealed by God can come about should not deter us from believing it because a finite intelligence ought not expect to understand the nature or causal power of an infinite being.

Arnauld's formulation of PDI (quoted in the third paragraph of this essay) is quite close to that given by Descartes in *Principles of Philosophy*, I, nos 25 and 76. Where Arnauld says that what God reveals 'ought to take first place in our belief [*doit tenir le premier lieu de notre créance*],' Descartes says that we should make it 'the first rule [*pro summa regula*]' that 'whatever God has revealed to us ought to be accepted as the most certain of all things [*ut omnium certissima esse credenda*].' Arnauld's and Descartes's 'ought' means that it would be irrational to believe that something is revealed by God and yet to reject it. How we can tell that something is in fact revealed by God is, of course, another matter. In this connection, Descartes says, 'Even with respect to the truths of the faith, we should perceive some reason which convinces us that they have been revealed by God, before deciding to believe them.'[26] But once given that something has been revealed by God, it would be irrational not to believe. Arnauld and Descartes also express (b) in quite similar terms: Where Arnauld speaks of what God reveals 'about himself or about the extraordinary effects of his omnipotence,' Descartes refers to revelation about 'his immense nature' and 'the things created by him.' Again the point has to do with rationality in the formation of beliefs: once given that something is revealed by God, it would be irrational to take the fact that we cannot see *how* it is possible as a reason for not believing it.

Although Arnauld was happy to have Descartes's support for PDI, he does not treat the doctrine itself as a distinctively Cartesian one. He points out that it is a commonplace in the fathers of the church.[27] What is distinctive in Descartes's treatment is his claim that 'what an infinite power is capable of' includes making it possible that self-contradictory propositions be true and that what are in fact necessarily true propositions be false. Descartes's strongest assertion of this position is in a letter to Mesland:

> The power of God cannot have any limits, and ... our mind is finite and so created as to be able to conceive as possible the things which God has wished to be in fact possible, but not to conceive as possible things which God could have made possible, but which he has nevertheless wished to make impossible. The first consideration shows us that God cannot have been determined to make it true that contradictories cannot be true together, and therefore that he could have done the opposite. The second consideration assures us that even if this be true, we should not try to comprehend it, since our nature is incapable of doing so.[28]

Descartes addresses a related claim to Arnauld in his second letter of 1648:

> But it does not seem to me that it should ever be said of anything that it cannot be done by God. For since every aspect of the true and the good depend on his

omnipotence, I would not dare to say that God cannot bring it about that there is a mountain without a valley or that one and two are not three. But I say only that he has given me a mind such that I cannot conceive a mountain without a valley, or an aggregate of one and two which is not three, etc., and that such things imply a contradiction in my concept.[29]

But Arnauld does not accept this distinctively Cartesian position on divine omnipotence, and hence PDI does not have quite the same force for him as for Descartes. This is clear, I think, from his treatment of the Eucharist. Consider his statement, quoted above: 'only extension is the essence of matter, and impenetrability is merely one of its properties. But only the essence is inseparable from it; regarding the properties, nothing prevents our saying that they can be separated from it by the power of God ...'[30] This passage certainly *seems* to say that something does prevent our saying that the essence of matter can be separated from bodies by the power of God. Arnauld does seem to think that to bring it about that a body is really present somewhere without being extended would be to make a contradictory proposition true. The obvious explanation of the above text, then, is that Arnauld thought that extension cannot be separated from matter, even by the power of God.

Arnauld rejects Descartes's advice more openly a few years later while commenting on Malebranche's statement that God is 'powerless [*impuissant*]' to do certain things. Arnauld accepts Malebranche's formula that God is powerless to do certain things, and gives as examples of things God cannot do, 'to raise someone from the dead in answer to the prayer of a false prophet who would lead an entire people into a false religion by means of this miracle, or to commit a criminal action such as to make a person who holds a high position die in order to put himself in his place.' 'All the theologians,' he says, would accept these examples. Later on he adds the example that God cannot lie (*OA* 39, 213).

Of course, Descartes also holds that God is not a deceiver. But I know of no passage in which he says flatly that God is powerless to lie. The strongest Cartesian pronouncements on the matter that I know of are: 'I recognize that it is impossible that God should ever deceive me [*agnosco fiere non posse ut ille me unquam fallat*]' (*Fourth Meditation*, AT 7, 53); 'It is impossible to imagine that he [God] is a deceiver [*deceptor fingi non posset*]' (*Second Replies*, AT 7, 144); and 'The will to deceive ... cannot be attributed to God [*nunquam certè fallendi voluntas ... in Deum cadere potest*]' (*Principles* I, 29). If Descartes means in these places to say that lying is not within God's power, then he is acting contrary to his own advice to Arnauld in 1648. However, these passages to not force us to that conclusion. They say only that we recognize it to be impossible that God should lie, and hence cannot attribute lying to God.[31] But Descartes also seems to hold that God could make possible what we recognize to be impossible – indeed, that God could make it possible that contradictories be true together.

Arnauld disagreed with Descartes on this point from the very beginning of his philosophical career. Thus in the *Fourth Objections* he attacks Descartes's claim that God derives his existence, in a positive sense, from himself: 'I think it is a manifest contradiction that anything should derive its existence positively and as it were causally from itself' (AT 7, 208). Hence, he concludes, 'God cannot derive his existence from himself in the positive sense, but can do so only in the negative sense of not deriving it from anything else' (AT 7, 210). He adds that 'it will scarcely be possible to find a single theologian who will not object to the proposition that God derives his existence from himself in the positive sense, and as it were causally' (AT 7, 214). Arnauld cannot have been unaware of the fact that Aquinas also says that God cannot cause himself to exist, and includes this in his rather lengthy list, in the *Summa Contra Gentiles*, of things God cannot do (*SCG* 1, 25). Indeed Arnauld's notion of omnipotence is close to Aquinas's: For any action *A*, God can do *A* so long as neither the proposition that God does *A* nor the proposition that God wills to do *A* is self-contradictory.[32]

Arnauld's willingness, against the advice of Descartes, to speak about things God cannot do suggests a broader disagreement between the two regarding possibility and the status of necessary truths. These are large topics, well beyond the scope of this essay.[33] The point I want to make here is that Arnauld disagreed with Descartes on divine omnipotence, at least in part for theological reasons. Descartes's position brought him into conflict with the theological tradition, with 'all the theologians.' This was enough to make Arnauld suspect that the Cartesian position, as it stands, is mistaken and, once the suspicion was verified, to reject it.

Notes

1 Steven Nadler, 'Arnauld, Descartes, and Transubstantiation: Reconciling Cartesian Metaphysics and Real Presence,' *Journal of the History of Ideas* 49 (1988), 229–46. See also Nadler's 'Cartesianism and Port-Royal,' *The Monist* 71 (1988), 573–84.

2 *Fourth Objections, Points Which May Cause Difficulty to Theologians*, AT 7, 215–16. In response to Arnauld's misgivings, Descartes added a clause in the Synopsis of the *Meditations* to make clear that the work dealt only with

speculative truths knowable by the natural light, and not with matters of faith or morals. See AT 7, 16; Cottingham 2, 11. But I know of no passage in his later works in which Arnauld speaks favourably of the method of doubt.

3 I have discussed Arnauld's late (post-1680) views on free will in 'Grace and Free Will in Arnauld,' in *The Great Arnauld and Some of His Philosophical Correspondents*, Elmar J. Kremer, ed. (Toronto: University of Toronto Press 1994), 219–39. For Arnauld's rejection of the Cartesian doctrine that judgment is an act of will in favour of the Thomistic one that judgment is an act of intellect, see his *Humanae libertatis notio*, in *Causa Arnaldina*, Quesnel, ed. (apud Hoyoux: Leodice Eburohium 1699), 99–111. A French translation by Quesnel can be found in *OA* 10, 614–24.

4 Arnauld refers to Descartes as a 'Christian philosopher' in *Examen, OA* 38, 90. This work was written about 1680, and published for the first time in *OA* in 1780. Arnauld's reference echoes Descartes's self-description, in the letter dedicating the *Meditations* to Faculty of Theology of the Sorbonne, where he says that he had carried out the injunction of the Fifth Lateran Council (1513–17) that 'Christian philosophers' should try to prove the immateriality of the soul: AT 7, 3.

5 I quote Arnauld's formulation of the principle in *Examen, OA* 38, 90. Arnauld's words echo Descartes's *Principles* I, nos. 24 and 25.

6 *Examen, OA* 38, 137. Cf. 38, 145–6.

7 *OA* 38, 73. See Antoine Arnauld, *On True and False Ideas, New Objections to Descartes' Meditations and Descartes' Replies*, Elmar J. Kremer, trans. (Queenston: Edwin Mellen 1990), 187.

Descartes does not frequently use the expression 'local extension,' but he indicates in the *Second Replies* that the essence of a body is local extension: 'The substance which is the subject of local extension and of the accidents which presuppose extension ... is called *body*' (AT 7, 161). And again, in the *Third Replies*, he says, 'Now there are certain acts that we call "corporeal," such as size, shape, motion and all others that cannot be thought of apart from local extension; and we use the term "body" to refer to the substance in which they inhere' (AT 7, 176; CSMK 2, 124).

8 'Christ's body, however, is not supposed to be present in a place strictly speaking, but to be present sacramentally ...' (AT 7, 252). The editors of CSMK say that Descartes is quoting session 13 of the Council of Trent. But there is no reference to 'local presence' or 'presence as in a place' in the document approved in that session. However, the Catechism of the Council of Trent, produced under the authority of the council, states quite explicitly that the body of Christ is not present in the sacrament as in a place: 'Deinde vero docerant, Christum dominum in hoc sacramento, ut in loco, non esse.' *Catechismus ex Decreto Concilii Tridentini, ad Parochos*, Typographia Pontificia, Eq. Petri Marietti, 1900, Part II,

Chap. IV, #44, 215. This is almost a direct quotation from Aquinas, who had said, 'Unde, nullo modo corpus Christi est in hoc sacramento localiter,' *Summa Theologiae* III, 76, 5.

9 He had taken quite a different attitude towards the same question some three years earlier in a well-known letter to Mesland: 'As for the manner in which one can conceive the body of Jesus Christ to be in the Blessed Sacrament ... the Council of Trent teaches that he is there "with that form of existence which we can scarcely express in words" ... All the same, since the council does not lay it down that "we cannot express it in words", but only that "we can scarcely express it in words", I will venture to tell you here in confidence a manner of explanation which seems to me quite elegant and very useful ...' (To Mesland, 9 February 1645, AT 4, 165).

10 *Examen, OA* 38, 121. A similar attitude is present in Arnauld and Nicole's *Grande perpétuité de la foi sur l'eucharistie*, which was published in 1669–73 and is quoted extensively in *Examen*. It may be argued that Arnauld had changed his mind on this point between 1648 and 1669, but I see no reason to think that he had done so.

11 Descartes in fact gives this argument in his second letter, with which the exchange of letters comes to an end.

12 J.-R. Armogathe, *Theologia Cartesiana* (The Hague: Martinus Nijhoff 1977), 12. The Scotist theory was opposed to that of Aquinas, who held that, in transubstantiation, the substance of the bread and wine was not annihilated, but, rather, converted into the body and blood of Christ. The distinction is a subtle one, as can be seen by considering the following statement of Occam, who is usually said to follow the Scotist approach: 'I say that if by annihilation is meant that what is annihilated is brought back to nothing [*redigitur in nihilo*] and not converted into something else, then in this sense the bread is not annihilated. But if it is meant that what is annihilated is reduced to purely nothing [*reducitur in ita purum nihil*] such as it was before the creation of the world, then in this sense the bread is truly annihilated (*In IV Sent.*, Bk I, ordin, 1, Q. 1, A. 1 & 6).

13 *Examen, OA* 38, 100–24.

14 Ibid., *OA* 38, 101–4. The text can be found in *OC* 1, 459–66. This citation of Malebranche by Arnauld should serve as a reminder that the two Cartesian theologians and philosophers, despite their long and rather bitter controversy, had a great deal in common. On the friendship and subsequent controversy between Arnauld and Malebranche, see *OC* 17.

15 *Examen, OA* 38, 111.

16 *OA* 39, 147. Cited by A.-R. Ndiaye in *La Philosophie d'Antoine Arnauld* (Paris: Vrin 1991), 323.

17 'Dans le premier exemple [*que ce impossible que je ne sois pas, si je pense*], c'est une impossibilité absolue; parce qu'il y a contradiction, que je pense & que je ne

sois pas' (*Ecrit du pouvoir physique*, *OA* 10, 492).

18 Letter to More, 15 April 1649, AT 4, 342. See also note 9, above.

19 *Examen*, *OA* 38, 111–12.

20 *Principles* I, no. 26.

21 *Summa Theologiae* III, 736, 6, ad 2.

22 In the *Sixth Meditation* he argues that the 'active faculty' corresponding to our 'passive faculty of sensory perception' exists in corporeal things, which produce or bring about our sensory ideas: AT 7, 79.

23 Cf. 38, 150: 'It is certain, as we have already said, that our body cannot act on our soul as a physical cause.'

24 *Examen*, *OA* 38, 146, 160. It is clear, too, that Arnauld realized that Aquinas held that a material thing cannot prouce an immaterial effect (see Arnauld's *Dissertatio bipartita*, *OA* 40, 126–8).

25 *Règles du bon sens*, *OA* 40, 153.

26 Appendix to the Fifth Objections and Replies,' AT 9A, 208. In the following sentence, Descartes suggests that people who accepted the truths of the faith without having any reason to convince them that those truths have been revealed by God would 'be behaving more like automatons or beasts than men.'

27 *Examen*, *OA* 38, 114–15.

28 To Mesland, 2 May 1644, AT 4, 118.

29 My translation, 195.

30 See note 11, above.

31 Mersenne, in the *Second Objections*, says 'You [Descartes] say that God cannot lie or deceive [*Deum negas posse mentiri aut decipere*]' (AT 7, 125). But, when Descartes repeats the point before replying, he omits the 'cannot' and instead says, 'In saying that God does not lie and is not a deceiver, I think I am in agreement with all metaphysicians and theologians past and future [*cum nego Deum mentire, vel esse deceptorum* ...]': AT 7, 142.

32 See the discussion of Aquinas on omnipotence by Cyrille Michon in Olivier Boulnois, *La Puissance et son ombre, de Pierre Lombard à Luther* (Paris: Aubier 1944), 206–16.

33 But see the essays by Carraud, Ndiaye, and Solère in this volume.

7

Arnauld: A Cartesian Theologian? Omnipotence, Freedom of Indifference, and the Creation of the Eternal Truths

VINCENT CARRAUD

The history of philosophy attempts to give an account of what the authors think on the basis of what the texts say, and it is always dangerous to comment on matters about which the authors remain silent. None the less that is what I propose to do here, by raising the question: Why does the Cartesian primacy of omnipotence among the divine attributes not appear in Arnauld's philosophical works? In particular, why is the doctrine called 'the creation of the eternal truths' not present there explicitly? We know that when Descartes took the position that the eternal truths, though grasped by our mind as immutable and necessary, are created by God, he was opposing both the mathematicians, like Kepler, Mersenne, and Galileo, who referred the mathematical truths to the divine understanding as their absolute foundation, and the philosophers, who attempted to establish an ontology, that is, a common concept of *being as thought*, under which to include both God and creation, the infinite and finite.[1] Indeed, we can trace a series of attempts beginning in the twelfth century, always *in philosophy*, to submit God to our concept of the possible, i.e., to posit a single rationality for both divine and human understanding. The first figure in this large movement of thought is probably Abelard, who unhesitatingly submits God, not only to the principle of non-contradiction, but even to what we may call, anticipating Leibniz, the principle of reason: From the fact (noted by Augustine) that God cannot go against his own wisdom and his own rationality, or again, that he cannot cease following the order he has decided to follow, we jump to the assertion that God must obey reason. Thus God's freedom is limited by his wisdom, at least that is what Abelard's censors took his position to be. The questions that we find in the seventeenth century had already been raised in the twelfth, in particular: Can

God do anything but what he in fact does? Can God make anything other than the best? And from the beginning, it is clear that the discussion depends on the relation between theology and philosophy. It can be shown how this movement, begun by Abelard, is developed in the commentaries on the *Sentences* of Peter Lombard,[2] and how the thesis of the univocity of logical truths becomes dominant. Without doubt it culminates in Suárez, with the affirmation of the univocity of being, substance, and truth, both logical and mathematical.[3] To this affirmation, Descartes responds peremptorily: 'nulla essentia potest univoce Deo et creaturae convenire.'[4] Thus we see how Descartes, alone in his century, at least in *philosophy*, resists this dominant movement, by philosophizing, if I may say so, against the philosophers, i.e., by philosophizing in perfect conformity with the theological condemnations tirelessly reiterated from the twelfth century on, beginning with the condemnation of Abelard by the Council of Sens in 1141.[5] In sum, the history of the submission of God to logical necessity, beginning with the principle of non-contradiction, forces us to place Descartes on the side of the most official orthodoxy in theology, against the 'emancipation' of philosophy that gave rise, at the beginning of the seventeenth century, to the concept of ontology. After Descartes, it is obvious that the three great post-Cartesians, Spinoza, Malebranche, and Leibniz, complete the history of that emancipation: the possibles are imposed upon God; the truths that are in the divine understanding are independent of the divine will. This can have occurred only with the abandonment, by all of the great post-Cartesians, of the radical thesis of 1630, the so-called doctrine of the creation of the eternal truths, itself a consequence of the priority of incomprehensible omnipotence over the other predicates of God.[6] The historical question then naturally arises, whether there is a post-Cartesian theologian ready to support Descartes's new beginning, his decisive break with the philosophical trend, in 1630.

Since we mean to speak about Cartesian theology, not merely about Cartesian themes present in some work of theology or other, whether positive[7] or speculative, we cannot neglect the fundamental Cartesian assertion of the incomprehensible power of God. Can we speak of Cartesian theology where the fundamental and persistent Cartesian thesis that 'God is a cause whose power surpasses the bounds of human understanding' is ignored, or even where it is weakened?[8] Can we speak of a Cartesian theology where what is for Descartes the way 'to speak of God worthily' is abandoned?[9] In other words, that thesis ought to be found in anyone who is a theologian trying to develop a Cartesian theology, and not merely a theologian who happens to be Cartesian in philosophy. This is the first motivation for studying Arnauld, as well as Fénelon and Bossuet, figures whom no one will deny were major theologians.[10]

The complex history of the reading of Holy Scripture by philosophers could provide a second motive for such an inquiry. Against Malebranche, who refuses to take account of certain scriptural texts on the pretext that Scripture is 'full of anthropomorphisms,'[11] especially 'the passages from Scripture which say that God acts by particular volitions,' Arnauld does not fail to call attention to the texts which put his adversary in the wrong, especially concerning the submission of God to the principle of contradiction and to the notion of the possible – Luke, 18:27: 'What is impossible for human beings is possible for God';[12] and concerning the submission of will to wisdom in creation, Ephesians 1:11: '[God] ... who works all things according to the counsel of his will.'[13] We could show, as Arnauld does not, that the Cartesian doctrine of the creation of the eternal truths provides a rigorous metaphysical formulation of several of these basic scriptural passages, interpreted literally. We could begin with Genesis, cited by Descartes himself in no. 8 of the *Sixth Replies*: 'because [God] decided that certain things should be made, "they are good," as it is said in Genesis, because their goodness depends on the fact that he willed to make them.'[14]

But there is a third motivation, which makes our initial question pressing, and which will provide the context for its solution: Arnauld's critique of Malebranche after the publication of the *Traité de la nature et de la grâce* in 1680 (and the *Eclaircissements* and additions of 1683 and 1684). In the face of Malebranche's emphasis on the claim that truths are imposed upon God himself, that God is obedient to the single rationality of order, or again, that his power is subjected to his wisdom (even so far as to make the fantastic statement, in 1684, that 'his wisdom makes him powerless' – a statement he qualifies in 1712: 'his wisdom makes him, so to speak, powerless'),[15] the critical reaction of a theologian who (like Arnauld or Fénelon) counts himself a Cartesian, could, or perhaps must, be based on the doctrine of 1630, at least in its formulation in the *Sixth Replies*. Descartes had there replied, in advance, to Malebranche, using, in section 6, a set of three terms that Malebranche will also employ: 'Neque hic loquor de prioritate temporis [of an idea of the good or the true in the intellect over the determination of the will], sed ne quidem prius fuit *ordine*, vel *natura*, vel *ratione ratiocinata*, ut vocant [that is, the Scholastics] ita scilicet it ista boni idea impulerit Deum ad unum potius quam aliud eligendum.'[16] Malebranche, like the Scholastics referred to by Descartes, speaks of the priority of order, nature (that is, 'the inviolable law of creatures and even of the Creator'), and reason.[17] Similarly, in section 8, Descartes says, 'Attendenti ad Dei immensitatem, manifestum est nihil omnino posse, quod ab ipso non pendeat: non modo nihil subsistens, sed etiam nullum *ordinem*, nullam *legem*, nullamve *rationem* veri et boni ...'[18] In both cases we have the Malebranchian triad: order, law, and reason. But what we expect does not occur. Although the critique of Arnauld and Fénelon bear upon what seems to them to be Malebranche's denial of the omnipotence of God, they do not rely at all upon the strongest Cartesian thesis, and the one most opposite to Malebranche's position, not even in its formulation in the *Sixth Replies*. Thus we face the following situation: the Cartesian theologians, when refuting the *Traité de la nature et de la grâce*, *ought* to defend the doctrine of the creation of the eternal truths in order most effectively to oppose Malebranche, both as Cartesians calling attention to Malebranche's abandonment of a constitutive thesis of Cartesian philosophy, and as theologians upholding the primacy of omnipotence among the divine attributes.We would expect to see the Cartesian doctrine reappear, at least in this polemical setting, since it is the one Malebranche rejects most decisively because it threatens most directly the whole of his system. But what we expect does not occur. It is this silence that we would like to explain.

To this end, we will concentrate on the years 1685–7, the three decisive years that follow the publication of the great texts responsible for the post-Cartesian re-establishment of the univocity of being (or of substance) and the univocity of truth. The authors are Spinoza, with the *Ethics* in 1677 (but the 'danger' of Spinozism is not our concern here); Malebranche, with the publication of the *Eclaircissements* to the *Recherche de la vérité* in 1678;[19] and Leibniz, with the completion of the *Discours de métaphysique* in 1685. But we will concentrate on these three years above all because they contain Arnauld's *Réflexions philosophiques et théologiques sur le nouveau système de la nature et de la grâce* (published in 1685), which crystallizes his opposition to the *Traité de la nature et de la grâce*, and his correspondence with Leibniz.[20]

Philosophy and Theology

According to Arnauld, the relations between philosophy and theology are controlled by the Augustinian principle noted in the *Fourth Objections*: 'Quod intelligimus igitur debemus rationi; quod credimus, authoritati,'[21] a principle applied in the division of the *Objections* themselves into two parts. The question *de Deo*, in which Descartes returns to the *inexhausta Dei potentia*, belongs, of course, to the philosophical part of the *Objections* and *Replies*. Henri Gouhier is referring to this principle when he speaks of the 'separation' of theology and philosophy: 'Faith and reason, positive theology and philosophy – Arnauld is in profound agreement with Descartes about their separation as well as the caution that ought to be inspired by speculative theology. The difference between the two has to do with their situations. Descartes is a philosopher facing theology; Arnauld, a theologian facing philosophy.'[22] If these comments were true in 1641, do they remain true in 1685–7? Assuming the Augustinian principle, only the requirements of polemic will justify the intrusion of one domain into the other. Gouhier gives two examples: When Arnauld is forced to go beyond positive theology in order to do philosophy, as in Volume III of *La Grande Perpétuité*, he is clearly Cartesian; when, on the contrary, the identification of matter and extension is attacked in the name of theology, as it was by LeMoine in the *Traité de l'esssence du corps*, Arnauld, in *Examen d'un écrit qui a pour titre: Traité de l'essence du corps* ... accumulates references in positive theology in order to show that the Cartesian philosophy is not opposed to them. If the *Réflexions sur le nouveau système de la nature et de la grâce* are *Réflexions philosophiques et théologiques*, that is because Malebranche (and not Arnauld) acts sometimes as a philosopher and sometimes as a theologian, without any clear principle demarcating the two roles. Furthermore, says Arnauld (no doubt thinking of the *Méditations chrétiennes*), 'this extraordinary way of putting words into God's mouth, in his philosophical discussions, is capable of taking people off guard.'[23] The separation of philosophy and theology in the *Réflexions philosophiques et théologiques* does not have the same theoretical status as the division of difficulties in the *Fourth Objections*.[24]

Nevertheless, the last page of the *Examen* adds a complication to the principle noted by Gouhier. The examination of the question of the Eucharist, like that of the hypostatic union, allows Arnauld to conclude firmly: the incomprehensible object of a dogma cannot be the norm for the philosophical discussion of natural things. So neither the Eucharist nor the hypostatic union is acceptable as a model for conceiving the natural union of mind and body.[25] Thus he says, 'nothing would be more unreasonable than to hold that philosophers, who have the right to follow the light of reason in the human sciences, are required to take what is incomprehensible in the mystery of the Incarnation as a rule for their opinion when they attempt to explain the natural union of the soul with the body, as if the soul could do with regard to the body what *the eternal Word* could do with regard to the humanity he took on, even though *the power, as well as the wisdom, of the eternal Word is infinite*, while the power of the soul over the body to which it is joined is very limited.'[26] Arnauld concludes with a principle that goes farther than would have been necessary, in so far as it posits equivocity between the human and the divine, a principle which Descartes, no doubt, would have accepted: 'We would not have those thoughts which *mix up everything in philosophy and theology*, if we were more convinced of the clear and certain maxim that Cardinal Belarmine used against the quibbles of the Socinians: "No inference can be made from the finite to the infinite," or, as others put it, "there is no proportion between the finite and the infinite."'[27] This principle is of interest to us for three reasons: (1) it denounces as a confusion the attempt to use an incomprehensible object of theology as a norm in philosophy (I note in passing that this criticism goes directly against Pascal); (2) it takes it as basic that the power of God (here the power of the Word in the act of its own Incarnation), like the wisdom of the Word, is infinite. Hence, there is no priority of the wisdom over the power of God to justify a priority of philosophy over positive theology and the marvels that it explicates; (3) thus the two domains are kept separate in the name of the infinite power of God, and it is our perception of the incommensurability of the infinite and the finite that rules out an analogy between the two: 'There is no proportion between the finite and the infinite.' That is, the affirmation of the incomprehensible omnipotence of God is prior to and establishes the division of theology and philosophy from each other. Further, in the Cartesian problematic, the first proposition of the Creed introduces the notion of a power that goes beyond the truths of the sciences – in particular, here, the science of the union of mind and body. In sum, behind an apparently banal theory of the separation of philosophy and theology, Arnauld, as a rigorous Cartesian, points to the infinite power of God as the unconditioned condition of the exercise both of theology (whose object is the mysteries of the faith) and of philosophical rationality.[28]

Thus the above principle has a twofold epistemic function: against LeMoine, to separate the incomprehensible mysteries of revelation from the work of philosophy so as to prevent the former from becoming the conceptual models of the latter; against Malebranche, to prevent the application of philosophical propositions to the divine, that is, to prevent the unconditioned from being conditioned by finite rationality. For the same reason, Arnauld, this time confronting Malebranche, refuses to submit the divine will to causality. I cite the *Réflexions philosophiques et théologiques*, Book II, Chapter 3: 'if we are asked why God has created the world, we should only reply that it is because he wanted to; and ... if we are asked anew why he wanted to, we should not say, as the author [Malebranche] does, that "he wanted to obtain an honour worthy of himself." The idea of God does not permit us to accept Malebranche's proposition. We ought rather say that he wanted to because he wanted to, that is, that we ought not seek a cause of that which cannot have one.'[29] Arnauld here relies on a passage from St Augustine, and again on Estius's commentary on the same passage, in which the repetition of the question 'Why?' is declared 'impertinent, because there can be no cause of God's volition.'[30] Arnauld's refusal, here against Malebranche but also against Leibniz, to submit God to causality, that is, to submit his will to rationality in the form of a principle of reason, brings us back to the *Fourth Objections* and *Replies*, though without any mention of the concept of *causa sui*, a silence no doubt connected with our present concerns.[31]

Freedom of Indifference

I know of no text in all the writings of Arnauld that explicitly affirms the doctrine of the creation of the eternal truths, in any form whatever. This point is all the more remarkable in that one of the Cartesian passages which enunciate that thesis is addressed to Arnauld. In his letter of 29 July 1648, replying to Arnauld's question about the impossibility of a void, which seemed to Arnauld to detract from the omnipotence of God,[32] Descartes says: 'As for me, it seems to me that one should never say of anything that it is impossible for God; for since everything that is true or good depends on his omnipotence, I do not dare even to say that God cannot make a mountain without a valley, or that one and two do not make three; rather, I say only that he has given me a mind of such a kind that I cannot conceive a mountain without a valley, or that the sum of one and two do not make three, etc. And I say only that such things imply a contradiction in my thought.'[33] Here I will only add a note that I have never found in the commentaries on Descartes. In the case of the void, we are dealing with a reversal of the ordinary way of thinking, which is *not* to appeal to the omnipotence of God. Ordinarily, we think that one and two make three, and that there is no mountain without a valley, and it takes nothing less than an exaggerated, hyperbolic, meta physical doubt to shake us and to suspend our certainty. That is, it takes an extraordinary appeal to the omnipotence of God, the turning-point which allows us to pass from a sceptical doubt to a metaphysical doubt in the *First Meditation*. By contrast, the prejudice by which we think that a void is possible consists in thinking *too much* about the omnipotence of God, through which the void, to us unthinkable, would be possible. 'Furthermore, this difficulty arises from the fact that we count on the divine power [*ex eo quod recurramus ad potentiam divinam*]; and because we know that it is infinite, we do not notice that we are attributing to it an effect which includes a contradiction in its conception, that is, which cannot be conceived by us.'[34] The possibility of a void is a case in which we naturally think in a hyperbolic way, because our prejudice assumes the infinity of God's omnipotence. Thus belief in the possibility of a void, as an enduring prejudice, calls upon the same principle as the provisional hypothesis of a God who could permit me to be deceived, namely, his infinite power.[35]

On the other hand, in a passage in the *Defense ... contre la réponse au livre des vraies et des fausses idées*, Arnauld uses an analogous reason to prove against Malebranche that God is not extended and that he is not in an immense space. The point of interest to us here is that Arnauld cites articles 22 and 23 of the first part of the *Principles of Philosophy*, which explicitly contain the Cartesian doctrine of the creation of the eternal truths ('[Deum esse] omnis bonitatis veritatisque fontem'):[36] 'But, to add the philosophers to the theologians [Arnauld has just cited Denis the Areopogite], I think everyone will agree that what Descartes says on this point is more worthy of God than the new dogma of his disciple [Malebranche's dogma that God is extended]. It is found in the first part of the *Principles*, articles 22–23.'[37] To conclude this brief note: Not only is Arnauld, like all his contemporaries, perfectly well aware of the texts on the creation of the eternal truths, but one of these texts was addressed to him. In addition, he is not afraid to cite the passage from the *Principles* that expresses the doctrine clearly.

I now turn to the *Réflexions philosophiques et théologiques*, where Arnauld attacks the question that concerns us on the basis of God's freedom of indifference. Arnauld's reading of the first Discourse of the *Traité de la nature et de la grâce* can be summarized as follows: If God *wills* to produce any work whatever outside of himself, then he *is obliged* to produce the most perfect (and to produce it most perfectly). By making the simplicity of means necessary, thus by submitting power to order, that is, the Father to the Son, Malebranche denies God's freedom of indifference. Here we do not need to evaluate the accuracy of Arnauld's critique.[38] But we want to bring out the paradox of his argument: (1) The notion of God's freedom of indifference is basic in Descartes, a freedom of indifference that does not have to do with choice, since for God's will there is no question of choosing among possibles. Consider again this constant thesis of Cartesianism in points 6 and 8 of the *Sixth Replies*, which we have already cited: 'Repugnat enim Dei voluntatem non fuisse ab aeterno indifferentem ad omnia quae facta sunt aut unquam fient ...'[39] Again, '[Deus] fuisset plane indifferens ad ea creanda quae creavit.'[40] However, (2) when Arnauld attacks Malebranche, he relies, not on Descartes, the great theoretician of freedom of indifference, but on St Thomas. This is all the more strange in that, for St Thomas, there cannot be any indifference on God's part towards the things produced (or even towards truths) because there is no equality among creatures. Since things always differ in degree of being because of their essence, that is, since formal distinction always requires inequality ('distinctio autem formalis semper requirit inaequalitatem' – each form taking its place), all creation presupposes inequality, or again, inequality pertains to creatures ('creatura, cui competit inaequalitas').[41] Therefore, although the Father and the Son are equal within the Trinity, there is no inequality among creatures, and consequently no possibility of indifference on God's part towards what is created. Arnauld knows this very well, and hence there is a certain difficulty when he tries to justify qualifying the freedom of God as indifferent. He is able to do so only by opposing it to the necessity with which God loves himself. This appears in a text that is especially confused: 'It is well to note how little freedom and indifference the author [Malebranche] leaves to God, with regard to what he brings about outside himself. I have added, *and indifference*, for we know that the Scholastics believed that there was present in God a freedom without indifference and without contingency, as in the case of the love he necessarily bears for himself, and the production of the Holy Spirit, the outcome of that love ... I do not mean to speak of that sort of freedom, but rather of God's freedom with regard to what he brings about outside himself, *which must be accompanied by indifference* [my italics], because God 'loves only his own nature invincibly and necessarily.'[42] (3) Arnauld then cites I, 19, 3, *Utrum quidquid vult Deus ex necessitate velit?*, giving a translation/paraphrase: 'Since the divine will has a necessary relation to his goodness, which is its proper object, it loves it with necessity. But since it loves all other things only for the sake of his goodness, it does not love them with necessity because they do not have a necessary relation to the divine goodness, for that goodness can exist without them and receives no increase from them.' And after posing the difficulty that what is capable of producing opposite effects does not act unless it is determined by some other thing, Aquinas replies, 'That is true for a cause that is in itself contingent. But the will of God is God himself, and consequently is a necessary being, so that it determines itself to will with regard to the things to which it does not have a necessary relation.'[43] Nevertheless it is clear that for St Thomas the determination of the will by itself does not imply any indifference, for the reasons we have just given. Besides, when St Thomas says that the divine will determines itself to that which it wills ('voluntas divina, quae ex se necessitatem habet, determinat seipsam ad volitum, ad quod habet habitudinem non necessariam'), he does not mean to oppose it to the intellect, because the attributes of God must never be really distinguished, above all not temporally (a principle taken up by Descartes). But Arnauld uses the texts against Malebranche to emphasize the self-determination of the will and thus imposes a Cartesian reading, in terms of indifference, on what is said about the divine will: 'Note that he [St Thomas] does not say that it is the wisdom of God that determines his will, by proposing that to which the will ought to direct itself [Malebranche's position], but rather that the divine will determines itself, *freely and indifferently*, towards all the things to which it does not have a necessary relation, that is, towards everything that is not God.'[44] To be sure, the argument of St Thomas is entirely opposed to Malebranche, whose position we stated above: If God *wills* to produce something outside of himself, then he *ought* to produce the most perfect one (and ought to produce it most perfectly). This is exactly the opposite of the reply to the second objection in question 13, article 3: 'Deus ex necessitate velit bonitatem suam, non tamen ex necessitate vult ea quae vult propter bonitatem suam.'[45] But Arnauld puts a Cartesian construction on the argument of St Thomas by saying 'freely and indifferently.' For St Thomas, from the fact that God does not will necessarily what he wills in view of his goodness, it does not at all follow that he wills with indifference.

Two points are noteworthy here. First, the St Thomas that Arnauld opposes to

Malebranche is a strangely Cartesian one. Even if Arnauld is trying to show that Malebranche is not a good theologian – a rather easy task, after all[46] – that does not justify his Cartesian reading of St Thomas. Once more we look in St Thomas for answers to questions he did not ask.[47] Second, Arnauld does not make use of the self-determination of the will ('voluntas divina determinat seipsam') to call attention to the doctrine of the creation of the eternal truths, which he could have done without forcing the texts any more than he did when he introduced indifference. Everything takes place as if it is Descartes who is behind the text of Arnauld and who is the true origin of his criticisms of Malebranche, as if the reference to St Thomas were not by itself sufficiently anti-Malebranchian, and the Cartesian affirmation of freedom of indifference had to be added in order to bring the attack on Malebranche to completion.[48] But it seems that this presence of Cartesian theses must remain clandestine.[49]

In conclusion, it looks as if Arnauld does not want to object against Malebranche that the submission of the divine power to order, for example, to the simplicity of means, is a *direct* denial of the omnipotence of God. He limits himself to saying that it denies God's freedom of indifference, appealing to St Thomas but using the vocabulary of the *Meditations* (to strengthen his polemic). How should we understand this detour? The doctrine of the creation of the eternal truths does not seem to be connected, in Descartes, to one formulation rather than another, to freedom of indifference rather than to omnipotence (or vice versa). Does Arnauld want to maintain God's indifference with regard to the things created but to deny that the truths are among those things (in which case he would not have accepted the reasoning about the void in Descartes's letter of July 1648)? Or does he, by contrast, admit the creation of the eternal truths *in itself*, but not dare to defend it, limiting himself to what is necessary for his polemical purposes? That would be to suppose that Arnauld means to be a Cartesian without considering himself able to defend philosophically the most daring theses of Descartes, in the first instance that of the creation of the eternal truths, but close behind it the thesis that God is *causa sui*. The correspondence with Leibniz will enable us partly to clarify the question.

Arnauld's Silence

From the time he first received the summary of the *Discourse on Metaphysics*, Arnauld focuses on the central difficulty of paragraph 13: How to understand the proposition that 'the notion of each individual contains once and for all everything that will happen to him.' He calls attention to the fact that the freedom of God is once again in question: 'Therefore God is no more free with regard to all that [is included in the notion of the individual Adam], assuming that he willed to create Adam, than he would be not to make a being capable of thinking, assuming that he had willed to create me.'[50] The Leibnizian problematic has to do, not with distinguishing one individual from another (within a problematic of intersubjective multiplicity), but with understanding the relation of an individual to itself, as a matter of intention, that is, with calling attention to the 'intrinsic connection' between a possible individual and everything that will happen to it.[51] In this situation, Arnauld takes the problem to be that of analysing the subject as subject of representation and carries out a twofold change of direction: (1)'The true notions' are to be sought, not in God, but in myself. (2) When thinking about that intrinsic connection, we can compare it to another type of connection, that between a sphere and its properties. I shall summarize briefly.[52]

(1) God is not the one we should question in order to arrive at knowledge of an individual nature. 'I can hardly believe that we philosophize well if we try to find out what we ought to think by considering the way God knows things.'[53] God's way of knowing things is forever inaccessible to us: 'We ought to seek true notions not in God, who dwells in a light that is inaccessible to us ... but in the ideas that we find in ourselves.'[54] So it is necessary to separate the truth of things in themselves to which we have no access and the truth of things for us, or, to speak with Descartes, in relation to our conception. 'The divine understanding is the rule of the truth of things *quoad se*; but it does not seem to me that it is the rule *quoad nos*, as long as we are in this life. For what do we now know about God's knowledge? We know that he knows everything, and he knows everything by a single, entirely simple, act, which is his essence. When I say that we know, I mean that we are sure that it must be so. But do we comprehend it? Ought we not recognize that however certain we are that we know that it is the case, it is impossible to conceive how it can be?'[55] There follows a wellknown criticism of the idea of 'purely possible substance.' We cannot represent to ourselves the possibles that God has not chosen because that would imply that we have at our disposal the very knowledge of God, and would imply that the possibles are not the effect of God's power, but of his understanding (which is the thesis of Leibniz, as of Malebranche: 'The place of possibles, that is ... his understanding'). So Arnauld takes up the Cartesian refusal of all representations of the divine decrees and applies it to the Leibnizian concept of the possible: 'I am strongly inclined to believe that those are chimeras that we form, and that everything that we refer to as possible, purely possible, substances, is nothing but the omnipotence of God which, as pure act, cannot contain any possibility.'[56] It would be hard to be more Cartesian than Arnauld is here. The possible is a concept which has value only with regard to my conception; it makes no sense in relation to God.

Since I cannot know 'in what way things are in the cognition of God,' I shall seek the notion of myself in myself. Once again, one could not philosophize in a more Cartesian way: 'But I find in myself the notion of an individual, because I find there the notion of myself. Therefore I need not look elsewhere ...'[57] The development of this important point is beyond the limits of this essay, and I pass at once to the second change of direction introduced by Arnauld.

(2) In thinking about this intrinsic connection of myself to myself, I can compare it with another type of connection: 'Therefore I need only consult this individual notion in order to know what it contains, just as I need only consult the specific notion of a sphere in order to know what is contained in it.'[58] With this astonishing comparison, Arnauld makes it appear that an individual has an essence (like the essence of the sphere as distinct from its dimensions). The application of 'the same rule to the individual notion of myself' allows Arnauld to use the hypothesis of a journey I can take or not take, thus to use the assumption of freedom, to reject the inherence of my life in my concept. In sum, Arnauld plays off freedom against individuality in the Leibnizian sense (all my life being in my concept). We know Leibniz's answer: it is incorrect to consider the same type of necessity with regard to a sphere and with regard to an individual: the notion of an individual substance and of a species differ totally.[59] At the level of the notion of a species, necessity has to do with eternal truths: 'The notion of a species includes only certain eternal or necessary truths, but the notion of an individual includes *sub ratione possibilitatis* matters of fact or what has to do with the existence of things and time, and consequently it depends on certain free decrees of God considered as possible.'[60] That is why we must 'philosophize differently' about the two notions. And that is what Arnauld did not do: 'I see that M. Arnauld did not remember or at least was not concerned about the opinion of the Cartesians, who hold that God establishes the eternal truths, like those that concern the properties of a sphere, by his will; but since I am not of their opinion, *any more than M. Arnauld*, I will only say why I think one ought to philosophize differently about the notion of an individual substance than about the sphere.'[61] The letter that was actually sent to Arnauld puts the point differently, not accepting Arnauld's initial silence: 'I will say a word about the reason for the difference ... between the notions of species and those of individual substances, in relation to the divine will rather than in relation to simple understanding. The highly abstract notions of species contain only certain necessary or eternal truths, which do not depend on the decrees of God (whatever may be said by the Cartesians, about whose position on this point it seems that you also are not concerned); but the notions of individual substances ... must include [*envelopper*] in addition ... the free decrees of God ...'[62] There can be no doubt that Leibniz repeats his point in order to challenge Arnauld to declare himself a Cartesian on this decisive point.

Thus, Leibniz concludes that Arnauld has abandoned, or has forgotten, the doctrine of the creation of the eternal truths, from Arnauld's comparison between the connection of the sphere and its properties and the connection of myself and what will happen to me, a comparison Leibniz himself rejects.[63] Starting from the fact that Arnauld tried to separate the essential from the inessential in the notion of the self, that is, the individual notion (to be myself) from that which is free or decreed (the journey) by comparing the self to a sphere, whose dimensions are inessential, Leibniz indicates to Arnauld that he has forgotten that, for a Cartesian, even what is essential or definitional for mathematical objects is decreed by God, and hence arbitrary and no doubt free. In other words, Leibniz is convinced that Arnauld has confused physical kinds with mathematical or metaphysical kinds,[64] and hence needlessly connects the two terms of Arnauld's comparison. I would like to conclude by showing that this treatment of Arnauld is unjustified, and that Leibniz has ignored the twofold change of direction that was introduced by Arnauld, as I noted above.

(1) In the letter of 26 September 1686, Arnauld writes: 'My only remaining difficulty has to do with the possibility of things, and with this way of thinking about God as having chosen the universe he created out of an infinity of other possible universes that he saw at the same time and that he did not will to create. But since that does not have to do with the notion of the individual nature, and since it would take me too far afield to explain what I think about it, or rather what I object to in the thoughts of others, because they do not seem to me worthy of God, it is better that I say nothing about it.'[65] Arnauld keeps his thoughts to himself, both his criticism of the (unworthy) conceptions of God (in Malebranche as well as in Leibniz) as needing to choose among possibles which are imposed on him, and his (Cartesian) refusal to distinguish faculties in God, *ne quidem ratione*: In God, wisdom is not prior to omnipotence, the understanding not prior to the will. Can we go so far as to say that he keeps to himself his basic agreement with the Cartesian doctrine of the creation of the eternal truths, the only way to 'speak worthily about God'?[66]

(2) Consider again the letter of 13 May 1686, more precisely the subtle passage, which Leibniz read perhaps too quickly, that articulates our inability to comprehend the how of God's knowledge (whence the distinction between *quoad se* and *quoad nos*) and the criticism of our representations of creation: 'We fancy that before willing to create the world, he [God] envisaged an infinity of possible things of which he chose some and rejected others.'[67] In this short passage, Arnauld wrote: 'Can we so much as conceive that God has knowledge of an infinity of things that he might not have known because they might not have existed, he whose knowledge is his immutable and necessary essence? The same point can be made about his will, which is also the same as his essence, in which there is nothing that is not necessary.'[68] God knows what he might not

have known because he knows what is. But what is and is known by God would not have been if God had not willed it. And yet it is necessary for us. Hence we propose to read this text as Arnauld's statement, discreet but exact, of the possibility of the Cartesian thesis of the creation of eternal truths. The inaugural Cartesian thesis remains an open possibility, at least.[69]

What was Arnauld's motivation for 'not going further,' in Henri Gouhier's words, and never maintaining explicitly the so-called doctrine of the creation of eternal truths? Two sorts of motivation suggest themselves to me. The first was recognized by Gouhier: the association of Cartesianism and Augustinianism is possible only if the doctrine of the creation of eternal truths is ignored.[70] As we have tried to show elsewhere,[71] because of Descartes a certain number of Augustinian texts and theses acquired a new *philosophical* status in the seventeenth century, and Arnauld contributed to this development. It is thus understandable that he wanted at all costs to avoid either directly contradicting St Augustine or showing a fundamental disagreement between Descartes and Augustine.

The second motivation is pointed out by Arnauld himself. It is what we called his first change of direction in his letter to Leibniz of 13 May 1686: It is not in God, who dwells in inaccessible light, that we should seek the true notions of things. There is too much *obscurity* and *difficulty* in that quarter.[72] Can this fundamental reserve be called Cartesian? Certainly, even if Descartes is not its only possible origin. Whatever the origin of the thesis that I must find in myself the true notions of things and of myself, it represents an authentically Cartesian way of philosophizing.

But behind the motives which are properly Arnauld's, I discern a more fundamental reason. When Arnauld falls back on the Cartesian concept of freedom of indifference, is this not a weakening of omnipotence itself? In the face of the priority of the divine understanding over the divine power, which characterizes all the great post-Cartesian systems, that is, in the face of the definitive submission of God, from that time on, to rationality, are the means still available, *in philosophy*, to consider omnipotence in all its radicalness and thus to uphold the creation of the eternal truths? I think not. Descartes, as I said at the outset, was the only one in his century to do so. He was also the last. To put the point differently, I see no *theological* reason that would stop Arnauld, or Bossuet or Fénelon, from holding the doctrine of the creation of eternal truths. What stops them is that they, like everyone else at the end of the seventeenth century, lacked the means or the audacity to contemplate *in philosophy* the proposition that essences cannot be attributed univocally to God and to creatures. Furthermore, the new problematic of theodicy (God summoned to justify himself according to the standard of common rationality) which will dominate the eighteenth century, requires a weakening of the unconditioned omnipotence of God. This weakening is anticipated, *malgré lui*, by Arnauld's silence.

Notes

It is my pleasant duty to thank Elmar J. Kremer on two counts: for translating this paper into English, and for comments that led to improvements in the final version.

1 See Jean-Luc Marion, *Sur la théologie blanche de Descartes*, 2d ed. (Paris: PUF 1991), especially Book I.

2 What is involved here is the application to theology of the methods used to study the history of long periods of time. See *La Puissance et son ombre. La Toute-puissance divine de Pierre Lombard à Luther: Sentences I, dist. 42 à 44*, introduction, translation and commentary under the direction of Olivier Boulnois (Paris: Aubier 1994). On the formula of Abelard that anticipates the principle of reason ('God does nothing with reason'), known by Odon de Soisson, see ibid., Introduction, iv.

3 See Jean Luc Marion, *Sur la théologie blanche de Descartes*, 110–39 and Jean-François Courtine, *Suárez et le système de la métaphysique* (Paris: PUF 1990), especially part II.

4 *Sixth Replies*, AT 7, 433, 5–6.

5 See Boulnois, *La Puissance et son ombre*.

6 See Jean-Luc Marion, 'De la création des vérités éternelles au principe de raison. Rémarques sur l'anti-cartésianisme de Spinoza, Malebranche, Leibniz,' *XVII*ᵉ *siècle* 147, 2 (1985), 143–64.

7 See for example the pages concerning Arnauld in Francisque Bouillier, *Histoire de la philosophie cartésienne*, 3d ed. (Paris: Delagrave 1968), vol. 2, 156–77.

8 AT 1, 150, 18–19.

9 AT 1, 146, 17.

10 Arnauld, Fénelon, and Bossuet, as theologians, are the great lacunae in the classic work of Henri Gouhier, *Cartésianisme et augustinisme au XVII*ᵉ *siècle* (Paris: Vrin 1978), as well as in the articles of Geneviève Rodis-Lewis in *Idées et vérités éternelles chez Descartes et ses successeurs* (Paris: Vrin-Reprise 1985). See especially the article 'Polémiques sur la création des possibles et sur l'impossible dans l'école cartésienne,' 139–57. Surely the study of this question in Arnauld, Fénelon, and Bossuet is more decisive than in those considered in these reviews of the Cartesian doctrine, such as Wittich, Calley, Desgabets, Poiret, or even Régis.

11 See *Réflexions*, *OA* 39, 186, 234–5, etc.

12 A reference already present in Descartes's letter to Arnauld of 29 July 1648: 'But it does not seem to me that we should say about anything that God cannot do it': AT 5, 223–4. Cf. the Gospel of Luke 1: 37 and Matthew 19:26.

13 First cited by Arnauld in *Réflexions*, *OA* 39, 219; St Thomas cites it in the *sed contra* of Ia, 19, 3. See also the *Summa contra Gentiles* II, 23.

14 AT 7, 435, 30; 436, 3. See Vincent Carraud, 'Descartes et la Bible,' in *Le Grand*

Siècle et la Bible, sous la direction de J.-R. Armogathe (Paris: Beauchesne 1989), 277–91.

15 *Traité de la nature et de la grâce*, I, XXXVIII, addition; *OC* 5, 47.

16 AT 7, 432, 5–9.

17 *Recherche de la vérité*, Eclaircissement X; *OC* 3, 140; *Traité de la nature et de la grâce*, *Eclaircissement* XIX; *OC* 5, 170; *Méditations chrétiennes et métaphysiques*, VIII, x; *OC* 10, 66; *Traité de morale*, I, I, 7 and II, 4, 10; *OC* 11, 19 and 182, etc.

18 AT 7, 435, 22–6.

19 Similarly, the third edition of the *Recherche* in 1678 contains the famous correction of the ambiguous formula about necessary truths 'immutable by their nature, and because they were fixed by the will of God': I, 2, no. 2; 1:63. See Gouhier, *Cartésianisme et augustinisme*, 160.

20 Bossuet's and Fénelon's opposition to Malebranche also occurred during these years: the *Réfutation du système du Père Malebranche sur la nature et la grâce*, as well as the second part of the *Traité de l'existence de Dieu*, probably date from the winter of 1687–8. See Henri Gouhier, *Fénelon philosophe* (Paris: Vrin 1977), 39 and 130. The present essay can therefore be seen as the first tablet of a dyptich of which the second will be the similar silence of Fénelon in his critique of Malebranche.

21 AT 7, 216, 24–5.

22 *Cartesianisme et augustinisme*, 130. See the end of Arnauld's letter to Du Vaucel, 29 April 1680: 'The philosophy of M. Descartes is the most reasonable of all' (*OA* 2, 245).

23 *Réflexions, OA* 39, 169.

24 AT 7, 197, 15–22.

25 *Examen, OA* 38, 156–7. According to Arnauld, the Athanasian creed says nothing about the way in which the soul is united to the body: 'Far from agreeing with the author that the words of the creed require us to believe that the soul and the body are united in the human being in the same was as the human and divine natures are united in Jesus Christ, the theologians declare the opposite, holding explicitly that to understand Athanatius' comparison between the human being and Jesus Christ in that way would be to fall into the error of Eutyches while trying to avoid that of Nestorius ...' On this question, see the first two parts of the classic work of Paul Galtier, *L'Unité du Christ* (Paris: Beauchesne 1939).

26 *Examen, OA* 38, 175.

27 Ibid.; emphasis added

28 If this Cartesian reading were not correct, we would have to say that the infinite could not in any case be the object of philosophy, which would seem difficult for Arnauld to defend.

29 *OA* 39, 433. From the refusal to submit the will of God to causality, we pass to

Malebranche's application of the same refusal to reason itself: 'When we think of order, of the eternal laws or truths, we do not naturally seek a cause, for they do not have one' (*Tenth Eclaircissement, OC* 3, 133).

30 *OA* 39, 434. See Augustine, *The City of God*, XI, XXI.

31 See AT 7, 213, 8–16.

32 'Id vero omnipotentiae divinae derogare videtur': AT 5, 190, 14–15.

33 AT 5, 223, 31–224, 9: 'Mihi autem non videtur de ulla unquam re esse dicendum, ipsam a Deo fieri non posse; cum enim omnis ratio veri et boni ab eius omnipotentia dependeat, nequidem dicere ausim, Deum facere non posse ut mons sine valle, vel ut unum et duo non sunt tria; sed tantum dico illum talem mentem mihi indidisse, ut a me concipi non possit mons sine valle, vel aggregatum ex uno et duobus quod non sunt tria, etc., atque talia implicare contradictione, in meo conceptu.'

34 AT 5, 223, 27–3: 'deinde ex eo quod recurramus ad potentiam divinam, quam infinitam esse scientes, effectum ei tribuimus, quem involvere contradictionem in conceptu, hoc est a nobis concipi non posse, non advertimus.' See also the letter to Mersenne of 27 May 1638, part 2, AT 2, 138, 1–15.

35 See F. de Buzon and V. Carraud, *Descartes et les Principes II: Corps et mouvement* (Paris, PUF 1994), 66–9. On the relation between the doctrine of the creation of the eternal truths and the question of the existence of a void, see A.-R. Ndiaye, *La Philosophie d'Antoine Arnauld* (Paris: Vrin 1991), 323–32.

36 AT 8A, 13, 19–20.

37 *OA* 38, 543. Arnauld cites the Picot translation of the first part of the *Principles*, and ties together articles 22 and 23.

38 The same reproach is made by Fénelon, in Chapter 6 of his *Réfutation du système de la nature et de la grâce*. Regarding the absence of divine freedom of indifference in Malebranche, see for example the *Méditations chrétiennes*, IX, as well as the *Entretiens sur la métaphysique*, IX: 'It is with complete freedom that God determines himself to create the world': *OC* 12, 202. Once the world is created, however, the very idea of freedom of indifference ceases to have any sense (we could add that it is doubly impossible, since there are no singular thoughts in the Word).

39 AT 7, 431, 27–432, 1.

40 AT 7, 435, 27.

41 *Summa Theologiae*, I, 47, 2, ad 2.

42 *Réflexions, OA* 39, 598.

43 I, 19, 3, ad 5.

44 *Réflexions, OA* 39, 599.

45 See also the reply to the first objection in the same article: '*Ad primum ergo dicendum quod ex hoc quod Deus ab aeterno vult aliquid, non sequitur quod necesse est eum illud velle, nisi ex suppositione.*'

46 Arnauld does not fail to note, *à propos* the *Traité de la nature et de la grâce*, that 'it is quite strange that a theological system, full of so many new thoughts on the most important questions of religion, has been printed four times without the approbation of any bishops or doctors [of theology]': *Réflexions, OA* 39, 847.

47 The same point can be made about the creation of eternal truths, I, 44, 1, ad 3. *The Third Objection* was the following: In mathematics nothing is demonstrated by reference to an agent cause. The reply requires that we distinguish *mathematica ut abstracta secundum rationem from mathematica* in so far as they have being (whether separate or not). If the *mathematica* have being, they have an agent cause in so far as they beings, since they are involved in matter. But if they are considered in so far as they are abstract, they are not created, hence they have no agent cause. But for St Thomas, God remains subject to the principle of non-contradiction.

48 The complete elucidation of this hypothesis would require a twofold evaluation that is far beyond the limits of this essay: on the one hand, an estimation of the relation of Malebranche to St Thomas with regard to creation (and with regard to the concept of order that is implicit here); on the other hand, the relation of Arnauld to St Thomas regarding the question of freedom. On the latter point, I should thank Elmar Kremer for having drawn my attention to *Humanae libertatis notio*, published in 1699 by Quesnel in the *Causa Arnaldina*. (A French translation by Quesnel can be found in *OA* 10, 614–24.) This 'small work in Latin' (written on the basis of a collection of Thomistic texts that constitutes the *Disquisitio* ..., *OA* 10, 625–40), which, according to Kremer, dates from 1688, seems to indicate a rather precisely Thomistic development in Arnauld on the topic of human freedom. (See the convincing contribution by Elmar Kremer, 'Grace and Free Will in Arnauld,' in *The Great Arnauld* ..., (Toronto: University of Toronto Press 1994), 219–39.) If we can believe a letter to Vuillaret of 21 June 1692 (*OA* 3, 498, cited by Kremer in n. 3, p. 232), Arnauld's basic work on the Thomistic theory of freedom would date from 1684–5 ('six or seven years ago'), hence immediately before the composition of the *Réflexions*, with which I am now dealing and in which Thomistic and Cartesian elements are combined into an ambiguous argument.

49 See also the classic discussion of the third *Eclaircissement* of the *Traité de la nature et de la grâce*, which breaks the Cartesian rule that we should never say that God *is not able* to do something: 'The wisdom of God thus renders him powerless in this sense, that it does not permit him to will certain things, or to act in certain ways' (*OC* 5, 181). The point is discussed by Arnauld in the *Réflexions*, where he mentions lying, causing miracles in order to authorize error, damning the blessed, etc.

50 G II, 15.

51 G II, 29.

52 Here I will only point out certain elements of the first letters in the correspondence. For a commentary on the entire debate (but one that does not deal with the point on which I am concentrating) see R.C. Sleigh, Jr, *Leibniz and Arnauld: A Commentary on their Correspondence* (New Haven, CT: Yale University Press 1990).

53 G II, 19.

54 G II, 32.

55 G II, 31. It is not necessary to insist once again on the Cartesian Thomism of Arnauld.

56 G II, 321.

57 G II, 32.

58 Ibid.

59 The compete notion determines an individual by the conjunction of all its essential and existential attributes: The notion of a circle is not complete if it contains only its essential predicates (see G. II, 39, 45, 52). That is why there is no complete notion of geometric figures, or of species of substance (see also the *Textes inédits*, published and annotated by Gaston Grua [Paris: PUF 1948], I, especially p. 311.) Recall that, for Leibniz, in contrast to Arnauld, the *cogito* does not give a complete notion of my individuality (G II, 32,33, 45, 52, etc.).

60 Remarks on a letter of Arnauld, in the letter of 21/31 May 1686 to the Landgraf Ernst von Hessen-Rheinfels, G II, 39.

61 G II, 38–9. These remarks of Leibniz have been noted and commented on, in a way close my own, by Ndiaye in *La Philosophie d'Antoine Arnauld*, 332–43, where he discusses a 'certain difficulty' of Arnauld's.

62 G II, 49.

63 This point all the more remarkable in that Leibniz himself began paragraph XIII of the *Discourse on Metaphysics* by comparing the consideration of the notion of an individual substance with that of the nature of a circle: 'by considering [the] notion [of an individual substance] one can *see* there everything that can be truly said of it, just as we can *see* in the nature of a circle all the properties that can be deduced from it.' The comparison has to do with vision (that is, with the intelligibility of the determinations), not with deduction (because the one consititutes a necessity *ex hypothesi* and the other an absolute necessity). But what is at stake in the correspondence is the contrast between the notion of a species and the notion of an individual.

64 G II, 131.

65 G II, 64.

66 AT 1, 146, 17.

67 G II, 31.

68 Ibid.

69 One might cite against this hypothesis, a difficult passage in the *Règles de bon*

sens, where Arnauld writes: 'Things, properly speaking, are the substances created by God; whereas truths, and propositions demonstrated in the sciences, are not things created by God ' (*OA* 40, 167). In response, two main points need to be made:

(1) The question Arnauld is dealing with here has to do first of all with the use of 'thing,' a notion strictly defined as 'substance'; and while Descartes grants to truths the same status as 'all the other creatures' (AT 1, 145, 9–10), and does not hesitate to say that God 'is the sole author on which all things depend' (AT 1, 150, 7–8), indeed, goes so far as to use the vocabulary of creation with regard to truths (AT 1, 152, 20 and 27, for example), he would clearly not say that truths are created things if by that is meant that they are substances, that is, existents; his intention is to assign the same ontological status to essences as to existents (AT 1, 152, 2–5, 28–9). This is the origin of the two types of eternity distinguished by Arnauld in the *Dissertatio bipartita*, which he uses to 'Cartesianize' a Thomistic thesis: that essences, in so far as they are possibles, do not have the same eternity as God.

(2) In 1693, the date of the *Dissertatio bipartita*, followed by the *Règles de bon sens*, Arnauld, faced with his new adversaries, Gommaire Hyygens and François Lamy, settles on positions that are ostensibly Thomistic, once again as a polemical strategy, at least at the outset, and the usual Augustinian *corpus* is, rightly or wrongly, conceded to his adversaries. The fact remains that Arnauld is silent precisely at the point where we might expect him to join battle, namely, at the point where, in order to set himself at once against what he will present as two parallel errors, he opposes Malebranche and Huygens. Malebranche's error is the vision of all creatures in God, because bodies are not visible through themselves, not the vision of truths in God, for truths are merely relations. (On this last point Malebranche 'is entirely right': *OA* 40, 158.) Huygens, by contrast, holds that we see *only* the necessary and immutable truths in God. In the face of these upholders of the vision in God, vision of things or vision of truths, Arnauld avoids both alternatives with the help of St Thomas, not Descartes. Nevertheless, it seems to me that a careful analysis of the *Dissertatio bipartita* would enable us to find there the same ambiguous Cartesian Thomism that we found earlier in the *Réflexions*.

70 *Cartésianisme et augustinisme*, 156. See also the illuminating remarks of Geneviève Rodis-Lewis in 'Augustinisme et cartésianisme,' *L'Anthropologie cartésienne* (Paris: PUF 1990), 101–25.

71 'Arnauld: From Ockhamism to Cartesianism,' in *Descartes and His Contemporaries*, R. Ariew and M. Grene, eds. (Chicago: University of Chicago Press 1995).

72 G II, 32.

8

Arnauld's Defence of
Miracles and Its Context

GRAEME HUNTER

The Background

It is sometimes supposed that, if a thing is to excite our wonder, it must be rare. In particular the wonderfulness of miracles has been attributed by some philosophers to their being seldom seen. But during the Middle Ages this inverse law seems not to have held, for, as is well known, miracles at that time were both highly regarded and frequently attested.[1] Moreover, at the zenith of that age, St Thomas Aquinas provided the philosophical background against which miracles could credibly be said to be both commonplace and provocative of wonder. The crux of his account is his definition of miracles as events which it exceeds the power (*facultas*) of nature to perform.[2] Paraphrasing him, we could say that miracles are natural events with supernatural causes.

This definition raises the question of what is meant by nature. St Thomas understands it to be the order of what he calls 'secondary causes,' an order created and presided over by the primary cause, God.[3] All creatures are secondary causes, endowed by God with characteristic powers according to their kind. Within a stipulated range, the use of these powers is left up to the discretion of creatures, at least of animate ones. A dog, for instance, can bark or not when a rabbit runs by. The rabbit can increase its pace or dodge into a hole. A completely natural event is then a transaction among creatures which can be wholly explained by reference to their creaturely powers. Now, since God is free to suspend, limit, or enhance his creatures' powers from time to time as it suits his purposes, when he does so, by definition, a 'supernatural' event occurs. And such events are what are properly called 'miraculous,' because they depend on a power outside the natural order of secondary causes.

Yet to confine miracles outside the natural order is not to banish them from experience. On the contrary, St Thomas's account of them could be called 'centripetal,' for it drives miracles right into the middle of things. Miracles always occur just when intervention is least expected, right in the midst of ordinary events. That is why they are sources of wonder. Miracles so understood are also by the same token local events. If, for example, Lazarus is raised from the dead, it is not a victory over death everywhere and forever. It is a reversal of the process of bodily decay in only a single human body, and only for a season. Some theologians distinguish therefore between resurrection, which is global, and resuscitation, which is local. For St Thomas, resuscitation, so understood, would be a model of miracles generally. They are mainly local disruptions in the natural order.

This is why miracles can be simultaneously frequent and wonderful. It is not their rarity, but the intrinsically awesome fact of supernatural intervention in ordinary life, which is the object of human wonder.[4] Thus the proliferation of miracles in late medieval practice finds a basis in rigorous Thomistic theory. I shall refer to that happy combination of theory and practice as the Catholic status quo.

In the modern period the Catholic status quo was under attack on two fronts. Protestants were proposing a more stringent criterion for miracles, namely, that they not merely be wonderful but in addition pass the test of conformity to the teachings of scripture. Calvin refers to this *desideratum* as 'the test of Doctrine,'[5] and Luther formulates it as follows: 'the rule is this: Regardless of their size and number, no wonders or signs are to be accepted contrary to established teaching ... The only preventive is to have a good grasp of doctrine and to keep it before your eyes continually.'[6]

The reasons given by the reformers themselves for their more demanding criterion were not accepted by their Roman Catholic critics. The reformers said that they were trying to purify the church of superstition and idolatry; the counter-reformers alleged that the Protestants were only attempting to make less conspicuous their own lack of miraculous confirmation, or, as Luther himself put it in his inimitable parody of their attacks, the fact that 'the Lutherans had never even cured a lame horse.' A neutral way of characterizing the Protestant doctrinal test of miracles would be to say that it grew out of Luther's general principle: *sola scriptura*.

The second attack on the Catholic status quo originated with the apologists for the modern scientific outlook and was due to the new science's reconception of nature. What for the medievals had been a community of creatures (secondary causes) came to be understood by the moderns as a vast system of matter in motion, obedient to simple physical laws and describable in mathematical terms. Divine power seemed to be the only motor either necessary or sufficient to account for the motion of matter, and accordingly the doctrine of secondary causes plummeted into disrepute.[7]

Some of the early moderns wished to explain miracles away altogether. This seems to be pretty clearly the case with men like Spinoza, Hobbes, and Thomas Burnett. Others were willing to keep them, provided they were rare and decorously absent from local events of concern to the sciences. To the latter group of philosophers must be counted such figures as Malebranche, Leibniz, and Samuel Clarke. Of course these very different thinkers differed also in the detail of their accounts of miracles. Robert McRae has recently clarified the extent to which Clarke's (and hence, Newton's) understanding of miracles, which could be called 'statistical,' was at odds with Leibniz's power-based account.[8] But they were able to agree at least that there is a general order of things which, due to God's foresight, holds no (or negligably few) miraculous surprises for the practising scientist. Even those of the moderns who are sympathetic to miracles do their best to confine them to the periphery of experience. This centrifugal account is prefigured, like so much of modern philosophy, in Part V of Descartes's *Discourse on Method*. The only reference to miracles made in that place is to the 'miracle of creation,' which, though conceded to be a fact, is compared unfavourably from the scientific point of view with a kind of universal, mechanical evolution which, Descartes says, was a possible blueprint of our origins, though not the one actually chosen by God.[9]

It is instructive to note in this connection that St Thomas does not recognize creation as a miracle at all, since it establishes, and hence cannot contravene, the natural order.[10] Yet creation is the only miracle that the advocates of the new science can comfortably admit. These philosophers demand a tame, predictable first mover who initially will oblige them by getting things off to a good start and thereafter will govern in undeviating adherence to a scientifically detectable pattern. Such a creator has the twin virtues of accounting metaphysically for the order of nature and of guaranteeing its permanence. And he accomplishes both of these tasks without any of the erratic intrusions on the system of matter in motion which caused the God of Abraham, Isaac, and Jacob to fall from the scientists' favour.

Arnauld

Antoine Arnauld had some of the right credentials for being on the modern team. As one suspected of sympathies with the Reformation he might have been supposed to share some of the reformers' concerns about medieval excesses in the matter of miracles. Since he was a Cartesian, one would anticipate his allegiance to the demands of the new science. But Arnauld surprises us on both counts. He defends instead the church's historic position on miracles, holding them to be interventions of God in the normal course of events, and allowing them to be frequent, local, and confirming of doctrine, rather than dependent on it. The questions to be examined in this essay are, first, why Arnauld defended the Catholic status quo, and, second, how well his defence of it holds up in the modern setting.

La Sainte Epine

To guess at thinkers' motivations is often a risky business, but it is less so in the present case. The circumstances of Arnauld's life easily explain his dissent from the modern consensus on miracles. He was personally involved with a sequence of miracles which fascinated Paris, rocked the Jesuit establishment, and determined to a large extent the fortunes of Port-Royal, beginning with the so-called miracle of the holy thorn. From the viewpoint of posterity, the most significant achievement of this miracle was undoubtedly that it inspired Pascal's *Pensées*. But it also led Arnauld to defend it against the polemics which it excited and so awakened his philosophical interest in the question of miracles. In order to evaluate his apologetic position, it is important to be familiar with the main circumstances of this story.

On 24 March 1656 Mademoiselle Marguerite Perrier was just approaching her tenth birthday. She was a pupil in residence at one of the 'petites écoles' attached to Port-Royal, probably so that she could be under the supervision of her uncle, Blaise Pascal. Mlle Perrier was originally from Clermont, where her family still resided. At the age of six she had developed in the corner of her left eye, next to the nose, what the doctors of the day called a 'fistula lachrymosa,' which means literally a conduit out of which tears (and other fluids) continually leaked. Pascal, who had seen his niece in Clermont, at the beginning of her illness, described it as having originally consisted in 'some drops of water which fell out of the corner of the said left eye next to the nose, the discharge rapidly growing more frequent and viscous and eventually changing into something like mud [*boue*].'[11]

She was seen by some of the best doctors of France, who unanimously recommended cauterization, though they could not guarantee that the eye, or even the child, would survive the ordeal. They knew, however, of no other treatment. It is not difficult to see why this severe and risky recommendation led the family to try first some of the gentler remedies proposed by doctors of lesser stature. These were pursued right up until August 1655, with the result that the eye got continually, though slowly, worse. By that time Mlle Perrier was a pupil at Port-Royal, and her father recommended, by the intermediary of Pascal, that all treatment be discontinued, to see whether unaided nature might not effect a cure. Instead a tumour about the size of a filbert nut developed, and the girl began to lose her sense of smell. In addition the fluid, which by now gave off such an odour that Mlle Perrier had to be segregated from the other girls, was also flowing into her nose and mouth. She had grown weak, pale, and emaciated and had difficulty sleeping because of the constant discharge. Once again the unanimous recommendation of the doctors was cauterization. Pascal was alarmed about his niece's condition and wrote a letter to her father in Clermont, requesting that he come as soon as possible to Paris for the operation. The latter set out for Paris on 29 March 1656, still believing that his daughter would be operated on when he arrived.

Meanwhile, the monastery of Port-Royal had received on loan from a certain M. de la Potterie, a high-ranking Parisian churchman, a relic from his collection, said to be a thorn from the crown of Christ. Apparently it had been making the rounds of some monasteries prior to its arrival at Port-Royal. It was delivered there on the Friday of the third week of Lent, 1656, which in that year was the 24 March. The poet Jean Racine, in his account of the miracle, notes that the introit of the prescribed mass for that day was drawn from the words of Psalm 86: 17, 'Fac mecum signum in bonum ...,' in the King James version: 'Shew me a token for good; that they which hate me may see it, and be ashamed: because thou, Lord, hast holpen me, and comforted me.'

To the members of the community of Port-Royal, these words would have been deeply significant, because their monastery was under steady and bitter attack from the Jesuits on points of doctrine. The community was thus collectively hoping for a sign of some kind to vindicate them in what they regarded as the unjust attacks of their enemies, one thrust of which, incidentally, was to demand the closure of the very school which the Perrier girl attended.

Following vespers that evening all the schoolgirls filed past the relic and, when it came the turn of Mlle Perrier, the school-mistress said to her: 'Commend yourself to God and touch the thorn to your eye.' She did as bidden. Following the ceremony the girls returned to their rooms. Scarcely had Marguerite Perrier reached her room when she said to one of her companions: 'My sister, I am no longer in pain. The holy thorn has cured me.' Someone, who may have been Arnauld, responding to a later Jesuit attack on the miracle, describes the rapid sequence of events as follows:

The source of the mud [*boue*] which was flowing continually from her eye, her nose and her mouth, and which had still been flowing on her cheek a moment before the miracle, as she herself declared later in her statement, was completely dried up. The bone, which had been decayed and rotten, was restored to its original condition. All the stench which had been associated with her wound, and which was so intolerable that the girl had to be separated from the others by order of the doctors and surgeons, was changed into breath as sweet as an infant's. At the same time she recovered her sense of smell, and none of the ills which were a result of the main one returned. Even her colour, which had been pale and leaden, became as lively and clear as it ever had been.[12]

The miracle of the holy thorn became a *cause célèbre* in Paris, to such a degree that the Queen Mother and the King sent their personal physicians to join the large party of other prominent doctors and religious authorities investigating it. The physicians examining Mlle Perrier after the event included several who had also attended her before it. They concluded unanimously that there were no medical causes for the cure. Even the hostile Jesuits were forced to recognize that a miracle had occurred, and they confined their criticisms to saying that there can be miracles which vindicate neither sects nor doctrines.[13]

The fact that the Jesuits took up this typically Protestant position in attacking the miracle of the holy thorn meant, of course, that anyone setting out to defend it would have to occupy different ground. And it is not surprising that advocacy of the miracle fell to the lot of Arnauld, it being a crucial event in the life of the Port-Royal community, to whose defence Arnauld had consecrated his life. Against this background, then, it is understandable that the entire argumentative strategy of Arnauld's apologetical essay on the authority of miracles consists in proving that the Jesuits have taken up the cause of the Calvinists, while he (Arnauld) is defending, not merely the Port-Royal Community, but the church and God himself.[14]

Circumstances thus determined not only that Arnauld would defend local miracles, but also that his apologetic would take the traditional theological slant that it did. Furthermore, the fact that the miracles connected with the holy thorn seemed to come dramatically at the moment of Port-Royal's greatest need would certainly have encouraged Arnauld to look upon them as doctrine-confirming, rather than as in need of doctrinal testing. He writes: 'Since these miracles occurred in the middle of the worship services and in such propitious circumstances, there was no one who failed to recognize them as marks of God's protection of this community ...'[15] In short, Arnauld's deep commitment to the monastery of Port-Royal led him to understand the events connected with the holy thorn as local miracles and to see them as direct interventions of God intended for confirming doctrine, specifically the Jansenist doctrines which informed both the religious life of Port-Royal and the teaching at the *petites écoles*.

A defence of particular miracles is unlikely to advance very far, however, in the absence of a general account of them. The writing of the Port-Royal *Logic* in the years following the healing of Marguerite Perrier gave Arnauld an opportunity to formulate just such a general account.

Miracles in the Port-Royal Logic

The Art of Thinking[16] was, of course, co-authored by Arnauld and Pierre Nicole. However, we have it on the authority of Racine that Arnauld was singlehandedly responsible for its fourth part, concerning method, and it is there that the chapter devoted to miracles is found.[17] Briefly, Part IV of the *Logic* studies each of the three ways in which belief can qualify as knowledge. If a belief is self-evident, it is knowledge of the type called in French *intelligence*; if it is arrived at by sound proof, then the conviction so produced is called in French *science*. In the third place, if the belief in question is based on authority, then the knowledge it produces is called 'testimonial' (in French *foi*).[18]

The chapter on miracles is found within Arnauld's discussion of this third branch of knowledge, the one that is based on authority. That setting militates against a correct understanding of the chapter for two reasons, which ought to be noted in passing. The first is that we tend, by an inveterate modern prejudice, to regard all appeals to authority as suspicious, if not actually fallacious. With sufficient attention, that prejudice can be overcome, but the second difficulty is more serious: we are likely to be led astray by a deceptively ambiguous term which is pivotal in Arnauld's discussion of this type of knowledge.

The word in question is *foi*, which, in some contexts, must be translated as 'faith' and, in others, as 'testimony.'[19] What makes it treacherous in the present setting is that in a number of cases both translations make sense, though each leads in a different direction. The sentence with which Arnauld introduces the third (authority-based) type of knowledge is a good example. The original French says: 'Si c'est l'autorité qui fait que l'esprit embrasse ce qui est proposé, c'est ce qu'on appelle foi.'[20] This has been translated as: 'If it is authority which leads the mind to embrace what is proposed to it, this is what is called faith.'[21] So translated, it yields a not implausible definition of faith: faith is believing on the authority of another. But the word 'testimony,' or its adjectival derivative 'testimonial,' fits here just as well. In fact, when I paraphrased the same French sentence above, I said that, when belief was based on authority, the knowledge it produced was called *testimonial*. When the sentence is translated in this way, it becomes, not a definition of faith, but instead a classification of knowledge. Although the sentence taken in isolation makes the translation of 'foi' by 'faith' look, if anything, more plausible, its context, which is precisely a classification of types of knowledge, makes 'testimony' (or 'testimonial') a better translation. Similarly, in Chapter 12 of Part IV of the *Logic*, when Arnauld returns to this matter, the same decision must be faced time and again by the translator. The title of that chapter ought to read (in English): 'Of what we know through testimony, whether human or divine.' However, a usually reliable English translator, the one with whom I have already quarrelled regarding an earlier occurrence of 'foi,' once again puts 'faith' where 'testimony' should be, despite the fact that no literal sense can be made of the idea of 'divine faith.' 'Foi' is a small word, but this is not a small point. The proprieties of translation have to be established already, because the discussion of the connection between knowledge and testimony in Chapter 12 is the first step on the way to Arnauld's discussion of miracles in Chapter 14.

In the intervening chapter (IV, 13), Arnauld formulates rules for the acceptance of human testimony. Where they are followed, Arnauld suggests, it is possible to attain to moral certainty in matters of this kind. In Arnauld's concise discussion, one can discern three rules for reasoning well about testimony. The first rule is to recognize a realm of merely contingent matters, including paradigmatically those which depend on free human decisions. To call them contingent is to say that they are not necessary, and therefore to imply that it is futile to expect apodictic certainty in any belief which we may form concerning these events. Arnauld understands such contingency (or non-necessity) to include independence of physical, as well as logical necessity, as he explicitly says.[22] Rule two is to recognize that the fact that we abandon the search for necessity does not mean that we have to settle for bare possibility. Testimony does not become credible merely because the events it describes are possible. Rule three is formulated against the background of its predecessors: To know whether or not to believe testimony concerning a certain purportedly contingent event, we must first examine both the internal and the external circumstances of that event. By 'internal circumstances' Arnauld means what belongs to the event itself, such things as its consistency and plausibility; by 'external circumstances' he means especially the testimony which leads us to believe that such an event took place, and the reliability of the witnesses who are responsible for that testimony. If our examination reveals both the internal and the external circumstances to be such that falsity in similar cases would be very rare, then we can have moral certainty that the witness's testimony is true. This is the highest degree of certainty which we are able to attain, since, by hypothesis, we are dealing with matters of contingent fact.

An example is desirable at this point, and one is provided by Arnauld in the subsequent chapter, entitled 'Application of the foregoing rule to the belief in miracles.' Miracles are paradigm cases of events which are (in Arnauld's sense) contingent with respect to the order of nature, and of which we become aware by testimony. Arnauld, of course, did not intend to exclude the possibility of one's being an eyewitness of a miracle, and hence not needing testimony for it, but, for all the miracles on which the Christian faith depends, reliance on human testimony is necessary and the same would apply to any contemporary miracle, if it were to be widely used for the confirmation of doctrine. In considering when testimony concerning miracles should be accepted, and when not, we must apply the rules discussed in the previous chapter.

It must be remembered that the general aim of the Port-Royal *Logic* is to 'form our judgment' in such a way that we will exhibit 'good sense and accuracy of thought, in discriminating between truth and falsehood.'[23] In the case of miracles, then, this places us under a twin obligation. The first is to avoid unwarranted scepticism in the consideration of miracles. They cannot be ruled out *a priori*, because the events they describe are not logically impossible. To try to eliminate them in this way is to fail to recognize the domain of the contingent, to which the previous chapter of the *Logic* carefully laid claim. But, in the second place, one must also avoid the opposite extreme of credulity, the vice of believing things on the strength of their possibility alone. Where scepticism perversely overlooks the rightful inhabitants of the realm of contingency, credulity populates it with fabulous ones.

The key to avoiding both extremes lies in observing the third rule from the previous chapter, the one concerning the examination of the internal and external circumstances surrounding a miraculous event and the testimony in its favour. In order to permit his readers to apply this rule, Arnauld mentions several miracles and recounts at length the details of one performed by St Augustine and described by him in *The City of God* (BK. 22, ch. 8). The purpose of the itemized description is to enable the reader to decide whether there is any *a priori* reason why the events could not have happened precisely as Augustine described them. Briefly and neutrally, the facts are that a brother and a sister on two public religious occasions, which followed each other in close succession, were released from a condition of convulsive trembling, common to their entire family. Augustine was the eyewitness of the second miracle, which occurred while he was conducting a service of thanksgiving for the first. There is, Arnauld assumes, no *a priori* reason why such things could not have happened. And if they happened in the religious context described, Arnauld claims, 'no reasonable person could fail to recognize the finger of God in them.'[24]

With the internal circumstances of these miracles thus satisfactorily examined, Arnauld turns to the external ones, that is, the reliability of Augustine's testimony. Arnauld first points out the psychological improbability of any sober person's lying about so public an event. In the second place he reminds us of the general probity of Augustine in particular as a witness to anything, of his hatred of lying as a crime and his fear of it as a sin. The conclusion of Arnauld is that 'every reasonable man, even if he is not pious, must recognize as true the miracles that St. Augustine describes ...'[25]

No further study of chapters 13 and 14 is necessary to see that Arnauld's interest in the problem of miracles is an epistemological one. He stipulates the existence of a general field of contingent events, which would include any that were miraculous, i.e., any which were inexplicable by reference to secondary causes alone. The philosophical task, as Arnauld conceives it, is only to show that testimony presenting the details of a putatively miraculous event must be evaluated according to the criteria usually applied to testimony about contingent matters of any kind. Presumably this would entail such things as making sure that our informants are not providing the description for frivolous or obviously self-serving ends. Of course, even a testimony which was self-serving or frivolously given might still be true, but it would clearly be unworthy of belief by a third party. Next we must ascertain such things as whether the witness's general integrity and competence is a matter of established fact and whether there are corroborating witnesses. If the answer to all such inquiries is affirmative, then we have grounds for believing that the event attested to really occurred. If, in addition to that, the event (which by hypothesis is scientifically inexplicable) occurred in appropriate religious circumstances, such as those in which it appears to be an answer to prayer, or to obvious needs of a religious community, or to unresolved questions of doctrine, then we may be morally certain that it is a miracle. Such, essentially, is Arnauld's apology for miracles in the Port-Royal *Logic*.

One thing may puzzle us about this account of miracles and several aspects of it may trouble us deeply. The puzzling thing is why Arnauld never directly mentions the miracle of the holy thorn, though some of what he says strongly suggests that he is thinking of it. The most likely explanation for the omission is that any testimony he had given in favour of the holy thorn would have appeared to be self-interested.[26] It is a less straightforward matter to reply to the philosophical reservations which many may have about his account of miracles. To them we now turn.

It is not necessary to be creedally opposed to miracles in order to be hesitant about Arnauld's defence of them. In the first place it is disconcerting to see him approach the matter as a logician or epistemologist, rather than as a metaphysician or philosopher of science. For, if the critics of miracles in the seventeenth and eighteenth century agreed upon anything, it was surely that the possibility of miracles, as tradition conceived them, meant the impossibility of science as they understood it. Thus it is hard to think any treatment of miracles complete that does not discuss them in scientific terms. A second (related) difficulty with Arnauld's account is that he seems to evaluate testimony concerning miracles as if it were no more intrinsically problematic than testimony on any other contingent subject. We post-Humeans, on the other hand, have been conditioned to think that we have *a priori* reasons for being particularly suspicious of such testimony, reasons which derive from the *a priori* improbability of miracles as such.

The criticism of Hume's which touches more than any other on both these points is the one in which he says: 'no testimony is sufficient to establish a miracle unless the testimony be of such a kind that its falsehood would be more miraculous than the fact which it endeavors to establish.'[27] What Hume implies is that, since a miracle is 'a violation of the laws of nature,'[28] it has a probability of 0.[29] And, of course, no testimony in favour of anything, let alone miracles, will ever have a probability of 1. As Hume says: 'it appears that no testimony for any kind of miracle has ever amounted to a probability, much less to a proof; and that, even supposing it amounted to a proof, it would be opposed by another proof derived from the very nature of the fact which it would endeavor to establish.'[30] Thus even a testimony that could be faulted from no other angle would be disqualified for the very reason that it was attesting to a miracle. In other words, miracles, according to Hume, can be ruled out *a priori*, and therefore can never be fit subjects of testimony in the first place. The cultural persuasiveness of this argument is one factor, I suspect, in the hesitation many people would feel about Arnauld's account of how knowledge of miracles is possible.

Though Hume's probabilistic criticism of miracles and Arnauld's epistemic discussion of testimony have quite different thrusts, it is not impossible to express their differences in a common idiom. The basis of their disagreement is that Arnauld affirms what Hume denies, namely, that there can be events, contingent with respect to physical laws, the cause of which is a direct act of God.

Hume, by insisting on the exceptionless regularity of nature, seems to be stating only a scientific truism, and therefore to be in a more defensible position than Arnauld, who allows for scientific anomalies. However, on closer scrutiny, Hume loses his advantage. Let us see why.

First, an assumption in Hume's account can be challenged. He assumes that the witness to a miracle must be claiming that a miracle occurred. But this is not so. The witness need only be testifying to the occurrence of a naturally inexplicable, i.e., contingent, event, such as happened with the application of the holy thorn. That the sequence of events there described could occur, and could do so in the order described, is not a logical impossibility. And it is not primarily the witness, according to Arnauld, but the events themselves, which testify to their being miraculous. Regarding the miracles of the holy thorn, I have already quoted

Arnauld as saying: 'Since these miracles occurred in the middle of worship services and in such propitious circumstances, there was no one who failed to recognize them as marks of God's protection of this community ...' Likewise, concerning the miracles described by Augustine, Arnauld was quoted above as saying that every reasonable man would have to recognize them as miraculous.

If we now shift the focus away from the events and onto the testimony about them, it is Arnauld's account that is universal and regular, and Hume's which admits of exceptions. To stipulate the exceptionless regularity of nature, as Hume does, thus comes at the cost of introducing differential rules for testimony. In other words, Hume cannot countenance any general theory for the evaluation of testimony, but must evaluate it *ad hoc*, according to its subject. Arnauld inverts that pattern. All testimony is evaluated by him according to its internal and external circumstances. This admits the possibility of there being true testimony regarding irregularities in nature, such as would lead any reasonable person to conclude that a miracle had occurred.

The miracle of the holy thorn must have strengthened Arnauld's conviction that such testimony was possible. And, indeed, there have been few events in all of recorded history which are attested to simultaneously by the best doctors (*pace* Sainte-Beuve),[31] philosophers and poets of an era, and witnessed in addition by a convent full of women of renowned probity. Should a rational person with an antecedent belief in the existence of God not conclude that the testimony is accurate and that it likely betokens a miraculous event? Only the unsupported (and even on Humean assumptions unsupportable)[32] assertion that there are no contingent events of the sort that Arnauld describes could rule this out *a priori*. Thus Arnauld's assumption of the regularity of the rules of testimony in the *Logic* is no more intrinsically controversial than Hume's assumption of the regularity of the laws of nature in the *Inquiry*. And Arnauld has a distinct advantage in his account of nature. He need only maintain that contingent events, as he defines them, are possible, whereas Hume must either defend the stronger claim that they are impossible, one for which he has no evidence, or else lose his *a priori* argument against miracles. Arnauld's general doctrine of miracles, though conceived in a limited apologetic context, thus proves defensible, even against the assaults of the ablest of the later modern sceptics.

Malebranche and Frequent Miracles

The miracle of the holy thorn thrust upon Arnauld the task of defending miracles as local interventions of God, useful for the confirmation of doctrine. The writing of the Port-Royal *Logic* gave him the opportunity of securing that position within a larger framework of epistemology. But neither occasion required Arnauld to take a position as to the remaining aspect of what I have been calling the Catholic status quo – the frequency of miracles. An opportunity to do so was provided, however, in 1684, with the publication by Nicolas Malebranche of an expanded fourth edition of his *Treatise on Nature and Grace*.

A major novelty of that edition was an added fourth *Eclaircissement* with the title 'The Frequent Miracles of the Old Law in no way mean that God often acts by Particular Volitions.' Malebranche ingeniously argues that the frequent biblical miracles can all be accommodated without supposing that God willed each one separately. God could, instead, have made a general resolution to act on every occasion as demanded by the intended interventions of his angels in human affairs. In this way God would remain the sole real cause in the universe, creatures would be only occasional causes, the world would be governed only according to general laws, and yet frequent miracles would still be possible. The ingenuity of this arrangement lay in its potential for satisfying several seemingly irreconcilable parties. Modern metaphysics, as we have seen, had no place for real secondary causes. This account of miracles satisfied its demand that God be the sole efficacious cause. Modern science's requirement that the universe be exceptionlessly regular was also satisfied by Malebranche's position, since it permitted God to act only according to general laws. Finally, a minimum demand of theological orthodoxy was that the miracles recounted in the Bible be deemed to have happened, and Malebranche was able to satisfy that too, yet without jeopardizing modern metaphysics and science. The key to this elegant solution obviously lays in the proof that there could be frequent miracles without frequent particular volitions on the part of God.

Arnauld lost no time in attacking it. In fact, he couldn't wait for his attack to be published in its natural place within the two book-length studies of Malebranche's *Treatise* which were in preparation in 1685, and so he brought it out separately in that year under a windy title, which began: 'Dissertation of M. Arnauld, Doctor of the Sorbonne, on the manner in which God performed the frequent miracles of the Old Law by the Ministry of Angels ...' In that work he was able to produce no knockdown conceptual argument against Malebranche's position, though he exhibited his wonted acumen in finding logical difficulties with it. His principal contention, however, reminiscent of Pascal, was that Malebranche's conception of divine concourse was a philosopher's pipe-dream and quite at odds with anything to be found in scripture or in the traditions of the church.

A.-R. Ndiaye has shown, in his study of Arnauld's thought, that the latter's doctrine of general providence entails that God acts by particular volitions.[33] It is not surprising, therefore, that his doctrine of special providence, or miracles, should make the same claim. And if God acts by particular volitions, then the dreams of the new science are not true, for the general laws it seeks will not be a comprehensive guide to all that happens in the universe.

Though the attack on Malebranche is philosophically the weakest of Arnauld's writings on miracles, it is of a piece with the others and adds a theological and biblical dimension desirable in dealing with a question of this nature. It is also important in being the only writing of Arnauld explicitly to defend the traditional understanding of the frequency of miracles.

The three texts on miracles examined here were written over a period of a quarter of a century and in different contexts. Yet they display sufficient continuity to form a unified defence of what I have called the Catholic status quo. It is characteristic of Arnauld to have mounted such a defence at a time when every aspect of the thing defended was under attack, and yet to carry it off with such aplomb that it challenges the most formidable sceptics. Nevertheless, to reason well is sometimes to do no more than spit against the wind. A defence of the Catholic status quo, however well executed, was not what was called for in the age of reason. Neither has subsequent history looked kindly upon it. If there is a time for Arnauld's theory of miracles, it must therefore be still to come.

Notes

1 See Benedicta Ward, *Miracles and the Medieval Mind* (Philadelphia: University of Pennsylvania Press 1982), 1f.
2 St Thomas Aquinas, *Summa Theologica*, I q. 105, a. 8, resp.
3 Ibid., I, q. 105, a. 6, resp.
4 Ibid., I, q. 105, a. 7, resp.
5 Jean Calvin, *Institutes of the Christian Religion*, vol. 1, J.T. NcNeill, ed., F.L. Battles, tr. (Philadelphia: Westminster Press 1960), 'Prefatory Address,' 15.
6 Martin Luther, cited in *What Luther Says*, vol. 2, E.M. Plass, ed. (Saint Louis: Concordia 1972), #3006, p. 957.
7 See for example Malebranche's critique of secondary causes in *Eclaircissement* 15 of the *Recherche de la vérité*.
8 Robert McRae, 'Miracles and Laws,' in *The Natural Philosophy of Leibniz*, K. Okruhlik and J.R. Brown, eds. (Dordrecht: Reidel 1985), 171–81. See p. 176.
9 Descartes, AT 6, 45. It is possible, of course, that Descartes is speaking ironically here and that his real meaning was that the evolutionary course was the true one.
10 Thomas, *Summa*, I, q. 105, a. 7, ad 1.
11 Quotes in Tetsuya Shiokawa, *Pascal et les miracles* (Paris: Nizet 1977), 79.
12 The editors of the *Oeuvres* of Antoine Arnauld give some very convincing reasons

for thinking that the author of the article from which this excerpt is taken entitled 'Réponse à un écrit ...' is indeed Arnauld (See their introduction in *OA* 23, viii ff.) Modern scholars however are not convinced (see Shiokawa; *Pascal*, 106). The cited passage at any rate is found on p. 11 of the 'Réponse ...'

13 The sources of the account given here are Arnauld (or Pseudo-Arnauld) ('Réponse ...,' iii–10); the historical and critical preface to the 'Réponse ...,' vi; Racine, *Abrégé de l'histoire de Port-Royal* (Paris: Editions d'aujourd'hui 1981), 81–90; Pascal (see Shiokawa), and Shiokawa, *Pascal*, ch. 3.

14 Arnauld, 'De l'Autorité des miracles,' *OA* 23, 33–86, esp. 35.

15 Ibid., 67: 'Mais puisque ces miracles ne sont arrivés qu'au milieu de leurs [i.e., of the religious] adorations & de leurs hommages, & dans les conjonctures si étranges, qu'il ny a personne qui ne les ait pris pour des marques de la protection de Dieu sur cette maison.'

16 All citations of this work are according to the critical edition of it entitled *La Logique ou l'art de penser*, Pierre Clair and François Girbal, eds. (Paris: Presses Universitaires de France 1965).

17 Jean Racine, *Abrégé*, cited in Arnauld, *Logic*, 365.

18 *Logic*, IV, 1, 291f.

19 The problem here is analogous to that faced by the French translator in translating different occurrences of 'you.' To the English speaker they seem univocal; to the French speaker some of them seem to mean 'tu,' others 'vous.' The word 'foi' may appear to French speakers to be used univocally throughout the passages in question, but the work demands different English translations in different contexts and remains perplexingly ambiguous in some.

20 *Logic*, 292.

21 This is the translation given by the usually reliable translator Thomas Spencer Baynes in *The Port Royal Logic*, 5th ed. (Edinburgh: Sytherland and Knox 1861), 300.

22 Arnauld, *Logic*, IV, 13, 339: 'J'entens tout ceci selon leurs causes prochaines, ...'

23 Ibid., Premier Discours, 15.

24 Ibid., IV, 14, 346: 'il n'y a point de personne raisonnable qui n'y doive reconnoître le doigt de Dieu.' I assume that Arnauld would counter the claim that atheists are reasonable people who would not recognize God's finger in the events by saying either that such events would convert a fully rational atheist or that there are no fully rational atheists.

25 Ibid., IV, 14, 345: 'Mais je soûtiens que tout homme de bon sens, quand il n'aura pas de pieté, doit reconnoître pour veritables les miracles que S. Augustin raconte ...'

26 Sainte-Beuve makes this point in general about the Jansenist use of this miracle, in spite of disconfirming instances like the present one (see *Port Royal*, v. 3, ch.

XII [Paris: La Connaissance 1926], vol. 3, ch. 12, p. 52).

27 Hume, *Enquiry* §10, part 1 (Indianapolis: Library of Liberal Arts 1976), 123.

28 Ibid., 122.

29 I am aware that weaker interpretations of Hume's meaning in this chapter are possible. I do not believe them more conformable to Hume's text, however, and of course they would be of less use in the present context, where Hume is to act as a foil for Arnauld.

30 Hume, *Enquiry* §10, part II, 137.

31 Sainte-Beuve regards the miracle as a 'fait naturel' exploited by the Jansenists in order to save themselves from extinction (*Port Royal*, vol. 3, ch. xii, p. 52). However, the case he makes for this is so slight that it is better seen as an expression of his own struggles with orthodox Catholicism.

32 Within the scope of Hume's general sceptical treatment of causality a denial of the possibility of miracles is ruled out, because it allows for exceptions to the causal order. But, even within the chapter on miracles in the *Inquiry*, Hume seems only to want to prove their *a priori physical* impossibility. It is as if Hume wanted to say that miracle stories contain synthetic *a priori falsehoods*.

33 A.-R. Ndiaye, *La Philosophie d'Antoine Arnauld* (Paris: Vrin 1991), 259.

9

Arnauld versus Nicole: A Medieval Dispute

JEAN-LUC SOLÈRE

Antoine Arnauld was known as a fierce controversialist. At the end of his life, he fought, not only with his lifelong opponents, but even with his friends. Hence, we can read the report of his controversy with Pierre Nicole, Gommaire Huygens, and François Lamy. The first, Arnauld's longtime companion, needs no introduction. The other two were also sympathizers with what has come to be known as Jansenism; they belong, at least, to the Augustinian sphere of influence whose champion was the Master of Port-Royal.

Thus we will observe the persecuted quarrelling among themselves. Their inflexible theological theses will be found to rest on rather unexpected philosophical positions; we will find to our surprise that Arnauld has, at this stage, abandoned St Augustine in favour of St Thomas Aquinas. It will emerge, then, that whatever their enemies may have said, the 'Jansenists' did not form a doctrinally homogeneous group or 'party.' This may help us revise our historiographical categories, which we too often draw from the polemical vocabulary of the times, the summary labels proposed by one or another litigant, thus compromising our historical neutrality.

Nicole and General Grace

The dispute originated in Pierre Nicole's theory of general grace. Around 1688–9, in his XIIIth Theological Instruction, it became glaringly obvious that this eternal second to Arnauld had his own views on the matter.[1] Nicole is concerned to explain the following: Every descendent of Adam shares in the fall of human nature, yet any one of them *can* do good and save himself, though he will never actually want to do so unless he receives a special efficacious grace. No one who lacked a sufficient capacity to do good could be considered guilty of wrong doing. But the simple physical power to choose recognized by Jansenius and Arnauld is not enough; in the absence of the knowledge of good and evil, the simple power seems to Nicole 'like a healthy eye which is deprived of light, like healthy legs which are well tied up.'[2]

Thus Nicole proposes the hypothesis of a (non-Molinist) supernatural assistance *sine qua non*, given to all, a light from God shining on every person, whether Christian or not (even if he does not actually make use of it). This aid is a general grace, a reception of eternal truth in all minds: 'It consists in truths we do not have to learn from men'[3] because they are communicated directly to us by the Creator.

Is it likely that every person is enlightened in this way, even if he is not conscious of it and does not recognize the source of the enlightenment? So it would be for the vast number of non-Christians, and indeed for many Christians. Arnauld raises this issue in lemma 5 of his *Ecrit géométrique sur la grâce générale*. He objects that 'a soul has not been enlightened with regard to an object when it has not known it and has not a single thought of that object ...' In other words, for Arnauld, this 'general grace' is but a name: It is supposed to consist in knowledge bequeathed supernaturally and universally, whereas many minds have evidently never received it, since they have no notion or knowledge of true good and true evil. To know something is to think about it and to be aware of thinking about it.

Nicole admits that this is the main point, and that the doctrine of general grace assumes that a soul is never in the state of invincible ignorance with regard to moral truth or with regard to natural law. (He cites the teaching of the theologians of Louvain.)[4]

In reply to Arnauld's objection, he proposes a distinction between two types of knowledge: direct knowledge of an object or truth 'by means of an exact and distinct idea, which will make us know it distinctly, expressly and immediately,'[5] and indirect or shrouded knowledge, by dint of a general principle in which the truth is contained really but confusedly and implicitly. In the latter case, we can know the truth expressly by deriving it from the principle communicated to us by God, and we are prevented from doing so only by our passions and vices, which divert our attention from the principle, which is none the less always present in our mind.[6]

The question, then, is whether the implicit, confused, even unnoticed, apprehension of a truth in its principle is indeed knowledge. Nicole is not in doubt: 'We conceive many truths without tying them to words, without noticing that we know them, and many people who have never heard the principle that the whole is greater than its part have judged that a part is smaller than its whole ... This is not done by means of distinct propositions, but by intellectual perceptions that yield the same conviction.'[7]

Nicole identifies this kind of unformulated or implicit knowledge with the divine illumination taught by St Augustine.[8] The assumed 'intellectual perception' is a perception of God himself, or rather of the eternal ideas in God (equality, order, justice, piety ...). It is not the result of effort or research, which obviously could not be carried out by everyone; on the contrary, the ideas are unveiled by God, *qua veritas docens et illuminans*. Thus, 'God as truth, as justice, as light, shines forth in the spirit of infidels and of ungodly people.'[9] Again, 'since this illumination ordinarily takes place without words, the mind does not perceive it distinctly, and so we should pay no attention to the account of those who say that they have never had thoughts and illuminations of that kind, for they might have had them without knowing it.'[10]

In order to describe these notions, unnoticed yet given by God to every mind, Nicole proposes the category of 'imperceptible thoughts,' which is, thus, the keystone in the system of general grace. True knowledge and true thoughts differ from clear and distinct ideas in that they are not dressed in language and spread out in consciousness; these 'imperceptible thoughts' are in fact knowledge by feeling: 'that is to say, delicate thoughts, prompt, confused, indistinct, and afterwards forgotten.'[11] Nicole refers explicitly to Pascal's theses on the grasp of principles: many things are known by feeling alone, 'by which is meant that we do not have the fully developed idea of them ready to hand.'[12]

G. Huygens, Divine Illumination and Its Thomist Interpretation

In his discussion of lemma 5 in Arnauld, Nicole refers, we saw, to the teaching of the theologians of Louvain. More particularly, he refers to a thesis advanced by one of their number, Gommaire Huygens: *de veritate aeterna, sapientia et justitia aeterna*.[13] Wishing to undermine such a foundation for the doctrine of general grace, Arnauld went directly after Huygens's thesis. In this way he attacked one of the chief supporters of Jansenistic Augustinism in Louvain, one of his own allies, with whom he was well acquainted.[14] Worse still: Huygens was only repeating Jansenius's ideas, contained in the *De statu naturae purae* (I, c. 7–8). It is therefore against Jansenius that Arnauld waged war, and behind him, against St Augustine himself.

In that thesis, Huygens had held, first, that it is in uncreated truth, namely, God, that we see all necessary, immutable truths, and, second, that when we love a virtue for itself, we in fact love its archetype in God, so that it is God himself that we love. Hence, Arnauld attacked him in a *Dissertatio bipartita*, intended to combat those two assertions one after the other.[15]

The second assertion is a consequence of the first, and for Arnauld the more embarrassing theologically, for, like Nicole's general grace, it entails recognition of the virtue of pagans.[16] From his earliest works, Arnauld had taken a clear stand on that issue, one inspired by Augustine (or at least by certain of his writings): pagans cannot practise any genuine virtue, for they do not fulfil the condition for all virtue, which is to love God as the only end in itself; even in their heroic, outwardly disinterested, actions, they remain subject to the sin of pride, to self-love (love of their own glory, of their soul's beauty), for they lack the power to overcome concupiscence through faith and grace. If, by contrast, one supposes with Huygens that the pagans' love of virtue is an implicit love of God because it is directed, without their knowing it, to the idea of virtue which is in God and which is God, there would be no denying that their conduct was morally good and, finally, that they could be saved without faith in Jesus Christ and without grace.

The idea that grace might not be absolutely necessary is intolerable to Arnauld. He tries to undermine that claim by contesting the first part of Huygens's thesis, namely, the view that every person discovers in God, or in God's light, the necessary truths he perceives. Thus Arnauld, paradoxically, finds it necessary, in order to maintain the strictest Augustinism in moral theology, to break with another, no less characteristic, Augustinian thesis on the metaphysical level: the thesis of illumination.

To that end, and here is the surprise, he uses Thomas Aquinas against Augustine: 'Truth is principally in the intellect, and secondarily in things.'[17] Truths are so called only with reference to the intellect upon which they depend: to the divine intellect in some cases (one speaks of 'true gold' if the metal concerned is in keeping with its archetype in God, in accordance with which God created it), to the human intellect in others. Now, all true propositions are of the latter sort, even when they state necessary and immutable truths:[18] 'The truth of the proposition is not other than the truth of the intellect.'[19] Propositional truth (which is truth proper, 'secundum propriam rationem'), Arnauld comments, is not a thing. It is nothing other than a *relatio*, 'a simple relation,' between subject and attribute in the judgment of the intellect, in so far as it is consonant with the thing it judges. It should therefore not be sought elsewhere than in the intellect.[20] Hence, the truths perceived by different intellects are not reducible to one single, selfsame, subsisting truth, God himself: 'There are as many truths, properly speaking, as there are judgments formed about things whether by diverse minds or by one and the same mind.'[21]

This is a curious revival of a quarrel four centuries old, in which St Thomas undertook to reduce Augustine's illumination to the light of the agent intellect proper to each person:[22] 'For there is in each and every man a certain principle of science, namely the light of the agent intellect, through which certain universal principles of all the sciences are known at once, in principle, naturally.'[23]

Only *qua* cause of our cognitive ability, and not *qua* first known object, is God the source of all our knowledge: Instead of giving himself in an illumination, he gives us *our* inner light, our knowing *faculty*: 'By God we are given the interior light of the intellect, which is the principal cause of knowledge [*scientiae*].'[24]

Having conceded that man is endowed with his own knowing power, we must apply the principle of economy and eliminate every superfluous hypothesis, such as the hypothesis that we need direct divine illumination in order to acquire natural knowledge: 'It is useless to have recourse to eternal truth above our mind if we find in our mind itself all that is necessary in order that we should judge true those things that are demonstrated with necessity in the sciences.'[25]

Now, if it looks into itself, the mind finds in itself perceptions or ideas, the faculty to join these together and to separate them (judgment), and finally the faculty to link two judgments by means of a third (reasoning). 'Assuming only these things, we easily understand how the human mind can acquire the demonstrative sciences, such as geometry and arithmetic.'[26] For they proceed through definitions and demonstrations. Definitions merely awake in our mind the ideas of the terms, which it grasps by simple apprehension.[27] Demonstrations merely lay down relations among those ideas. That is enough for the discovery of any truth, even it is necessary and immutable: 'But here there is only created truth, which is in my mind: the ideas are in my mind, their connection is a work of the mind, as is the assent by which it adheres to that connection.'[28] Every intellect finds in *itself*, not its truth, but the truth; agreement among minds on the true does not result from contemplation of a common object, but from parallel processes. Accordingly, Arnauld rejects the classical Augustinian argument: 'If both of us see that what you say is true and we both see that what I say is true, where, I ask, do we see it? Certainly I do not see it in you or you in me, but both of us in the unchangeable truth that is above our mind.' To this Arnauld replies: 'That I do not see it in you or you in me, I agree ... For each of us sees it in his own mind: I in mine, you in yours.'[29]

One may with reason conclude that in God there exist eternal reasons for things, their archetypes, considering that God is the cause of all things and that things have not been formed at random. But it does not follow that we have knowledge of the archetypes themselves: they cannot be perceived by us in this life, but only by the blessed who see God face to face.

François Lamy and the Defence of Augustinism

We are told that, when Nicole read the *Dissertatio bipartita*, he 'had the sincerity to acknowledge that he could not see what could be said in reply.'[30] He showed Arnauld's work to Father François Lamy (the Benedictine). The latter, both an Augustinian and a Cartesian, was a close friend of the renowned members of that cultural milieu: Nicole, of course; Arnauld (whose friendship antedated his departure into exile); Bossuet; and Malebranche. But that did not deter him from entering into lively disagreements with them.[31]

The controversy would thus spread to include a person closely connected to the previous protagonists. In fact, Lamy hastened to Nicole's rescue. Not that he adhered to his views: quite the contrary, for after Nicole provided him with the manuscript of the *Traité de la grâce générale*, he wrote *Réfutation du système de la grâce générale!*[32] However, he felt it his duty to defend, against Arnauld, both the Augustinian doctrine of illumination and the consequences drawn from it by Huygens concerning the love of God. Therefore, he wrote an answer to the *Dissertatio bipartita*. It remained unpublished and seems today to have been lost.[33]

We are in possession, though, of Arnauld's reply to Lamy. In addition to an answer on the heart of the matter, it contains a reflection on the procedures it should be adopted in that type of discussion, so as to put an end to misunderstandings, sophisms, and endless disputes. This is the *Règles du bon sens, pour bien juger des écrits polémiques dans les matières de science, appliquées à une dispute entre deux théologiens touchant cette question métaphysique: Si nous ne pouvons voir les vérités nécessaires et immuables, que dans la vérité souveraine et incrée.*[34]

Arnauld and the Rules of Common Sense

Joining theory to the practice of controversy, the *Rules* state fifteen general precepts, each illustrated by discussion of Lamy's objections to the *Dissertatio*. Or, to put it more accurately, Arnauld picked out certain objections and prefaced his discussion of them with *ad hoc* methodological considerations. Once again the work is divided into two main parts, reflecting the two parts of Huygens's thesis: There is a purely metaphysical question, that of the knowledge of truth, and a moral question that depends on it. We shall inspect a few of the articles.

ART. I: Diverse kinds of disputes

FIRST RULE: 'Take good heed of the nature of the question being disputed: is it philosophical or theological? For if it be theological, it must be decided chiefly by recourse to authority; whereas if it be philosophical, it must be decided chiefly by recourse to reason ...'

The first reproach Lamy levels at Arnauld is that he abandoned St Augustine 'to follow St. Thomas, thus preferring the opinion of the Disciple to that of the

Master' (p. 154). But it is the very spirit of Augustinism that allows Arnauld to move away from its letter; while opposing Augustine on a particular point, he remains faithful to a deeper Augustinian principle: 'quod credimus, debemus auctoritati, quod scimus rationi.' On the matter here in dispute, nothing is revealed by God or decided by the church; hence, the light of reason alone can and must show what side to take. Augustinism itself is not an indivisible block, to take or leave. One must distinguish within it what belongs to the exposition of Catholic doctrine, and what belongs to philosophical speculation.

Besides, Arnauld notes, 'should one wish to stop at authority,' that of St Thomas is far from being 'as contemptible as our Friend would make us believe,' for 'he was a very great mind, and held St. Augustine in most special esteem and respect' (p. 154). Scholasticism is often believed to be dead and gone in the seventeenth century. We can see, on the contrary, that Thomas's teaching lives on and plays a role in philosophical reflection. Indeed, we see it defended and illustrated by someone who is not outmoded, but has, rather, fought repeatedly in favour of Cartesianism.[35]

ART. II: The state of the question

SECOND RULE: 'To consider carefully whether the state of the question has been well put, and to take care that it is not subsequently changed by passing insensibly from the point at issue to another point not at issue.'

Arnauld acknowledges that the state of the question has been well formulated by Lamy: 'Whether all necessary and immutable truths are seen in a sovereign and uncreated truth' (p. 156). But we need to consider what is and what is not contained in that formulation, and to 'sort out the equivocation which might lie in the words: "to see immutable truths in uncreated truth",' for this phrase may be taken in a more or a less proper sense. Now Lamy, according to Arnauld, kept changing the state of the question and passing from one problem to another, for want of a full elucidation of the content of that phrase.

Arnauld starts out with an important remark: He sets the present discussion apart from his famous controversy with Malebranche, which also had to do with 'vision in God.' Despite the apparent similarity, this is not in fact the same problem, or the same vision. For Malebranche, what we see in God are not truths, which, for him, are mere relations, but rather the creatures themselves. By contrast, Lamy expressly denies that 'those works of God ... are seen in God; that is to say in the ideas according to which those bodies were formed'; for him, only (necessary and immutable) truths are seen in God. His Augustinism is far more orthodox than Malebranche's (even though he was known as a disciple of

Malebranche). His case seemed less extreme to Arnauld, who saw nothing but wild imaginings in the Oratorian's metaphysics.

Nevertheless, the root of the error is the same. It is the confusion provoked by the attractive formula of the Augustinians: to see (truth or creatures) in God. Beneath the apparent clarity of the expression there are formidable ambiguities. Arnauld will dissect these with great skill.

Applying a principle of his own *Logic* (to have a clear and distinct idea of the meaning of the words one uses), Arnauld asks for the general meaning of such a formula. 'When we say, especially with regard to spiritual insight, that we see one thing in another, B in A, the proper, natural sense of those words is, that knowledge of the one gives us knowledge of the other' (p. 158). For instance, in the case of the 'demonstrative sciences,' theorems are known 'in their principles,' i.e., are known by means of axioms, which are known by themselves. 'It follows that A must be known, and better known than B, if we are to speak properly of knowing B in A, *tamquam in objecto cognito*' (p. 158).[36] A is the 'efficient cause of the knowledge of B,' or its '*condition sine qua non.*'

On the other hand, to say that we see invisible corpuscles with the naked eye *in* a microscope (an allusion to a recent invention) would be to speak improperly: we see them *through* the microscope, for we do not see the microscope itself or even its eyepiece, but only what it shows us. Likewise, we cannot say that we see objects in the sun, but rather, thanks to the sun, light coming from it enables us to see them; it is a cause of our seeing, but we do not necessarily see it. We should speak of seeing objects in the sun only with the qualification 'causaliter, non vero objective, seu tamquam in objecto viso' (p. 159).[37]

This being understood, let us now ask those who hold that we see certain truths in God: 'Do you mean that we see them in God, *tamquam in objecto cognito*, or only *causaliter*, and because God is cause of the fact that we see them?' (p. 159).

In the second case, they would be in agreement with St Thomas (and Arnauld), who accepts the Augustinian thesis of a vision of certain truths in God if it is taken to mean that 'God is the efficient cause of the knowledge we have of those truths, since the natural light of our mind, thanks to which we know them, is a participation of uncreated light' (p. 159).

But, as Arnauld points out, that is not in fact their thesis. Malebranche, in the quarrel 'on true and false ideas,' held that modifications in our minds are not of an essentially representative nature, i.e., are not really and formally our light, which implies that God is, not only the cause of our light, but formally our light. For his part, Lamy specifies that if we do not see contingent truths in God, but only immutable and necessary truths, it must be because we see his essence, not his decrees; in other words, he holds that we see the divine essence *tamquam objectum cognitum*.

ART. III: St Thomas's definitions

Lamy appears to have challenged the definitions of truth borrowed by Arnauld from St Thomas, on the grounds that they are 'all founded on purely arbitrary definitions, and on notions forged recklessly, offering to the mind no more than a pure scholastic jargon that has nothing solid in it' (p. 161). A special target is the idea that 'truth proper is only to be found in [human] understanding.' 'Why,' Lamy asks, 'can we not say, with just as much or more reason, that truth proper is to be found properly and chiefly in things only; that it consists in their relation to the originals, the eternal ideas of them, and that in all the rest it is only improperly to be found; and that our judgments are thus true solely in so far as they express the relations of things to their ideas and their originals?' (p. 162).

But that, says Arnauld, is transcendental truth, which lies in the correspondence between things and their model, namely, the divine idea for natural things, and the craftsman's idea or the copied model for artificial things (as when we speak of the true portrait of a man). St Thomas speaks of that truth also, but for him it is not truth proper. Truth proper is found primarily in our judgments (p. 162). The question then is whether the notion of truth primarily means truth in the latter, predicative, sense, or in the transcendental sense. Is truth primarily logical or ontological?

Lamy appears to have reasoned as follows: Since correspondence between things and divine ideas is far more noble than correspondence between our judgments and their objects, we have better reason to say that truth proper is that which is in things (p. 163). But the rule here invoked is wrong. The greater or lesser propriety of the use of a term hardly depends on the greater or lesser dignity of the subject it is applied to: Scripture speaks of the wrath of God or of his arm, but God's superiority to men does not entail that those expressions are said with greater propriety of God than of men – quite the contrary.

One should therefore return to a simple thesis regarding the origin and nature of language: Words are conventions for the expression of ideas, and the exact sense of words, especially in real definitions, is fixed by common usage, unless otherwise indicated.[38] 'Now one of the first things that men need to convey is whether they or someone else are mistaken in their judgments of the things they talked about' (p. 163).

The words for truth and falsehood in all languages first signified quite simply that we are or not mistaken, i.e., that our judgments correspond or not *to* things. And this original meaning remains the chief and immediate meaning. The real definition proposed by St Thomas rests on this fact about ordinary usage and is therefore well grounded in common sense.

Of course those judgments cannot be correct unless they also correspond to divine ideas, to which correspond in turn the things whose ideas they are. But it is not necessary to know these ideas in order to know things. Or again, arriving at truth consists, not in knowing the relation of things to their archetypes, but rather in judging of their nature 'through experience and conjecture' (p. 164). We are, says Arnauld, in the situation of someone who wants to unravel the true meaning of a coded message not intended for him. He does not have the key to the code, but he has guessed it 'by means of certain rules, found out by those whose profession it is to unravel letters of that kind' (p. 165). The world is like a cryptic letter, but we do not understand it from its archetypes in God, which would be to know its code in advance. We can only trace the scrambled message back to its code, or rather assume that we are deciphering according to the code when we obtain coherence and sense, like Descartes who 'having laid down very simple and very evident principles, ... very clearly deduced from them a great number of the most beautiful phenomena of nature' (p. 165).[39]

ART. V: Imperceptible thoughts

We now arrive at the crucial moment of the dispute, at which the plausibility of direct illumination of minds by God is now at stake.

We know that Nicole is the one who put forward the postulate of imperceptible thoughts to prop up his system of general grace. The same postulate is appealed to by Lamy to make it possible for us in fact to see every truth in God, even if we are not conscious of doing so. For, in order to make up for the lack of evidence for that thesis (since, as with Malebranche, most men have the vision in God unwittingly), we are forced to suppose that when we know geometrical truths, we are thinking of uncreated truth without being aware that we are thinking of it.

That hypothesis is purely and simply incredible, says Arnauld. How could anyone accept the claim that, having seen truths such as two and three make five 'a thousand and a thousand times' I have had uncreated truth present to my mind a thousand and a thousand times 'without my ever noticing that I was thinking of it' (p. 171)?

Arnauld thus uses the question of imperceptible thoughts to test of the Augustinian theory of illumination. The latter must be rejected if it can be held only at the expense of conceding an unacceptable hypothesis: in this case, the existence of imperceptible thoughts, i.e., of thought contents which, although they take place in thought itself (understood as substance), are not perceived by it.

That postulate is not acceptable, for it goes against other well-established principles, whose suppression would ruin Cartesian gains in philosophy and the sciences. Indeed, the very cornerstone of the new science would thus be attacked, namely, the transparency of thought to itself, the possibility of evident knowledge of oneself as a thinking substance. The Cartesian soul, once it defined as *res cogitans*, is freed from the obscurity involved in the assumption that it animates the body. It is this possibility of knowing oneself completely which, after the *cogito* and the end of hyperbolic doubt, authorizes the mind's self-certainty as pure thought (it is not in myself that I see the notions that make me think I am a body), and authorizes the second proof of God through effects (there is not within me an unconscious power to give myself being). It also enables us to proceed through clear and distinct ideas.[40] The metaphysics of Cartesianism has as much horror of imperceptible thoughts as its physics has of occult qualities.[41] Thought is pure consciousness, and cannot admit to its fold any foreign element, anything opaque to it, which it could not perceive within itself: in short, nothing unconscious within consciousness itself; that would be a contradiction in terms. This important point, among others, set the seal on Leibniz's break with the Cartesians (in his theory of small perceptions) as well Malebranche's (in his thesis that the soul is obscure to itself).

By contrast, Arnauld relies on the Cartesian principle of the total transparency of thought to itself.[42] According to this principle, I am certain, thanks to the witness of my conscience, that I have seen many necessary and immutable truths of geometry and arithmetic with the the eyes of my mind, even though I did not have the slightest thought of a sovereign and uncreated truth. Now, 'to say that I think of a thing is the same as to say that the thing is present in my mind' (p. 170).[43] To entertain a thought is to have it present in the mind, so that it, like every other content of consciousness, is *ipso facto* an object of consciousness. When I think of something, I know at the same time that I think of it. Now I can have knowledge of truths without thinking of uncreated Truth. Therefore, I can have that knowledge without having uncreated Truth present in my mind, for if I did consider it in any way I would be conscious of seeing it.

Arnauld emphasizes that his critique is concerned only with *entirely* imperceptible thoughts: 'Certainly some thoughts are less perceptible than others, and we are far more aware of clear and distinct thoughts than of thoughts which are obscure and confused, more aware of thoughts on which we reflect deliberately than of those on which we reflect only virtually, a sort of reflection that must be judged inseparable from thought' (p. 172). But an *unperceived* or fugitive thought is not for that reason *imperceptible*.[44] Virtual reflection, i.e., the capacity to make thought an object, is inseparable from thought because it constitutes the very nature of consciousness. What makes us say that no natural or artificial body, however well organized, is endowed with intelligence, is the fact that no such machine is aware of what it does: *non est conscia suae operationis* (p. 173).[45]

Arnauld seems to weaken his position, however, when he gives the following argument: Everyone allows that it is really possible for a person to be of good faith, to know and to state the very core of one's thought. 'But how could a man swear that he has not had the slightest thought of this or that thing, without risking perjury, since he could have had imperceptible ones' (p. 173)? Psychologists would doubtless fault Arnauld here. There appears to be a misunderstanding between Arnauld, at ease with epistemological problems and logical dilemmas, and his two adversaries, Nicole, author of the famous *Essais de morale*, and Lamy, author of a treatise *De la connaissance de soi-même*, who are accustomed to probing the innermost recesses of the heart and the subtleties of feeling, of muted and clandestine thoughts.[46] Are they really talking about the same thing? As a matter of fact, Nicole invokes 'the example of certain secret feelings which we have in the heart and which the soul does not discern; for this reason its own depths are unknown to it and what swims on the surface of thought is quite often different from what dominates the heart, as St. Gregory the Great says.'[47] Does not Arnauld suffer a setback on this terrain?

Yet Nicole adds: 'Those secret feelings are always accompanied by secret knowledge because those feelings are loves, and there is no love without knowledge.'[48] It would seem, then, that he is the one in a weak position, since he goes back to the level of knowledge, of intellectualism, of thought, and therefore of consciousness. If secret feelings belong to the domain of knowledge, they might be *unperceived*, but they cannot be imperceptible. Besides, however profoundly self-love might be hidden under apparent virtues, La Rochefoucauld would not have written his *Maximes* had he not succeeded in tracking it down, i.e., in making it pass into conscience. Arnauld could then send the psychologist back to the preceding paragraph.

Finally, Arnauld reminds us that 'we must acknowledge the presence of mechanical acts in man, which take place without thought, and which cannot therefore serve as proof that there are imperceptible thoughts.' If Lamy is a Cartesian, he believes that beasts do not think and that they do an infinity of actions 'solely by the disposition of their machine.' He must admit, Arnauld concludes, that the same holds for many human actions, which assume no thought, not even imperceptible thought, such as chewing or walking, or even writing. The mechanicistic physics of Descartes renders useless the hypothesis of a psychological unconscious. To suppose an imperceptible thought guiding thoughtless action is to appeal to an occult quality, a hypothesis that is superfluous, given the capacities and the autonomy of the corporeal machine.

Having proved that imperceptible thoughts have no reality whatsoever, Arnauld goes on to show that, even if they existed, they would be of no use to a system of general grace. An imperceptible thought would be an ineffectual thought, since, not being conscious, it could not give me knowledge of any sort. 'Is there a difference between saying nothing at all to me about my danger of falling into an ambush, and warning me in a language I do not understand' (p. 182)? Hence 'imperceptible thoughts' cannot be used to accuse men before God.

ART. XIII. The Iroquois' conception of God as justice

The second part of the work is aimed at the moral corollary of Huygens's thesis: that one cannot sincerely love a virtue without loving that virtue's eternal form and reason, which is in God, so that to love a virtue is to love God. As we have seen, this assertion seemed to Arnauld even less tenable than what was said about truth, because it had the consequence that even pagans are capable of loving God.

Of course, Arnauld acknowledges, one may say that God *is* justice itself. But one may not draw the consequence that anyone who has some notion of justice has the notion of God. Arnauld cites the case of the Iroquois. Although they knew full well whether a contract was just or unjust, they had, according to the missionaries, no idea of any divinity whatsoever, whether true or false; indeed, they did not even possess a word for a divinity in their language (p. 239).[49] If it is replied that they may have known God without being aware of it, one could just as well say that they may have been geometers or astronomers without being aware of it (p. 240).

ART. XIV: On the love of justice

This article gives us the rare spectacle of Arnauld attacking Jansenius. Augustine, the doctor of Port-Royal reminds us, often says that one must do good for love of justice, and not for fear of punishment. What is this justice one must love while doing good? Jansenius has successfully shown against Vasquez that it is not merely the justice of the action itself, but God himself. 'But when he wants to explain how that justice is God, he resorts to Platonic thoughts that Augustine did not use when giving his excellent explanation of the nature of the genuine virtues' (p. 241).

Indeed, in his *Contra Julianum* (III, 4), Augustine shows that we must distinguish, within virtue, between the duty and the end, between what must be done and the motive for doing it ('Officium est quod faciendum est; finis, propter quod faciendum est'). Pagans may have done good works *secundum officium*; but those works, though good, were badly done, because they had no knowlege of God and so failed to link them to their genuine end. The first principle of Christian morality is that, since God alone is our sovereign good, he must also be the ultimate end of all our actions (p. 242–3).

That demonstration is sufficient. Hence, Arnauld confesses, Jansenius's additions 'are painful to me.' Indeed, in the *De statu naturae purae* (I, 8), Jansenius claims that we see the eternal rectitude, the immutable and eternal rule of justice which radiates within us and, thanks to which we form our judgments, not only through faith, but also through an intuitive insight (p. 243). But if that is true, the love of justice as Jansenius understands must be found 'in all men, including infidels and the impious, because that primitive and eternal form of justice is exposed to the spiritual insight of all men.' Now Jansenius himself proves in the *De statu naturae purae* (I, 5) 'that such a love of justice can only be had by a true and supernatural grace of God, which is not common to all men, and which is certainly not to be found in infidels or in the impious' (p. 245).

Conclusion

What lessons should be derived from the controversy we have seen unfold?

First, it is clear that internal tensions existed in the 'Jansenist' milieu, whose fundamental components, Augustinism and Cartesianism, allow for many individual variations. Though they fought together for years against common enemies, Jesuit or Protestant, Nicole and Arnauld are far from having identical convictions.

Next, let us pass in review the essential traits of the thought of Antoine Arnauld, chief among the protagonists. On the theological level, he holds strict, Augustinian positions on the separation between nature and grace (on account of original sin there is no room for pagan virtue), predestination (both universal actual grace, i.e., grace moving the intellect and the will, and 'sufficient grace' are rejected), and human guilt.

On the philosophical level, whose autonomy he upholds, Arnauld puts considerable distance between himself and the Platonism of Augustine and Jansenius, which he thinks he can dissociate from their theological positions. Depending heavily on Thomas Aquinas, whom he studied very closely, he pleads for the functional independence of the human intellect (it is the human individual who thinks), i.e., for the individual's capacity to produce ideas (instead of receiving or discovering them). Accordingly, he asserts its limitation: We can know God and the archetypes only indirectly. We have no vision of God or in God at all.

At the same time, Arnauld comes out as a defender of pure Cartesian doctrine. Some of these positions are in agreement with Thomistic ones, such as the individuality and independence of thought. Others are new, such as the identification of thought with consciousness and the transparency of the soul to itself, but do not seem to Arnauld irreconcilable with Thomism. In his eyes they are decisive, complementary gains. Hence it is that, in spite of his adherence to new ideas, Arnauld was able to keep Thomistic theses alive and functioning in the midst of the seventeenth century.[50] This observation gives us reason to revise the oversimplified view of that century as divided between innovators, on the one hand, and diehards, on the other: There existed intermediate positions.

Notes

I wish to express my warm thanks to Professor Thomas De Koninck of Laval University, Quebec, and Professor Elmar Kremer, for their contribution to the translation of this paper. Extant inaccuracies are mine.

1 Cf. *OA*, the 'Préfaces historiques et critiques' to vol. 10 (xix ff.), and to vols. 19, 38, and 39; the preface to Nicole's *Traité de la grâce générale* (1715). See also J. Laporte, *La Doctrine de Port Royal*, vol. 2: *La Doctrine de la grâce chez Arnauld* (Paris: Presses Universitaires de France 1922), 214–23; G. Lewis, *Le Problème de l'inconscient et le Cartésianisme* (Paris: Presses Universitaires de France 1950), 200–18, and A.-R. Ndiaye, *La Philosophie d'Antoine Arnauld* (Paris: Vrin 1991), 344 ff.

2 *Traité de la grâce générale* I, 501–2.

3 Ibid., I, 210.

4 Ibid., I, 83–4.

5 Ibid.

6 This is what Nicole calls 'to know a truth in its principle' (ibid., 83).

7 Ibid., I, 87.

8 Cf. *Ennar. in Ps.*, 61, 21: 'Ubi, inquam, vides hoc justum, quo viso reprehendis injustum? Unde illud nescio quid, quod aspergitur anima tua ex multis partibus in caligine constituta, nescio quid hod quod coruscat menti tuae ... vade illuc ubi semel locutus est Deus, et ibi invenies fontem justitiae ...' Also, De Trin., XIV, 15: 'Ubi sunt istae regulae scriptae, ubi quid sit justum et injustum agnoscit, ubi ergo scriptae sunt in libro lucis quae Veritas dicitur, unde omnis lex describitur?' Many other passages are quoted by Nicole in II, 71 ff. He also finds this opinion in other Fathers of the church, and assimilates it to the 'sufficient grace' of modern Thomists.

9 *Traité de la grâce générale*, I, 91.

10 Ibid., II, 85. 'Those reasons are known; but few know that they know them.' (I, 88). Arnauld will contest this very claim: that one can know without being aware that one knows.

11 Ibid., I, 463–4. Conversely, 'what is called feeling is only a lesser perceptibility.'

12 Ibid. Concerning the importance of the notion of feeling in seventeenth-century

Augustinian thought, see Ch. Chesneau (alias Julien-Eymard d'Angers), *Le P. Yves de Paris et son temps*, vol. II (Paris: Société d'histoire écclésiastique de la France 1946), 33 ff.

13 *Traité de la grâce générale*, I, 88.

14 The *Dictionnaire de Théologie catholique* (Paris: Librairie Letouzey et Ané 1922), vol 7, col. 351, describes him as a friend of Arnauld and Quesnel. He was born in 1631 and died in 1702. As a professor of philosophy and theology at Adrian VI college in Louvain, his scholastic career (in particular his admission to the 'strict faculty of theology,' in which resided the controlling authority in the university) was compromised by his Jansenist opinions, which he defended against M. Steyaert, one of Arnauld's opponents, and against the Jesuit fathers G. Bolck and De Vos (especially on freedom and grace). The Inquisition in Toledo condemned his treatise on penitence, and two collections of his theses were put on the *Index* in 1685 and 1691. See *Biographie nationale de Belgique* (Bruxelles 1886–7), vol. 9, col. 729–46. Arnauld tried to support Huygens's candidature to the strict faculty in a letter to Neercassel (25 June 1684, *OA*, 42: Supplément aux lettres, p. 46) and voices his disappointment at Du Vaucel (letter of 15 October 1684, *OA*, 42, 48–9). He mentions the matter again in his letter of 28 December 1691 (*OA*, 3, 421) and undertakes Huygens's defence against a libel in his letter to Du Vaucel of 21 December 1691 (*OA*, 3, 414–16).

15 As can be seen from his letter to Arnauld of 5 August 1693 (*OA* 3, 669), Lamy had read the *Dissertatio* a year and a half earlier; therefore, this work was completed as early as February 1692. So the date of 1693 given in *OA*, 40, and in the chronology of *OA*, 42, xvi, is false (as it is for the *Règles de bon sens*: see below.)

16 A document of the 'archives de Port-Royal' in Amersfoort (#3217, 15, quoted by G. Lewis, *Le Problème de l'inconscient* ..., 204, n. 1) specifies that Huygens was 'tormented by the bull of Pius V which condemns the proposition that all actions of the faithless are sins.'

17 'Veritas principaliter est in intellectu, et secondario in rebus.' *Dissertatio*, Art. 1, quoted from *Summa theologiae*, Ia, 16, 1, c. Huygens first tried to draw support from St Thomas, but Arnauld corrects his interpretation.

18 Likewise, the so-called eternal truths are eternal inasmuch as they are contained in the divine intellect, because it is itself eternal; in so far as they are in our intellect, they are not eternal. 'Veritas propositionum, quae dicuntur aeternae veritatis, non est aeterna, et ubique, proprie loquendo, sicut Deus est aeternus, et ubique, sed tantum improprie, quia non est alligata cero tempori, et loco' (*Dissertatio*, Coroll. VI).

19 'Veritas enuntiabilium non est aliud quam veritas intellectus': Thomas Aquinas, *Summa*, I, 16, 7, c.

20 *Dissertatio*, Art. II, Coroll. II and III, 119–20.

21 Ibid., Coroll. IV.
22 See E. Gilson, 'Pourquoi saint Thomas a critiqué saint Augustin,' in *Archives d'Histoire doctrinale et littéraire du Moyen Age* 1 (1926). In the *ad primum* of *Summa theologiae*, I, 16, 6, which Huygens quoted on his own behalf, St Thomas, as Arnauld remarks judiciously, only wants 'infringere auctoritatem Augustini doctrinae suae oppositam, quam pro sua in Augustinum observantiam, perrumpere nec audebat, nec volebat': 'S. Thomas hic obscurior est, quia occultare maluit quam prodere suam ab Augustino dissensionem' (Art. III, 125).
23 *Summa*, I, 117, 1, c. Cf. I, 84, 5, c. and 88, 3 ad 1 and ad 2.
24 *Dissertatio*, Art. III, 130.
25 Ibid., Art. IV, ratio II, 134.
26 Ibid.
27 Here Arnauld refers to Cartesian innate ideas, in order to prove that ideas are not transcendent: 'opus tantum habet [mens nostra] ut attendat ad ideas claras et simplices, quas in se ipsa reperit, ex quarum connexione illa judicia efformata sunt' (ibid.)
28 Ibid., 134–5.
29 Ibid., Art. V, reply to Objection I, 136–7.
30 *Avertissement* of the editors of the *Règles du bon sens*, *OA* 40, 115. Cf. *Lettres de M. Nicole* (1718), Vol. 2, no. 47, 13 January 1693, to P. Quesnel.
31 See the *Dictionnaire de théologie catholique*, vol. 8, col. 2552–5; *Dictionnaire de spiritualité*, vol. 9, col. 174–7; and Dom Jean Zehnder, 'Un Représentant de la vie intellectuelle française entre 1680, et 1710. Dom Fr. Lamy Moine bénédictin et religieux de la Congrégation de Saint-Maur 1636–1711. Essai d'introduction à sa vie et à son oeuvre' (thesis, University of Fribourg, Zoug; Imprimerie E. Kalt-Zehnder 1944). He was born in 1636 and died in 1711, was a Benedictine monk and professor of philosophy in Soissons in 1672–3. Himself a student of Rohault, he introduced Cartesianism into the congregation of Saint-Maur. This is perhaps why he was deprived of his office of Prior by royal order in 1687. His spiritual works seem to be influenced by Jansenism. However, he championed Fénelon's cause against Bossuet and Malebranche. (The latter answered him with the *Traité de l'amour de Dieu*.)
32 It remained unpublished, and is considered as lost by J. Zehnder, 'Un Représentant de la vie intellectuelle français ...,' 200, but it is reported under the title *Réflexions sur le traité de la grâce générale* by Lewis in *Le Problème de l'inconscient ...*, 276.
33 See J. Zehdner, 'Un Représentant de la vie intellectuelle français ...,' 91 and 200, and Lewis, *Le Problème de l'inconscient ...*, 212, n. 5, and 276. It was composed of fifty pages or so (cf. Lewis, ibid.) and was divided into remarks, as it appears from some passages of Arnauld's retort to Lamy (*Règles du bon sens*, *OA* 40, 157,

158, etc.) It was meant by Lamy for Nicole alone, but the latter committed the indiscretion of communicating it to Arnauld. When this came to Lamy's knowledge, he wrote to Arnauld to apologize for the sharp tone he used in his reply (letter of 5 August 1693, *OA* 3, 670). But Arnauld had already showed that he did not feel offended in his letter of 22 April 1693, to an anonymous correspondent (*OA* 3, 624), and confirmed it to Lamy on 12 September 1693 (*OA* 3, 676), after the latter had written to him on 31 August 1693 (*OA* 3, 673–4) to thank him for his leniency. (He had seen the letter to the anonymous correspondent.) Thus, despite their disagreement, Arnauld and Lamy remained good friends.

34 First published in 1715, in the *Recueil des ecrits sur la grâce générale*, I, by Fouillou and Petitpied, the work was completed in May 1693, as Arnauld informed Du Vaucel (letter of 22 May 1693, *OA* 3, 1693). It was reprinted in *OA*, 40. In what follows, I refer directly to page numbers in that edition.

35 In 1671, when Louis XIV forbade the teaching of the new philosophy, Arnauld addressed to the Parliament a memoir entitled *Plusieurs raisons pour empêcher la censure ou la condamnation de la philosophie de M. Descartes*. There he defended the freedom of thought (on subjects irrelevant to Catholic dogmas) and proved that it is dangerous to involve ecclesiastic and civil authority in such matters. He protested also against the censors who put Descartes on the *Index*, and not Gassendi. Against some of his friends of Port-Royal, who thought that philosophy was a waste of time, he was convinced that Cartesianism (thanks especially to its sharp distinction between soul and body) was able to stop materialism and atheism. Again in the name of Cartesianism, he opposed the theories of Malebranche and of Nicole, as we shall see later.

36 Cf. Thomas Aquinas, quoted in *Dissertatio bipartita*, Art. IV: 'Illud propter quod aliud cognoscitur, erit magis notum, ut principia conclusionibus' (*Summa*, Ia, 87, 2, ad 3m).

37 Cf. Thomas Aquinas, quoted in *Dissertatio bipartita*, Art. III: 'Dicendum est quod aliquid in aliquo dicitur cognosci dupliciter. Uno modo sicut in objecto cognito, sicut aliquis videt in speculo ea, quorum imagines in speculo resultant: sic in rationibus aeternis cognoscunt omnia beati, qui Deum vident, et omnia in ipso. Alio modo dicitur aliquid cognosci in aliquo, sicut in cognitionis principio: sicut dicimus quod in sole videntur ea quae videntur per solem: et sic necesse est dicere quod anima omnia cognoscat in rationibus aeternis, per quarum participationem omnia cognoscimus. Ipsum enim lumen intellectuale quod est in nobis, nihil est aliud quam quaedam participata similitudo luminis increati, in quo continentur rationes aeternae ...' (*Summa*, Ia, 84, 5, resp.).

38 To speak is to explain one's thoughts by signs invented by man for that intention (A. Arnauld and C. Lancelot, *Grammaire générale et raisonnée*, *OA* 41, 5). The

discussion has to do with the *définition d'usage* of the term 'truth' and the real definition (*qua res*) of 'truth.' In the latter sort of definition, as the *Logic* explains, 'on laisse au terme qu'on définit, *comme homme* ou *temps*, son idée ordinaire, dans laquelle on prétend que sont contenues d'autres idées, comme *animal raisonnable* ou *mesure du temps*; au lieu que dans la définition de nom, comme nous avons déjà dit, on ne regarde que le son, et ensuite on détermine ce son à être signe d'une idée que l'on désigne par d'autres mots' (*OA* 41, 171). The nominal definition is free, for the signification of a sound is arbitrary, and one can set it *ad libitum*. But one is not free to enforce it in the discussion, instead of the *définition d'usage*: 'comme les hommes ne sont maîtres que de leur langage, et non pas de celui des autres, chacun a bien le droit de faire un Dictionnaire pour soi, mais on n'a pas le droit d'en faire pour les autres, ni d'expliquer leurs paroles par les significations particulières qu'on aura attachées aux mots. C'est pourquoi quand on n'a pas dessein de faire connaître simplement en quel sens on prend un mot, mais qu'on prétend expliquer celui auquel il est communément pris, les définitions qu'on en donne ne sont nullement arbitraires; mais elles sont liées et astreintes à représenter, non la vérité des choses, mais la vérité de l'usage; et on les doit estimer fausses, si elles n'expriment pas véritablement cet usage; c'est-à-dire, si elles ne joignent pas aux sons les mêmes idées qui y sont jointes par l'usage ordinaire de ceux qui s'en servent' (*OA* 41, 178).

39 Cf. Descartes, *Principles* IV, 205.

40 'Potui ... pro certo affirmare nihil in me, cujus nullo modo sim conscious, esse posse' (*Meditations* VI, AT 7, 81).

41 Using the same Cartesian principle (that unconscious thought is impossible), J.-P. Sartre will contest the Freudian theory of a psychological unconscious (or, more accurately, the description of the unconscious as an entity able to censure, disguise, use craft, etc. – in short, of acting as a genuine, but unconscious, consciousness).

42 However, Arnauld himself had objected to the *Meditations*: 'Quis non videt multa in mente posse esse, quorum mens conscia non sit' (*Fourth Objections*, AT 7, 214; 9, 167). Descartes answered: 'nous voyons fort bien qu'il n'y a rien en lui [l'esprit], lorsqu'on le considère de la sorte [comme une chose qui pense], qui ne soit une pensée ou qui ne dépende entièrement de la pensée: autrement cela n'appartiendrait pas à l'esprit en tant qu'il est une chose qui pense; et il ne peut y avoir en nous aucune pensée, de laquelle, dans le même moment qu'elle est en nous, nous n'ayons une actuelle connaissance' (AT 9, 190; 7, 246).

43 On discussions among Cartesians concerning the value of the testimony of consciousness, see Lewis, *Le Problème de l'Inconscient* ..., ch. II.

44 In Descartes, thought is defined by consciousness, though this does not always entail express reflection. So he can say that we have been actually thinking since

the beginning of our existence, even if we have no memory of it.

45 Cf. *Des Vraies et des Fausses Idées*, ch. II, repr. in *Corpus des oeuvres de philosophie en langue française* (Paris: Fayard 1986), 23.

46 Fr. Lamy, *De la Connaissance de soi-même* (Paris: 1694–8), vol. III, 361.

47 *Traité de la grâce générale*, I, 122–3.

48 Ibid.

49 Arnauld quotes the *Premier Etablissement de la foi dans la Nouvelle France* of Chrétien Le Clercq.

50 This appears also from his controversy with Malebranche and Bayle on the question of pleasure and happiness. See my contribution to the Antoine Arnauld Conference in Paris, October 1994: 'Tout plaisir rend-il heureux? Une polémique entre Arnauld, Malebranche et Bayle,' *Chroniques de Port-Royal* no. 44 (Paris: Bibliothèque Mazarine 1995).

10

'Tange montes et fumigabunt': Arnauld on the Theodicies of Malebranche and Leibniz

STEVEN NADLER

In a century full of brilliance and great personalities, Malebranche, Arnauld, and Leibniz deserve credit for shining particularly brightly. Arguably three of the seventeenth century's most important thinkers after Descartes, they none the less were gifted in different ways: Leibniz was blessed with sheer natural brilliance and a vision both broad and penetrating; Arnauld's talent lay in keen analytical skills and was perhaps the most acute critical mind of his time; and Malebranche, while slow at times, was the great and pious synthesizer (of Augustine and Descartes) and system builder. What makes these three philosophers particularly fascinating as a group is their mutual relations. The Arnauld–Malebranche debate is one of *the* intellectual events of the century; the Arnauld–Leibniz correspondence proves crucial in the development of Leibniz's mature metaphysics; and Leibniz's admiration for Malebranche is evident even when the two are deeply engaged in polemic. Sometimes the fray was bloody, and tangling with Arnauld could be a dangerous affair. Leibniz, for one, knew what he was getting into, but was none the less taken aback when Arnauld trashed the outline of the *Discours de la métaphysique* (1686; hereinafter *Discours*) that Leibniz had sent for his perusal. To paraphrase Leibniz: 'It's no wonder you don't have any friends left.'[1]

The philosophical issue I focus on here, as a way of bringing the three thinkers together, is the theodicy problem – that is, the problem of justifying God's ways in the face of the apparent imperfections and evil in the world, and of the apparent unfairness in the distribution of grace. What is initially remarkable (but not surprising) is a similarity: in this case, it concerns the general theodicean strategy adopted by both Malebranche and Leibniz. But what I will show is not that there are no differences between Leibniz's and Malebranche's theodicy. In fact, in the course of my argument, I take note of some important differences between their respective accounts, differences which are recognized both by recent scholars and by Malebranche himself. Rather, I argue that, *for Arnauld*, whatever differences there may in fact be between the two accounts would be outweighed by some crucial similarities, not just in general theodicean strategy, but also in the mechanics of the divine *modus operandi* in the realms of nature and grace. And using Arnauld's perspective in this way aids us in identifying those more particular but less obvious similarities.

I

In 1680, Malebranche published his *Traité de la nature et de la grâce* (herein-after, *Traité*), the work that ignited Arnauld's wrath and that caused Arnauld to reconsider his earlier mild judgment of Malebranche's *De la recherche de la vérité* (1674–5). The *Traité* elaborates on themes previously discussed in the *Recherche* and the *Conversations chrétiennes* (1676). Malebranche explains how God's omnipotence, benevolence, and perfection can be reconciled with the persistence of evil and imperfections in the world (including the balance of human pleasure and pain) and with what appears to be an unjust, and even haphazard, distribution of the grace required for everlasting happiness.

Our concept of God tells us that God is infinitely wise, good, powerful, and perfect. God's knowledge and benevolence are without bounds, and God's will and power are necessarily efficacious.[2] Moreover, God wishes, with respect to the realm of nature, to make the most beautiful and perfect world possible, the better to express and honour the qualities and perfections possessed by God himself. None the less, the world which God has, in fact, created certainly appears to us to be quite imperfect in its details and full of disorders of every variety. Monsters and deformed creatures are born; there is sin and misery among human beings; even the rain regularly falls on the sea, where it is not needed, rather than on fertile soil.[3] As Theodore, Malebranche's spokesman in the *Entretiens sur la métaphysique*, exclaims, 'The Universe then is the most perfect that God can make? But really! So many monsters, so many disorders, the great number of impious men – does all this contribute to the perfection of the universe?'[4] Aristes, his interlocuter, is led thereby to wonder either about the efficacy of God's will or the benevolence of God's intentions: 'God wishes to make a work that is the most perfect possible. For, the more perfect it is, the more it will honor Him. This appears evident to me. Yet I understand that the work would be more accomplished if it were free of thousands upon thousands of defects which disfigure it. Here is a contradiction that stops me quite short. It seems that God did not accomplish His plan, or that He did not adopt the plan most worthy of His attributes.'[5]

The resolution of this conundrum, as presented in both the *Entretiens* and the *Traité*, is to be found in the consideration, not just of the details of the visible universe, not just of the particular effect wrought by God, but also of the means undertaken to achieve and sustain this product. According to Malebranche, God, when creating, looks not only to the final result of the creative act (that is, to the goodness and perfection of the world *per se*). God is honoured, not just by the *creatatum*, but also by his work or ways. And the activity or means most expressive of God's nature are of maximum simplicity, uniformity, fecundity, and universality.[6] God does not accomplish by complex means that which can be accomplished by simple means; and God does not execute with many particular volitions that which can be excecuted by a few general volitions. This holds true even if it means that the world created by God could be spared some imperfections were God to compromise the simplicity and generality of his operations. That is, the perfection of the world in its details as a product is completely relative to the mode of activity that is most worthy of God. God might increase the absolute perfection of the world, perhaps by decreasing the number of defects or evils therein. But this would entail greater complexity in the divine ways. God might, for example, keep the rain from falling on anything but fertile and inseminated soil. But this would involve departing from the general laws of nature established at creation.

> In a sense, it can be said that God wants all his creatures to be perfect; that he does not want infants to perish in their mothers' wombs; that he does not like monsters, and that he has not made the laws of nature in order to engender them; and that if he had been able, by equally simple ways, to create and conserve a more perfect world, he would not have established laws from which so many monsters necessarily result. But it would have been unworthy of his wisdom to multiply his volitions in order to prevent certain particular disorders.[7]

Thus, the world that God has created is the one out of the infinitely many possible worlds that best reconciles perfection of design with simplicity and generality of means of production and conservation.[8] By a number of 'particular volitions [*volontés particulières*]' – volitions that are *ad hoc* and not occasioned by some prior event in accordance with some law of nature – God could correct deformities of birth, keep fruit from rotting on trees, prevent physical disasters about to occur by the regular course of the laws of nature, and forestall sin and wickedness. But, Malebranche insists, 'we must be careful not to require constant miracles from God, nor to attribute them to him at every moment.'[9] God, in other words, only acts by 'general volitions [*volontés générales*]' – volitions that are in accordance with some law and whose operation is occasioned by a prior event, as dictated by that law – and the most simple ways (*les voies les plus simples*), and never by particular volitions (*Dieu n'agit point par des volontez particulières*). The solution to the problem of evil, then, is found in the simplicity and uniformity of God's causal conduct in the world, in the generality of the divine will.

Similar considerations apply to the problem of grace. A benevolent God wills, with what Malebranche calls a 'simple volition,' that sinners convert and that all humans should be saved. But clearly not all humans are saved; many are lost. And not all those who receive grace appear to be ready to receive it, or even worthy of salvation. The anomaly is again explained by the generality of God's volitions. The distribution of grace is, like the events of nature, governed by certain general laws willed by God, and the occasional causes responsible for the actual distribution of grace in accordance with those laws are the thoughts and desires in the human soul of Jesus Christ. Because Jesus *qua* human is not omniscient, at any given time he never knows with full awareness all the relevant facts about the agents upon whom grace is to be bestowed – for example, whether they are ready to make proper use of it. Thus, as with the distribution of evil and imperfection in the natural world, God allows grace to be disbursed unevenly, and even inequitably, by the laws of grace in combination with the occasional causes that activate them.[10]

Leibniz was generally impressed by Malebranche's insights,[11] and this is reflected in Leibniz's own solution to the problem of evil. God, Leibniz claims, does everything in the most desirable way, and cannot have made things any better than they are. This is, he insists, the best of all possible worlds. But what makes it best is obviously not the total absence of pain and other apparent evils. Nor is it that these are simply outweighed by a great abundance of pleasures and other good things. Rather, God has chosen the one out of the infinitely many possible worlds that best combines simplicity of laws or 'hypotheses' and richness of phenomena. The world must contain the greatest amount of possibility or essence, but be governed by laws which are of maximum simplicity.[12] God is like a good architect who 'utilizes his location and the funds destined for the building in the most advantageous manner,' or like an 'excellent Geometer who knows how to find the best construction for a problem.'[13] The world we experience may not seem perfect to us in its details; it may be full of apparent irregularities and suffering. But, Leibniz says, 'I do not believe that that which is best and most regular is always convenient [*commode*] at the same time for all creatures.'[14] These unpleasant features of the world belong to the course of nature as determined by its laws, laws which are themselves few, simple, universal, and fertile. Evil and misfortune are permitted by God, but not positively willed, since they occur 'by means of the laws of nature that he has established';[15] they are a part of the rich variety of phenomena that, following from and in combination with those laws, constitute the best overall result.

One cannot help but notice striking similarities here with Malebranche's account. For both Leibniz and Malebranche, God in creation chooses from an infinity of possible worlds, and pays particular attention, not just to the created theatre itself, but especially to its relationship with the laws of nature and grace, laws that must be of maximum simplicity. Malebranche and Leibniz agree that evil and sin occur because God *allows* them to occur as a result of the ordinary course of nature as governed by the laws God has chosen (for Leibniz, there is a sense in which God actually wills or intends the evil, but only with what he calls a 'permissive will'). And they agree that God could (theoretically) diminish, or even eliminate, the apparent imperfections in the world – the quantity of pain and unhappiness or inconvenience – but only by interfering with the laws, and thus violating the simplicity of the divine ways (as Malebranche would put it) or by detracting from the overall and maximum metaphysical goodness or perfection of the world (as Leibniz would say). These points of agreement have been well catalogued by others, most notably Catherine Wilson[16] and Robert C. Sleigh, Jr.[17] As general theodicean strategies, then, the Malebranchian and Leibnizian accounts share some important substantive features. On both accounts, creatures are allowed to suffer, the needs and desires of many are unsatisfied, there is sin, and not all humans are saved, because God must satisfy some higher value – for Malebranche, that higher value is simplicity of law/means; for Leibniz, it is a best overall world that is simplest in laws and richest in effects.

Does this mean that Leibniz's theodicy and Malebranche's theodicy are, in all practical respects, equivalent? One recent scholar suggests as much, saying that 'even if they do not agree on all points, one is led to believe that they are to all intents saying the same thing.'[18] Catherine Wilson presents a more nuanced view. While noting that 'Leibniz's original rationale for optimism was Malebranchian,' and that 'he continued to think of the justification of evil in Malebranchian terms,' none the less she concludes that 'he never succeeded in integrating the Malebranchian solution with his own theory of individual substance.'[19] And Sleigh insists that there is a fundamental difference between Leibniz and Malebranche on the ranking of values that God must coordinate in the choice of the world, and concludes that they 'appear to differ on details, albeit details of substance.'[20]

Donald Rutherford takes the analysis even deeper. He recognizes a fundamental difference in the way in which Malebranche and Leibniz conceive of God's wisdom and of how it gets played out in God's aim in creation. For Malebranche, God acts only for the sake of his own glory,[21] which he finds reflected in a work that is sanctified by a divine person (Jesus Christ) and that is created and sustained by sufficiently worthy means. Leibniz's God, on the other hand, aims to produce the maximum amount of goodness possible, and this goodness is an inherent feature of the world itself. Rutherford notes that, 'within [Leibniz's] scheme, the issue of the worthiness of the created world vis à vis God receives a completely different treatment than in Malebranche. Quite simply, we can say that the only possible world worthy of God is that world which contains, in and of itself, the greatest perfection or reality.'[22] God's wisdom for Leibniz, then, consists in the 'knowledge of the good,' and it is wisdom so understood that guides God in choosing the best. For Malebranche, on the other hand, God's wisdom is expressed in the simplicity of his ways. As Rutherford concludes, Malebranche's position is thus fundamentally at odds with the main tendencies of Leibniz's thought.[23]

But now consider Leibniz's own assessment of the situation:

> The ways of God are the most simple and uniform: for he chooses rules that least restrict one another. They are also the most *productive* in proportion to the *simplicity of ways and means* ... one may, indeed, reduce these two conditions, simplicity and productivity, to a single advantage, which is to produce as much perfection as is possible: thus, Father Malebranche's system in this point amounts to the same as mine.[24]

Upon reading this in 1711, Malebranche demurs, and suggests to Leibniz that there is an important difference in their respective views:

> I am persuaded, as you are, that God has produced for his creatures all the good that he can produce for them, acting nonetheless as he must act, that is to say, acting according to his law which can only be the immutable order of his divine perfections, which he invincibly loves and which he can neither violate nor neglect. And thus his work [*son ouvrage*] is the most perfect it can be, not absolutely, however, but in relation to the means in accordance with which it is executed. For God is honored not only by the excellence of his work, but also by the simplicity and the fecundity, by the Wisdom of his ways.[25]

A month later, Leibniz in effect acknowledges that he may have oversimplified things a bit, and explains to Malebranche the ground of the difference Malebranche is describing:

> In effect, when I consider the work [*l'ouvrage*] of God, I consider his ways as a part of the work, and the simplicity joined to the fecundity of the ways form a part of the excellence of the work, for in the whole the means form a part of the end [and the simplicity of means form a part of the excellence of the work].[26]

But towards the end of the letter, Leibniz goes on to recap some important points of agreement, and I wonder if he is not suggesting that the difference between them is really just a nominal one: Leibniz says that God creates the best of all possible worlds; Malebranche says that God does *not* create the best of all possible worlds – but this is only because Malebranche uses the term 'world' (or *ouvrage*) more narrowly than Leibniz does to refer only to the created product, exclusive of the laws governing it. This is what allows Malebranche to declare that the goodness of the world is only relative to God's means, or the laws. Leibniz's point could be that, terminological differences aside, they agree that the composite of product design and laws is, taken as a whole, the best overall and the most worthy of God's wisdom and benevolence, even if the product design itself, exclusive of the laws, seems fraught with imperfections.[27]

And yet, in an addition to the *Traité* made in the fourth edition (1684), it becomes clear that, in Malebranche's eyes, at least, the differences must be more substantial than Leibniz seems willing to allow. For Malebranche's God is not concerned with producing as much good as possible, as is Leibniz's God. Malebranche's God is not trying to balance or even maximize two values to produce the best outcome. Rather, for Malebranche, the simplicity of God's ways takes precedence: 'His wisdom in a sense renders him impotent; for since it obliges him to act by the most simple ways, it is not possible for all humans to be saved [as God would like], because of the simplicity of his ways ... God loves his wisdom more than his work ... because his wisdom prescribes means which most bear the character of his attributes.'[28] One can characterize the difference as that between Malebranche's God the deontologist, for whom a particular value must be pursued no matter what the consequences, and Leibniz's God the consequentialist, who chooses means in order to produce as much overall good as possible.[29]

II

There are important differences, then – noted both by recent scholars and by Malebranche himself – between the theodicies of Malebranche and Leibniz, especially regarding how God's wisdom is conceived and the goals and details of his operations. And these differences are not inconsistent with the general (but not abstractly trivial) similarities in theodicean strategy that I (partly taking my cue from Leibniz) describe above.

I would now like to approach the issue from another perspective, and here is where Arnauld comes in. In 1686, when commenting on Leibniz's outline of the *Discours*, Arnauld has just finished his masterful and massive critique of Malebranche's *Traité*, the *Réflexions philosophiques et théologiques sur le nouveau système de la nature et de la grâce* (1685; hereinafter, *Réflexions*).

Arnauld never directly comments on Leibniz's theodicy strategy, especially proposition five of Leibniz's summary, whose terms are certainly reminiscent of Malebranche's account: 'In what the principles of the perfection of the divine conduct consist and that the simplicity of the means is in balance with the richness of the effects.'[30] And yet we can ask the following speculative but relevant question: Is Leibniz's theodicy subject to the same criticisms that Arnauld levels at Malebranche? Must it, in Arnauld's eyes, suffer from the same flaws; or, on the other hand, are there substantial-enough differences between Leibniz's account and Malebranche's account for Leibniz to escape Arnauld's charges? These are important questions. While I do not intend to claim that Arnauld's perspective on the similarities and differences between Leibniz and Malebranche is in any sense a privileged one, none the less in the seventeenth-century context of Leibniz's and Malebranche's discussions of theodicy, Arnauld's point of view is rather crucial. First, Arnauld is one of the period's leading thinkers on the issue of grace, and the theodicy problem arises in the seventeenth century mainly over a problem of grace: how is it that not all humans are saved when Scripture tells us that God wants to save all?[31] Second, Leibniz is himself trying to earn Arnauld's approval and thus win him over to his ecumenical project[32] – and in this he will certainly not succeed unless he can, in Arnauld's eyes, distinguish himself from Malebranche. I argue that, through the lens of Arnauld's critique of Malebranche, we can discern some further differences in detail between the two theodicean accounts. Yet in the end, *through that same lens*, and even at the level of detail – especially with respect to the way God's omnipotence is treated, a crucial consideration for Arnauld in assessing a theodicy – the differences turn out to be less important than some essential similarities.

Prima facie, it looks as though Leibniz does escape some of Arnauld's criticisms. Consider Arnauld's complaint that Malebranche humanizes God's mode of acting. He accuses Malebranche of limiting God's omnipotence by insisting that God *must* choose the simplest means, and therefore must proportion his work to fit those means. Thus, God chose the world which he could produce and conserve by the simplest laws. Now it may be true, Arnauld says, that human beings often have to tailor their work to fit their means. An architect might not be able to make the building he really wants to make, the absolutely best building of its design, if the funds available are limited. But, he argues, this kind of reasoning cannot possibly apply to an omnipotent God, for whom all means are equally easy and available. 'All means for executing his designs are equally easy for God ... and his power so renders him master of all things and so independent of the need for help from others, that it suffices that he will for his volitions to be executed.'[33]

Leibniz, when composing the *Discours de la métaphysique*, certainly had

Arnauld's *Réflexions* in mind.[34] And it may be precisely this criticism that Arnauld directs at Malebranche which occasioned Leibniz to say in the *Discours* that 'nothing costs God anything, just as there is no cost for a philosopher who makes hypotheses in constructing his imaginary world, because God has only to make decrees in order that a real world comes into being.'[35] This kind of remark should satisfy Arnauld's demand that any theodicy respect God's omnipotence, and perhaps Leibniz is on better ground here than Malebranche. After all, Leibniz's God aims to create as much perfection as possible, or a world that is absolutely the best, and necessarily succeeds in doing so; whereas Malebranche's God would like to create the best world but cannot execute that desire. More-over, unlike Malebranche's God, who must sacrifice perfection of effect for the sake of simplicity of means and universality of law, Leibniz's God apparently gets to maximize all his values: simplicity of laws *and* richness of effect. As Malebranche notes, simple laws have unfortunate consequences (*La simplicité des lois ... a, nécessairement, des suites fâcheuses*),[36] whereas, for Leibniz, the most simple laws are also the ones that produce the richest effects. The point of Leibniz's theodicy is simply to explain that a world that is simplest in laws and richest in effects – that is, the best of all possible worlds – will not necessarily be a world that is the most convenient for all the particulars it contains; it will not necessarily be a world in which each individual being enjoys its highest perfec-tion and all humans are saved.

Finally, both Arnauld and Leibniz appear to agree on the moral character of God's creation. Arnauld accuses Malebranche of granting to the enemies of religion that the world really is imperfect, and claims that now Malebranche's project is simply to explain this as a necessary and unavoidable consequence of the simplicity and generality of the laws.[37] This entails, as well, that, for Malebranche, the irregular and imperfect aspects of the world which are sup-posed to detract from its beauty and goodness are parts of creation not 'posi-tively and directly' willed by God. The true view, Arnauld insists, is that of St Augustine and St Thomas: the imperfection of the world is only in appearance. God desired to create a world which is on the whole entirely good and beautiful. And each thing in that world was positively and directly chosen by God because it contributes to the world's goodness and beauty. To be sure, there are events we regard as unfortunate, and beings whom we consider monstrous. But we must not allow these to adversely affect our assessment of the whole, for our view of the whole is necessarily restricted and incomplete. Even monsters contribute to the beauty of the world.

Nothing seems more contrary to music than dissonances, or what we otherwise call false agreement; and yet a dissonance, mixed with many consonances, is what makes for a most excellent harmony. And do we then say that, this dissonance being a false agreement, it was not positively and directly put in the composition by the composer? Similarly, a monstrous animal is a kind of dissonance in the harmony of the universe; but it does not fail to contribute to the overall harmony.[38]

There are no faults in God's work, Arnauld concludes (*il n'y a aucun défaut dans les ouvrages de Dieu*). It is all a matter of perspective. If somehow our vision could be expanded to take in the whole – and by 'whole' Arnauld means both the visible elements of the world and its principles or laws – we would see the beauty of the universe and the contribution each part makes to that beauty.

Now, if this is Arnauld's view, how could he fail to appreciate Leibniz's almost verbatim approach? When arguing that the world is both metaphysically and morally the most perfect, Leibniz insists, to those who would deny this by pointing to the misfortunes and confusions that seem to predominate, that 'it is truly unjust to render a judgment without having studied the whole ... Great composers very often mix dissonance with harmonious chords to stimulate the hearer [so that he may be pleased].'[39] In the *Theodicée*, too, Leibniz says that the imperfection of the world is only apparent, and a function of our limited insight.

> God, by a wonderful art, turns all the errors of these little worlds to the greater adornment of his great world. It is as in those devices of perspective, where certain beautiful designs look like mere confusion until one restores them to the right angle of vision or one views them by means of a certain glass or mirror. It is by placing and using them properly that one makes them serve as adornment for a room. Thus the apparent deformities of our little worlds combine to become beauties in the great world, and have nothing in them which is opposed to the oneness of an infinitely perfect universal principle: on the contrary, they increase our wonder at the wisdom of him who makes evil serve the greater good.[40]

One is tempted to conclude that, in fact, it is Arnauld and Leibniz who share the same theodicean strategy, and not Malebranche and Leibniz.

It would appear, then, that Leibniz's theodicy should, from Arnauld's perspective, fare better than Malebranche's. And yet, I suspect that such a conclusion would be based on a fairly superficial comparison, and that, ultimately, at a deeper level, Arnauld should be no more pleased with Leibniz's system than with Malebranche's.

Let us go back to Arnauld's critique of Malebranche. As we saw, what particularly bothers Arnauld is the way in which Malebranche's theodicy diminishes God's omnipotence and freedom. Malebranche claims that God's wisdom and simplicity constrain his power: although God would have liked to create a world that is absolutely the best, he cannot. God, for Malebranche, necessarily follows the principles of Order; that is, God's power is regulated and limited by his wisdom, and this wisdom prescribes to God certain means. As Malebranche puts it, 'the immutable Order of Justice is the essential rule governing the will of God.'[41] But, for Arnauld, God's will has no rule other than itself: this is the very meaning of omnipotence and divine freedom.[42] According to Arnauld, on Malebranche's view 'God is impotent in that he cannot choose means that are unworthy of his wisdom and that, instead of bearing the character of his wisdom, goodness, constancy, and immutability, bear a character of less intelligence, of malevolence, inconstancy, and lightness of mind.'[43]

We can put all this another way by focusing on a particular case of the theodicy problem in the realm of grace. Malebranche takes seriously and literally the words of St Paul: God wants all humans to be saved.[44] But, of course, not all humans are saved; many souls are lost. This is because God wills all humans to be saved only with what Malebranche calls a 'simple volition' – a volition or preference that does not necessarily get carried out, for some reason or another. Just because God has a simple volition for something does not mean that that thing or state of affairs obtains. In this case, the reason lies in God's wisdom, that is, immutable order and the simple laws of grace. In other words, not all of God's volitions are efficacious: 'When it is claimed that all the volitions of God are efficacious, this refers only to practical volitions [*volontés pratiques*]. For there are things God wants but does not do.'[45]

Arnauld has two serious problems with this account, both of which have their ultimate ground in his Jansenism. First, he cannot accept the claim that God literally wills all individual humans be saved. Nothing could be farther from Jansenist doctrine, which stipulates in no uncertain terms that God in his mercy has decided to save some humans and deliver them to glory by infallible means, while deliberately leaving others to perdition.[46] The phrase 'God wills that all humans be saved' is Scripture, to be sure, but Arnauld insists that it needs to be properly interpreted.[47] Malebranche, however, takes the phrase in a strong literal sense, and this, to the Jansenist Arnauld, is *per se* unacceptable. Second, the Jansenist doctrine of predestination aside, there is an obvious tension between the claim that God wills the salvation of all and the evident fact that not all are saved. If God's volition to save all is taken literally and is a *real* volition (as Malebranche would have it), then this implies, as Malebranche willingly grants, that not all of God's volitions are efficacious. And this, too, Arnauld (or any Jansenist) cannot accept. It is absurd to say that a divine volition, the volition of an omnipotent being, is not accomplished. As Arnauld states, 'if God willed that all humans be saved, then they would be.'[48] Or, more generally, 'it suffices that [God] will in order for his volitions to be carried out.'[49] This issue is, of course, intimately bound up with the Jansenist doctrine of efficacious grace.

Similarly, if, as Malebranche insists, God wills that the world be absolutely the best but this volition cannot be carried out, then not all of God's volitions are efficacious, and God's omnipotence is undermined – by his own wisdom, to be sure, but undermined none the less.

Turning to Leibniz, we find that in Arnauld's eyes his theodicy must appear to undermine God's omnipotence in similar ways. Leibniz's God, it is true, necessarily accomplishes his plan to create the best. But it is also the case that, for Leibniz God's will to create the best, and thus his power to do so or otherwise, is determined (albeit with a moral but not a metaphysical necessity) by his wisdom and goodness: 'Moral necessity ... constrains the wisest to choose the best.'[50] Or, in other words, Leibniz's God does not will the world 'freely and indifferently,' as Arnauld would have it, but is, like Malebranche's God, constrained by reason and principle: 'The highest liberty [is] to act in perfection according to the sovereign reason.'[51] Once again, wisdom wins out over power, *sagesse* over *toute-puissance*. I agree entirely with Sleigh's judgment here: 'Had Arnauld grasped the full scope of the principle of sufficient reason in Leibniz's philosophy, in particular its application to God's will in every single act of that will, even creation, Arnauld would have been convinced that Leibniz's scheme fared no better than Malebranche's with respect to a proper account of God's freedom in creation. The fact is that Arnauld saw ... the idea that there must be some reason for God's decision to create, other than simple appeal to his will, as the real culprit.'[52] The deep concern for safeguarding God's freedom that Arnauld demonstrates in his correspondence with Leibniz over metaphysics would, I am certain, simply carry over to the theodicy question as well.[53]

Arnauld would not be pleased, then, with Leibniz's use of the distinction (adopted from St Thomas) between an antecedent will and a consequent will, which is basically equivalent to Malebranche's distinction between a simple volition and a practical volition.[54] God wills only good for each and every thing, but only with an antecedent will. These antecedent wills do not necessarily get carried out, for the sake of the consequent will to create the best overall.

> Taking it in the general sense, one may say that will consists in the inclination to do something in proportion to the good it contains. This will is called antecedent when it is detached, and considers each good separately in the capacity of a good. In this sense it may be said that God tends to all good, as good, *ad perfectionem simpliciter simplicem*, to speak like the Schoolmen, and that by an antecedent will. *He is earnestly disposed to sanctify and to save all men*, to exclude sin, and to prevent damnation. It may even be said that this will is efficacious of itself (*per se*), that is, in such sort that the effect would ensue if there were not some stronger reason to prevent it: for this will does not pass into final exercise (*ad summum conatum*),

else it would never fail to produce its full effect, God being the master of all things. Success entire and infallible belongs only to the consequent will, as it is called. This it is which is complete; and in regard to it this rule obtains, that one never fails to do what one wills, when one has the power.[55]

Note that Leibniz has God will the salvation of all humans, albeit only with an antecedent and inefficacious volition. (Apparently the best of all possible worlds must allow for the eternal loss of many.) It was exactly this that brought Arnauld's wrath down upon poor Malebranche, and I see no reason to think that it wouldn't equally bring it down upon Leibniz as well. There is suffering and sin, and humans are lost, because God is, in some sense, impotent to carry out his (antecedent/simple) volitions which are geared to the individual good of each creature and would effectively save all humans. Arnauld may have had a fine mind for fine distinctions, but even the 'moral' and non-metaphysical necessity that constrains Leibniz's (and Malebranche's) God would be too much for him. It is still a rule higher than God's power, and one that renders some of his volitions inefficacious.

III

By putting Leibniz's theodicy in the context of the Arnauld–Malebranche debate, we gain an illuminating perspective on what may be the similarities and differences between his and Malebranche's account. We see that in addition to the general strategical similarities between the Malebranchian and Leibnizian theodicies, there are also, for Arnauld, deep and substantive similarities of detail regarding the nature of God's operations in the realms of nature and grace, similarities that emerge in the light of Arnauld's criticisms of Malebranche. I do not at all intend to minimize the important differences between the two theodicies that recent scholars have brought to our attention. Yet I have argued that from Arnauld's perspective – a not insignificant perspective when it comes to issues of grace and God's *modus operandi* – these differences, however *real*, are outweighed by some essential similarities. The overriding issue for Arnauld is safeguarding God's omnipotence, which, to his mind, both Leibniz and Malebranche fail to do in similar ways.[56]

Notes

1 See Leibniz's letter to Count Ernst von Hessen-Rheinfels, 12 April 1686: 'Je ne scay que dire à la lettre de M.A., et je n'aurois jamais cru qu'une personne dont la

reputation est si grande et si veritable et dont nous avons de si belles Relexions de Morale et de Logique, iroit si viste dans ses jugemens; apres cela je ne m'etonne plus, si quelques uns se sont emportés contre luy': G II, 16. See also the letter of the same date, where Leibniz says that 'I am not surprised now that he has so easily fallen out with Father Malebranche and others who used to be his fast friends': G II, 22.

2   *Traité*, Discourse I, article 12, in *OC* 5, 27.

3   Ibid., articles 13 and 14, *OC* 5, 28–30.

4   *Entretiens sur la métaphysique* (hereinafter, *Entretiens*), IX.9, *OC* 12, 211. The translation is from *Dialogues on Metaphysics*, Willis Doney, tr. (New York: Abaris Books 1980), 211 (hereinafter, D).

5   *Entretiens*, IX.9, *OC* 12, 211; D 211.

6   *Traité* I.13, *OC* 5, 28.

7   Ibid., I.22, *OC* 5, 35.

8   Ibid., I.13, *OC* 5, 28.

9   Ibid., I.21, *OC* 5, 34.

10   For the discussion of God's ways in the realm of grace, see ibid., discourses II and III.

11   See, for example, Leibniz's *Theodicée*, Essay II,.§ 204, G IV, 238; and his letter to Malebranche, 22 June/2 July 1679, G I, 337.

12   See *Discours de la métaphysique*, §§ 3–7; and 'On the Radical Origination of Things,' G VII, 303–4.

13   *Discours*, §5.

14   *Theodicée*, II, §211, G VI, 244.

15   *Discours*, §7.

16   'Leibnizian Optimism,' *Journal of Philosophy* 80 (1983), 765–83; and *Leibniz's Metaphysics: A Historical and Comparative Study* (Princeton, NJ: Princeton University Press 1989), ch. 8.

17   *Leibniz and Arnauld: A Commentary on Their Correspondence* (New Haven, CT: Yale University Press 1990), 43–7.

18   A.-R. Ndiaye, *La Philosophie d'Antoine Arnauld* (Paris: J. Vrin 1991), 221.

19   'Leibnizian Optimism,' 774–6.

20   *Leibniz and Arnauld*, 45.

21   See *Traité*, I.1, *OC* 5, 12–15.

22   Rutherford, 'Natures, Laws, and Miracles,' in Steven Nadler, ed., *Causation in Early Modern Philosophy* (University Park: Pennsylvania State University Press 1993), 156.

23   Ibid.

24   *Theodicée*, II, §208, G VI, 241.

25   Malebranche to Leibniz, 14 December 1711, in André Robinet, ed., *Malebranche et Leibniz: Relations personelles* (Paris: J. Vrin 1955), 417.

26 Leibniz to Malebranche, January 1712, in ibid., 418.

27 Then again, as Donald Rutherford has suggested to me, it could be that Leibniz has particular motives for exaggerating their agreement – for example, to win Malebranche's approval.

28 *Traité* I.38–9, additions, *OC* 5, 47. See also *Traité* I.13, *OC* 5, 28. As far as I know, Sleigh is the only commentator who picks up on this significant difference; see *Leibniz and Arnauld*, 45.

29 For further discussion of this, see Charles Larmore, *Modernité et morale* (Paris: Presses Universitaires de France 1993), ch. 5.

30 Leibniz to Count Ernst von Hessen-Rheinfels, 1/11 February 1686, G II, 12.

31 See St Paul, I Timothy 2: 5–6. Jansenius himself gets things going when he attacks the Pelagian and semi-Pelagian (i.e., Molinist) way of reconciling these two claims, and Arnauld then spends the rest of his life defending Jansenius.

32 This is why Leibniz had Arnauld sent a summary of his *Discours de la métaphysique* in the first place.

33 *Réflexions* I.2, *OA* 39, 189–90.

34 It is often assumed that Leibniz's *Discours* was intended for Arnauld as a part of Leibniz's ecumenical project. For an amplification of this, see Leroy E. Loemker, 'A Note on the Origin and Problem of Leibniz's *Discourse* of 1686,' *Journal of the History of Ideas* 8 (1947), 449–66.

35 *Discours* §5.

36 *Méditations chrétiennes* VII.13; *Traité* I.43.

37 Malebranche does, in fact, say that 'I do not agree that there is evil only in appearance. I think that there is evil, that God permits it ...,' *Entretien d'un philosophe chrétien et d'un philosophe chinois*, Avis, *OC* 15, 53.

38 *Réflexions* I.2, *OA* 39, 205.

39 'On the Radical Origination of Things,' G VII, 306–7.

40 *Theodicée*, II, §147, G VI, 197–8. As Catherine Wilson has pointed out, the broader perspective needed here is not simply a larger experience of the visible world, its past and present, but some insight into its hidden dimensions, 'an aspect of the world which is not directly available to perception' (i.e., the laws governing it); see her 'Leibnizian Optimism.'

41 *Traité* I.20, *OC* 5, 33.

42 See *Réflexions* II.26, *OA* 39, 599: 'The divine will determines itself, freely and indifferently, to all things to which it does not have a necessary relation; that is, to all things outside of God.'

43 Ibid., I.3, *OA* 39, 212. And Malebranche seems to accept this characterization: 'God's wisdom renders him impotent, so to speak, since his wisdom obliges him to act by the simplest means ...' (*Traité* I.38, addition, *OC* 5, 47). For a discussion of this, see Ndiaye, *La Philosophie d'Antoine Arnauld*, 230.

44 *Traité* I.38, *OC* 5, 47. See I Tim. 2: 5–6.

45 *Réponse aux Réflexions philosophiques et théologiques*, I.1.iv, *OC* 8, 655. See also
   *Réponse à une dissertation de Mr. Arnauld contre un Eclaircissement du Traité de
   la nature et de la grâce, OC* 7, 527: 'Not all of God's volitions are practical.' For a
   good discussion of the distinction between simple and practical volitions, see
   Sleigh, *Leibniz and Arnauld*, 154ff.
46 See the article 'Jansénisme' by J. Carreyre in the *Dictionnaire de théologie
   catholique*, vol. 8, part I, 318–529; and Jean Laporte, *La Doctrine de Port-Royal*,
   vol. 2: *Exposition de la doctrine (d'après Arnauld): Les vérités de la grâce* (Paris:
   Presses Universitaires de France 1923).
47 Arnauld's preferred interpretation is that 'all humans' refers to all *kinds* of human
   beings: kings and peasants, old and young, wise and ignorant, etc. See *Réflexions*
   II.23, *OA* 39, 572–3.
48 *Apologie pour les Saints Pères, OA* 18, 108. Arnauld (following Thomas) does
   grant the distinction in God between antecedent volitions and consequent
   volitions, where antecedent volitions are basically what Malebranche calls 'simple
   volitions'; see *Réflexions* II.23, *OA* 39, 572ff. Thus it looks as though even
   Arnauld recognizes non-efficacious volitions in God. Yet he also insists that such
   antecedent volitions are not *real* volitions; rather, he claims that they are volitions
   only metaphorically, being mere *velléités*; see *Apologie pour les Saints Pères, OA*
   18, 111.
49 *Réflexions* I.2, *OA* 39, 190: 'Il suffit que [Dieu] veuille afin que ses volontés soient
   executés.'
50 *Theodicée* II, §367, G VI, 333.
51 *Discours* §3. See Ndiaye, *La Philosophie d'Antoine Arnauld*, 239–40.
52 *Leibniz and Arnauld*, 46–7.
53 In fact, the specific concern for safeguarding God's freedom that Arnauld
   demonstrates in criticizing Leibniz's account of substance in their correspondence
   is framed in almost exactly the same terms as it appears a year earlier in his attack
   on Malebranche's theodicy. In the *Réflexions* (II.26, *OA* 39, 599), Arnauld notes
   that, for Malebranche, 'God must produce the most perfect [world]. And the
   design being formed, he is no longer free to choose the means by which he will
   execute it: for he *necessarily* chooses general ways, which are the most worthy of
   his wisdom, his greatness, and his goodness. Thus, the design being taken, and the
   means fixed, he [Malebranche] often calls what follows from this "the *necessary*
   consequences of the general laws". God is thus free only in having willed to create
   something, but everything else has been the effect of a more than Stoic fatality,
   with the exception of the miracles he brings about by means of particular
   volitions.' As Sleigh notes (*Leibniz and Arnauld*, 46), Arnauld wrote this passage
   just before receiving the outline of the *Discours* from Leibniz. Compare it with the
   following from Arnauld's letter to Leibniz of 13 May 1686: '"The individual

concept of each person involves once and for all, all that will ever happen to him"
... Whence I thought that we could infer that God was free, in so far as the creating
or not creating of Adam, but supposing that he had wished to create him, all that
has since happened to the human race has come and must come by a fatal
necessity ...' (G II, 27). Sleigh's comment seems apt: 'The necessity has gone from
stoical to fatal, its source is different, but from Arnauld's point of view the same
unacceptable consequence is involved in Leibniz's scheme as in Malebranche's'
(*Leibniz and Arnauld*, 46).

54 See note 49, above.

55 *Theodicée* I, §22, G VI, 115–16, emphasis added.

56 I am very grateful to Vincent Carraud, Charles Larmore, Don Rutherford, and
Catherine Wilson for their helpful comments on an earlier draft of this paper; and
to audiences at the University of Toronto and the Sorbonne (both commemorative
gatherings on the occasion of the three-hundredth anniversary of Arnauld's death)
for their questions and suggestions.

11

Arnauld on Efficacious Grace and Free Choice

ROBERT C. SLEIGH, JR

In a letter written on 21 June 1692,[1] Arnauld advised those interested in assessing his views on freedom that they ought to examine what he had written on the subject in the last seven or eight years (i.e., since 1684), rather than what he wrote earlier, in his apologies for Jansen. With respect to the latter, he noted that he was then obliged to defend Jansen. In the same letter, Arnauld suggested that his later views on freedom resulted from a careful examination of St Thomas's writings relevant to freedom, and, in particular, from his having noted the respects in which the views expressed in Thomas's later writings are superior to those expressed in his earlier writings.[2] In concluding the letter of 21 June 1692, Arnauld listed five advantages of the account of freedom to be found in St Thomas's later works, one of which is that the account offered makes it easy to reconcile the efficaciousness of grace with freedom.[3] A major aim of this essay is to specify what forms of compatibilism are consistent with Arnauld's mature account of freedom. This attempt involves an examination of Arnauld's mature thought about freedom and the nature of efficacious grace. In order to keep track of the forms of compatibilism Arnauld accepted, I contrast Arnauld's position with a Catholic position that is as incompatibilist as the faith allows. Actually, Malebranche's position would do, but his central metaphysical tenet – that God is the only true cause – produces static on the line. So I use the Molinist position for contrast.

In preparing these remarks, I have had the advantage of studying two items from the secondary literature that are models of good work in the history of philosophy: Jean Laporte's book on Arnauld on grace, and Elmar Kremer's recent article 'Grace and Free Will in Arnauld.'[4] My remarks are really no more than footnotes to those two studies. With Laporte and Kremer as predecessors, definitive results are a reasonable expectation; but none is forthcoming. In their place, I record various doubts and hesitations, accompanied by divagations on metahistory, in this case on why it is so hard to reach firm conclusions about what an author, now dead three hundred years, meant by what he said, even when that author wrote clearly and employed those clear writings to express the thoughts of one of the sharpest minds of a period in the history of philosophy noted for sharp minds.

In section I, I record various theses concerning efficacious grace and free choice to which Arnauld was committed in his mature period. Then, I highlight the controversial aspects of the theses recorded, in order to prepare the way for discussion of the primary topics of the essay. In section II, I discuss the basic change in Arnauld's conception of efficacious grace. And, in section III, I consider features of the Thomistic conception of freedom to which Arnauld committed himself after 1684, and their relation to various forms of compatibilism

I

On the score of grace, Arnauld seems to have held the following in his mature period:

a) That fallen man is incapable of performing supernaturally meritorious actions unaided by grace;

b) That efficacious grace is efficacious in virtue of its own intrinsic nature – 'par elle-même,' as Arnauld often put the matter;

c) That an action is supernaturally meritorious only if it is free;

d) That an action's being done under the influence of efficacious grace is consistent with its being done freely;

e) That the freedom with which efficacious grace is consistent, and which is required for supernatural merit, requires, in turn, that the agent could have done otherwise; and

f) That no operative actual grace need be posited other than efficacious grace, even in fallen man, i.e., no merely sufficient grace need be posited, even though fallen man lacks the capacity to perform supernaturally meritorious actions unaided by grace.[5]

Much of Arnauld's writing on grace is devoted to sustaining (f) against, for example, the neo-Thomists and Nicole.[6] I plan to discuss Arnauld on thesis (f) in a separate paper; here it is not considered. I believe that Arnauld would claim that theses (a), (c), (d), and (e) are *de fide* for Catholics and, hence, non-negotiable. Thus, according to Arnauld, the only thesis from (a) through (e) that is up for serious philosophical discussion is (b).[7] Here is a remark on (e) that has obvious applications with respect to the other theses: what the agent could have done otherwise is elicit a volition. There is no effort here to purchase freedom on the cheap by arguing that freedom fundamentally applies to first-order bodily actions that the agent could have done otherwise, meaning no more than that the agent would have done otherwise had the agent so chosen.[8]

(b) is where the seas of philosophical theology rise high. I approach it with considerable trepidation. There is a primitive notion that is helpful here – the idea that each actual (as opposed to habitual) grace that occurs *is aimed at* contributing to bringing about some volition v in some agent a. The admittedly imprecise locution 'is aimed at' is employed rather than, for example, 'is intended as,' because what God intends absolutely (all things considered) comes about. So, by 'is aimed at' I mean something like 'is intended to contribute to ... , other things being equal (which they may not be).'

Consider the following two propositions:

1) Necessarily, for any grace g, volition v, and agent a, if grace g aims at volition v in agent a, and grace g occurs and is efficacious, then a elicits v.

2) For any grace g, volition v, and agent a, if grace g aims at volition v in agent a, and grace g is efficacious, then necessarily, if g occurs and agent a exists, then a elicits v.

The first is a proposition that all parties to these disputes would accept; its necessity is a simple consequence of the rather humdrum fact that 'efficacious' is a success-adjective. The second is where the action is. Molinists (e.g. Malebranche) reject it; Thomists, neo-Thomists, and Arnauld in every one of his phases accept it. I focus the debate somewhat by noting one thing that is *not* at stake. All sides would agree that, if grace g aims at v in a, then, necessarily, g aims at v in a. So the issue boils down to the truth-value of the following:

3) If grace g is efficacious, then, necessarily, grace g is efficacious.

Molinists reject (3), the others mentioned accept it, and, then, conjoining it with other items not in dispute, derive (2). This third proposition is a way of capturing the claim (b), i.e., that efficacious grace is efficacious in virtue of its own intrinsic nature – 'par elle-même' – as Arnauld was wont to put it.

It is important to have a grasp of what Arnauld took to be the main enemy here. It is the Molinist claim that whether a grace supplied by God to agent a, aimed at volition *v*, *is* or is not efficacious, is ultimately up to *a* and not to God. If *a* freely elicits *v*, then *g* is efficacious; otherwise not. Furthermore, whether *a* freely elicits *v* under the influence of *g* is ultimately up to *a* in the sense that there is nothing God can do that is either metaphysically or causally or naturally sufficient for *a*'s freely eliciting *v*. Of course, it is within God's power to bring it about that *a* elicits *v*, but it is *a*'s *freely* eliciting *v* that matters here. And, of course, God has it in his power to choose circumstances, both external and internal to *a*, that will contribute towards *a*'s freely eliciting *v* when under the influence of *g*. None the less, it is crucial to see how radical the Molinist position is. It has these consequences: in accounting for the ultimate sufficient conditions of the events that occur in a world that contains creatures who elicit free choices, you must mention those choices as well as God's. Put another way: there are possible worlds that God can not create. There are mainline, traditional conceptions of theological determinism, theological compatibilism, and predestination with which these consequences are incompatible.

Authors often claim that the relevant conceptions of theological determinism, theological compatibilism, and predestination are *de fide* for Catholics. But that is rash. The *Congregatio de auxiliis* ended with a formal decree proclaiming, among other things, that the relevant aspects of Molinism are not incompatible with anything that is *de fide* for Catholics.[9] I believe that Arnauld had these points in mind in contrasting his position with Malebranche's: he wrote:

> The grace that I maintain as the foundation of gratuitous predestination, and that I claim has the consequence that the merits of the Saints are the gifts of God, is not a grace of the sort that some theologians imagine it to be, which has, or lacks, effect according to whether it is agreeable to the will; rather, it is grace that is efficacious *par elle-même*; i.e., that does not rely on our willing, but that brings it about that we will.[10]

Molinism may offer a less than robust notion of predestination, but it clearly has advantages, in virtue of its denial of (3), with respect to establishing the consistency of (a) through (e). By contrast the affirmation of (3) generates a problem for Arnauld and his ilk. Consider the following, which is a consequence of (2):

4)   Let *g* be some efficacious grace that aims at volition *v* in agent *a*; it is not possible that *g* occurs and *a* does not elicit *v*.

Isn't (4) inconsistent with (e)? Of course, as a chorus, those non-Molinists who accept (4) say no. To the rescue comes the notorious distinction between the composed and the divided senses. It is sometimes explained in the following way. Consider:

5) Let g be some efficacious grace that aims at v in agent a and let g occur; nonetheless, it is possible that a does not elicit v.

According to the explanation I am now considering, (4) affirms of a certain compound state of affairs that it can not obtain – the composed sense; whereas (5) says that, even if one component of this compound state of affairs does obtain, it remains *possible* that the other component does as well – the divided sense. The explanation grants that in virtue of affirming (3) the non-Molinist is saddled with (2), and, hence, (4), but claims that disaster does not ensue because (5) is all that is required in order to establish the consistency of (a) through (e).

It is primarily a defence of (e) that requires this convoluted escape mechanism. In turn, (e) is required by the following from the Council of Trent: 'If someone says that the free choice of man, moved and excited by God, in no way cooperates with the exciting call from God, by an assent in virtue of which man disposes and prepares himself to obtain the grace of justification; and that man can not dissent, even if he wills to, ... let him be anathema.'[11] Suppose we take the 'possible' in (5) as standing for metaphysical possibility. Then, surely, it crosses the mind that (5) is simply no match for this robust canon from the Council of Trent.

I believe that Arnauld did not rely on anything so tepid as (5); that, in place of (5), he offered the following elongation of (4):

6) Let g be some efficacious grace that aims at volition v in agent a; it is not possible that g occurs and a does not elicit v. But it is possible that g occurs and a retains the power not to elicit v and also the power to elicit some volition v' other than v.

Focusing on what (6) says is impossible and what (6) says is possible yields a more robust and useful contrast between the composed and the divided senses. It also introduces us to Arnauld's convoluted thought on the topic of power, a topic beyond the scope of this essay.

II

In a letter to Nicole (28 August 1685) Arnauld noted that there are three non-Molinist, but Catholic candidates for the role of efficacious grace: the physical predeterminations (*prédétermination physique*) of the neo-Thomists;

the victorious pleasure (*délectation victorieuse*) of the Jansenists; and the inspiration of love (*inspiration d'amour*) of Estius, which Arnauld attributed to Thomas, and which Arnauld favoured in his later phase.[12] For ease of reference, I identify each candidate via a champion of that candidate noted as such by Arnauld: physical predetermination, with Alvarez; victorious pleasure, with Jansen; and the divine inspiration of love, with Estius.

In a letter of July 1693, to Bossuet, Arnauld claimed that there are two accounts of actual grace, one of which identifies actual efficacious grace with the combination of God's mercy in the form of a divine volition concerning creature *a* and a resulting form inherent in the soul of *a*; the other of which identifies actual efficacious grace solely with God's mercy in the form of a divine volition concerning creature *a*.[13] In the letter to Bossuet, Arnauld referred to an early work of his, the *Dissertatio Theologica*, published in 1656, which contains a discussion of these issues.[14]

I think that the difference in count here – are there two theories or three? – is of no consequence. By Arnauld's lights there are two fundamental distinctions to note. All the relevant theories of grace claim that a given case of actual efficacious grace involves at least these two items: first, a volition on God's part concerning a free motion (volition) of some creature's will; second, the free motion (volition) of that creature's will. The first fundamental distinction is between those theories that posit some intermediary entity in *a*'s soul (intellect or will) that serves to execute God's volition and those that do not. In their theories, Alvarez, Jansen, and even Molina postulate such an intermediary entity. In the cases of Molina and Jansen, the alleged intermediary entities function like any other motive for choice in a human agent, i.e., they make a causal contribution to choice along with, and often in competition with, other secondary causal contributors. The second fundamental distinction concerns the type of determination (or lack thereof) that holds in the theory between the item identified with grace and the resulting free choice. In Jansen's theory, the determination involved seems close to a causal determination; in the theories of Alvarez and Estius, the determination seems to be metaphysical but not causal; and, in Molina's theory, there is no determination in the relevant sense at all.

Arnauld had a variety of reasons for preferring the theory of Estius to its competitors.[15] I take note of a pair of those reasons. Arnauld claimed that, on Estius's view, 'it is much easier to explain the efficaciousness of grace and to reconcile this efficaciousness with freedom.'[16] The reconciliatory point is twofold: (i) *prima facie*, there is a difficulty in explaining how a created entity, e.g., a victorious pleasure, operationg on the will without benefit of the agent's rational deliberation, can bring it about that the agent elicits a choice without harming the will's freedom; and (ii) *prima facie*, there is a difficulty in explaining how the occurrence of a created entity in the will, distinct from the elicitied choice of the agent, can metaphysically determine that the agent elicits a specific choice. The first difficulty applies to Jansen's account; the second, to Alvarez's account.

On the positive side, there is a clear advantage to Estius's view with respect to (ii). It is metaphysically determined that if God wills p with a consequent will, then p. So, if each occurrence of efficacious grace is identified with some consequent willing of God, there is no problem in explaining the resulting metaphysical determination. But does this account not exacerbate Arnauld's problem with respect to (i)? True, on Estius's view, efficacious grace does not involve a created entity operating on the will without benefit of the agent's rational deliberation. Still, it involves an uncreated entity, God's will, which is not subject to the agent's deliberative powers, apparently metaphysically determining that the agent elicit a specific choice.

What Arnauld wrote on this point is standard fare. For example, in his *Instruction sur l'accord de la grâce avec la liberté*,[17] Arnauld argued as follows: (a) we know, in virtue of God's omnipotence, that he has the power to bring it about through an exercise of his consequent will that a created agent freely elicits a specific choice; (b) we know that it is metaphysically necessary that what God consequently wills occurs; and (c) we know that we are free. This line of reasoning is weak. We can skip (b) and (c); (a) is the whole ballgame. The issue is: is the state of affairs consisting in God's bringing it about that an agent freely elicits a specific choice possible? Molina thought not; Arnauld simply asserted that it is in this text.

Perhaps I am being unfair. Arnauld often wrote about God's will *determining* a created agent's will, not about God's will bringing it about that the agent elicits a specific choice. Elmar Kremer, in the essay mentioned above, notes that there are divine determinations that metaphysically determine an agent's choice without threatening freedom, e.g., divine foreknowledge. We need another intuitive notion here. Philosophers in the seventeenth century recognized various varieties of determination: semantical, in virture of a true prediction; epistemological, in virture of someone's foreknowledge; and, of course, causal determination, among others. Some of these were seen as bringing about the item they determined; others were not. I call the former 'the category of quasi-causal determination.' The question to be answered is this: Did Arnauld have a rational basis for claiming that, although divine efficacious grace metaphysically determines the state of affairs it aims at, it does not involve quasi-causal determination? I do not know the answer to that question; if Arnauld had such a rational basis, he was a master at hiding it.

I have some confidence on one point here: If Arnauld had such a basis, it turned essentially on features peculiar to grace and free choice. It was not a general denial such as the following principle involves:

7) For any x and y, if x metaphysically necessitates y, then it is false that x causally necessitates y.

Suppose Arnauld had been attracted to (7). He knew that Malebranche was attached to the following:

8) For any x and y, if x causally necessitates y, then x metaphysically necessitates y.

Now from (7) and (8) we can deduce:

9) It is false that there is an x and y such that x causally necessitates y.

So had Arnauld accepted (7), he would have had the tools to establish that Malebranche's fundamental thesis concerning causality, i.e., (8), has the consequence that there are no causal connections. Had argumentative, abrasive Arnauld possessed those tools, he would have applied them. But, to the best of my knowledge, there is no such argument in Arnauld's lengthy exchange with Malebranche. But that must be because Arnauld rejected (7).

III

I have noted that Arnauld accepted a version of theological compatibilism that Molina rejected. In this section I consider a form of compatibilism – infallible-determination compatibilism; Arnauld accepted it and Molina rejected it. I then consider, utterly indecisively, whether infallible-determination compatibilism and causal compatibilism amount to the same thing.

As noted previously, for Arnauld, the eliciting of a volition by a human agent is the central item in a proper conception of human freedom. Hence, a relevant form of causal compatibilism would be the following:

10) There is some human agent a, volition v, and time t such that: (i) a elicits v at t; and (ii) there are conditions $k_1 \ldots k_n$ that obtain at or prior to t and that are causally sufficient for a's eliciting v at t; and (iii) a is free in eliciting v at t.

So, if Arnauld rejected causal compatibilism, he denied that (10) is so much as possible. Well, did he? I do not know. Part of the point of this section is to provide some excuse for my ignorance.

My concern is with the relationships among three concepts of determination – natural determination (and, correspondingly, natural necessity); infallible determination; at last, causal determination (and, correspondingly, causal necessity). In his mature phase, Arnauld held that natural determination (natural necessity) is incompatible with freedom, whereas infallible determination is compatible with freedom. Taking 'causal determination' ('causal necessity') to refer to *our* concept of causal determination (causal necessity), my problem is how natural determination, infallible determination, and causal determination are related, according to Arnauld. My claims are these: (i) the texts make clear that if Arnauld's natural determination is our causal determination, then Arnauld denied the possibility of (10); and (ii) the texts do not settle the matter as to whether Arnauld's natural determination is our causal determination.

Here is a useful text for commencing discussion on this topic. In his *Instructions sur l'accord de la grâce avec la liberté*, Arnauld, intending to help the reader understand that an act can be free and yet done under the influence of efficacious grace, wrote: 'One has only to conceive properly what freedom is, and to get rid of the false idea that many have of it, who imagine that a person can only freely will something when that person is not determined to will it' ...[18] Arnauld then went on to note various cases of what sound like psychological causation that involve free choices, e.g., a prostitute who is infallibly determined to commit a sin freely in virtue of aspects of her reaction to the sum offered for her services.[19] After a number of such examples, the interlocutor asks if there is *any* necessity and *any* determination that is incompatible with freedom. Arnauld answered that there is indeed one such case: 'It is the case of natural necessity, or determination to one thing by nature. For our soul would not be free, if it were naturally determined' ...[20] He went on to add that, in the case of natural determination, the agent is not master of his own action, and the agent lacks *potentia ad opposita*, the power to do (choose) otherwise.[21]

Here are some remarks on the two passages quoted above. In the first passage, Arnauld claimed that, in order to conceive properly what freedom is, we must rid ourselves of a widely held, but false idea – namely, that a person can elicit a choice freely only when no variety of determination yielding the aforementioned eliciting, i.e., no quasi-causal determination, is present. I believe that the position Arnauld asked us to forgo here is the Molinist position. According to the Molinist position, various conditions, both internal and external to the eliciting agent, are germane to what choice the agent elicits, and, in fact, control over those conditions is, according to Molina, exactly how divine providence is exercised with respect to the free choice of creatures. This germaneness may be construed as a kind of counter-factual sufficiency that both Arnauld and Molina would view as something less than a determination – at any rate, something less than a quasi-causal determination. In the examples accompanying the first passage quoted, Arnauld assumed that what we might call 'infallible sufficiency' is a kind of quasi-causal determination, and, hence, is a stronger connection than mere counter-factual sufficiency and is compatible with freedom. Let (10') be the result of replacing 'causally sufficient' with 'infallibly sufficient' in (10). Thus, (10') formulates a version of compatibilism that Arnauld accepted and that he believed Molina rejected. Noting this fact is what first led me to consider the hypothesis that in his mature phase Arnauld may have accepted (10) after all.

Let (10") be the result of replacing 'causally sufficient' in (10) with 'naturally sufficient.' The second passage quoted above shows that Arnauld rejected (10"), and, of course, we know that Molina got off the compatibilism bus long before stop (10"). In general, a philosopher gets off the compatibilism bus as soon as that philosopher reaches a level of determination that he or she views as depriving the agent of *potentia ad opposita*, the power to choose otherwise. Molina's view, at least as Arnauld construed it, was that any quasi-causal determination leads to the relevant deprivation; Arnauld believed that infallible determination leaves the agent in possession of *potentia ad opposita*, whereas a natural determination does not.

Arnauld, intending to follow St Thomas here, took natural necessity (or the lack thereof) to apply to the exercise of a power (active or passive) by an agent in specified circumstances. There is considerable plausibility to the following claim: in the case of non-intelligent agents, the assertion that such an exercise occurs as a natural necessity is tantamount to the assertion that the state of affairs that obtains as a result of that exercise is causally necessary in the specified circumstances. My problem concerns how to understand Arnauld's talk about natural necessity in the case of exercises of powers peculiar to intelligent agents, i.e., agents with intellects and rational wills. According to Arnauld, again intending to follow St Thomas, when an intellect exercises its powers and comes to know a self-evident proposition, it does so as a natural necessity; in every other case, exercise of an intellectual power does not occur as a natural necessity. And when an intelligent agent wills something (its own happiness, as it turns out) that would utterly satisfy the agent, were it possessed, then, and only then, does the agent will as a natural necessity. My radical proposal is this: what we are getting here are extensions of the notion of natural necessity from its home base in non-intelligent agents; these extensions are in some measure stipulative. Hence, to say that a given volition v elicited by agent a does not occur as a result of a natural necessity just amounts to saying that even were v fulfilled, agent a would not be utterly satisfied. But that seems consistent with saying that, in the circumstances then obtaining, it was causally necessary that a elicit v – that, for example, a's high moral character, plus his beliefs about the circumstances then prevailing, causally necessitated that he elicit v. And that, according to my radical proposal, is exactly the content of the remark Arnauld might have made about a's situation, namely, that a was infallibly determined to elicit v.

My situation is this: I cannot convince myself that this radical proposal is false. There are numerous objections to it; I close by noting one. Elmar Kremer has drawn my attention to passages in the *Réflexions* in which Arnauld, in his mature period, stated that the thesis (which he attributed to Malebranche) that all human choices are 'a necessary consequence of natural laws ...' involves the mistake of Wyclif, since it deprives humans of freedom.[22] This surely sounds like a denial of causal compatibilism. It is, if Arnauld means by 'natural law' what we mean by it. However, there is the possibility that careful examination would convince us that in Arnauld's system the more basic notion is natural necessity, with natural law the derived notion, so that Arnauld understood a natural law as a universally quantified conditional that holds as a natural necessity. In that case we would be back to square one. And, in fact, the nearest preceding passage in the *Réflexions* in which Arnauld commented in detail on the character of laws of nature is this:

> General laws of nature include only a certain measure of motion, imprinted on all matter, and the rules of the communication of motion, by which a body which collides with another, determines a different motion in it, either by communicating a new motion to it, or by preventing it from continuing with the motion it had.[23]

Only a materialist would suppose that choices fell under laws of nature, so construed; only the strictest sort of epiphenomenalism would yield determinations of choices under laws of nature, so construed.

To this point, my investigation suggests that Arnauld was committed to at least two forms of compatibilism rejected by Molina – theological compatibilism and infallible-determination compatibilism. In fact there is some reason to suppose that Arnauld would insist that there is only one form of compatibilism here, under two descriptions. In describing Arnauld's views about the relation of efficacious grace to the will under the influence, I have allowed myself the woolly term 'metaphysical determination.' But when we examine Arnauld's efforts to explain the consistency of determination of the will by efficacious grace with freedom of the will so determined, the determination begins to look like infallible determination. Still, the really interesting question – how infallible – determination compatibilism and causal compatibilism are related – remains beyond my grasp.

Notes

1 *OA* 3, 497–8.
2 Arnauld did not have access to *De Malo*, with its important question on free choice.

3 The other alleged advantages are as follows: St Thomas's mature view of freedom is perfectly consistent; the authority of Thomas renders it above suspicion; it explains why freedom from necessity, and not just freedom from coersion, is required for merit and demerit; and, lastly, it explains just what is right, and what is wrong, about St Bernard's famous remark 'Ubi voluntas, ubi libertas.'

4 Jean Laporte, *La Doctine de Port-Royal. Tome deuxième: Exposition de la doctrine (d'après Arnauld). I – Les Vérités de la grâce* (Paris: Presses Universitaires de France 1923); and Elmar Kremer, 'Grace and Free Will in Arnauld,' in *The Great Arnauld and Some of His Philosophical Correspondents*, Elmar Kremer, ed. (Toronto: University of Toronto, Press 1994), 219–39.

5 See for example *Instruction sur la grâce, OA* 10, 401–34.

6 See for example *Écrit du pouvoir physique, OA* 10, 481–530.

7 See for example *OA* 39, 91–2.

8 See for example 'Humanae Libertatis Notio,' in *Causa Arnaldina*, Pasquier Quesnel, ed. (apud Hoyouxi: Leodici Eburonium 1699), 99–111. There is a French translation of this work by Quesnel in *OA* 10, 614–24. Elmar Kremer kindly supplied me with a copy of the Latin version.

9 I take it that at *OA* 39, 91–2, Arnauld agrees.

10 *OA* 39, 68.

11 Council of Trent, Session VI, ch. 4. In this quotation, the expression 'exciting call' refers to actual (prevenient) grace, which is the grace that concerns us, the grace that aids us in performing supernaturally meritorious actions. The grace of justification is an item that occurs, if at all, much later in the process, the end result of which, when things work out, is salvation.

12 *OA* 2, 558–9.

13 *OA* 3, 664.

14 *OA* 20, 232–39.

15 See *OA* 2, 558–9; *OA* 3, 573–4, 578, 636, 664; *OA* 10, 616, 620; *OA* 20, 232–9.

16 *OA* 3, 664.

17 *OA* 10, 436.

18 Ibid.

19 *Instruction sur la grâce, OA* 10, 437.

20 Ibid., *OA* 10, 438.

21 Ibid.

22 *OA* 39, 316 (cf. *OA* 39, 301).

23 *OA* 39, 258.

Notes on Contributors

Jill Vance Buroker is Professor of Philosophy at California State University at San Bernardino, and Adjunct Professor of Philosophy at Claremont Graduate School. Her publications include *Space and Incongruence: The Origin of Kant's Idealism* (Dordrecht and Boston: D. Reidel 1981) and a translation of the Port-Royal *Logic* (Cambridge: Cambridge University Press 1996) as well as articles on Kant and on Cartesian philosophy, including 'Judgment and Predication in the Port-Royal *Logic*,' in *The Great Arnauld and Some of His Philosophical Correspondents*, Elmar J. Kremer, ed. (Toronto: University of Toronto Press 1994).

Vincent Carraud is Maître de conférences en philosophie at the Université de Caen. His publications include *Pascal et la philosophie* (Paris: PUF, coll. 'Epiméthée,' 1992) and (in collaboration with F. de Buzon) *Descartes et les 'Principia' II: corps et mouvement* (Paris: PUF, coll. 'Philosophie,' 1994), as well as many articles in modern philosophy, including 'Arnauld from Ockhamism to Cartesianism,' in *Descartes and His Contemporaries*, R. Ariew and M. Grene, eds. (Chicago: University of Chicago Press 1995).

Graeme Hunter is Associate Professor of Philosophy at the University of Ottawa. His publications include the *Leibniz-Lexicon* (Olms: Hildesheim 1988) and 'The Phantom of Jansenism in the Arnauld-Leibniz Correspondence,' in *The Great Arnauld ...*

Elmar J. Kremer is Associate Professor of Philosophy at the University of Toronto. His publications include a translation of Arnauld's *On True and False Ideas and New Objections to Descartes'* Meditations *with Descartes' Replies* (Queenston: Edwin Mellen 1990); and two articles in *The Great Arnauld* ...

Thomas M. Lennon is Professor of Philosophy at the University of Western Ontario. His publications include a translation (with Paul J. Olscamp) and philosophical commentary of Malebranche's *The Search after Truth* (Columbus: Ohio State University Press 1980) and *The Battle of Gods and Giants: The Legacies of Descartes and Gassendi, 1665–1715* (Princeton, NJ: Princeton University Press 1993).

Steven Nadler is Associate Professor of Philosophy at the University of Wisconsin (Madison). His publications include *Arnauld and the Cartesian Philosophy of Ideas* (Princeton, NJ: Princeton University Press 1989); *Malebranche and Ideas* (Oxford: Oxford University Press 1992); and many articles on early modern philosophy, including 'Malebranche's Theory of Perception,' in *The Great Arnauld* ... He is currently working on a biography of Spinoza.

Aloyse-Raymond Ndiaye is Dean of the Faculty of Letters and Human Sciences at the University of Dakar. He is currently serving as the director of the Fonds International de Cooperation Universitaires, Montreal. He is a member of the steering committee of the International Federation of the Societies of Philosophy. His publications include *La Philosophie d'Antoine Arnauld* (Paris: J. Vrin 1991).

Alan Nelson is Associate Professor of Philosophy at the University of California, Irvine. His publications include 'Are Economic Kinds Natural?' in *Minnesota Studies in the Philosophy of Science* 14 (1991): 'Social Science and the Mental,' in *Midwest Studies in Philosophy* 15 (1991); and 'Cartesian Actualism in the Leibniz–Arnauld Correspondence,' in *Canadian Journal of Philosophy* 23 (1993).

Peter A. Schouls, formerly Professor of Philosophy at the University of Alberta, is Head of Massey University, New Zealand. His publications include *Reasoned Freedom: John Locke and Enlightenment* (Ithaca, NY: Cornell University Press 1992) and *Descartes and the Enlightenment* (Edinburgh: Edinburgh University Press; and Montreal and Kingston: McGill-Queen's University Press 1989), as well as many articles on modern philosophy.

Robert C. Sleigh, Jr, is Professor of Philosophy at the University of Massachusetts (Amherst). His publications include *Leibniz and Arnauld: A Commentary on Their Correspondence* (New Haven, CT: Yale University Press 1990) and an edition and translation of Leibniz forthcoming from Yale University Press.

Jean-Luc Solère is a member of the Centre National de la Recherche Scientifique, Paris. His publications include the sections on Guillaume d'Auxerre and Durand de Saint-Pourçain in *La Puissance et son ombre, de Pierre Lombard à Luther*, sous la direction d'Olivier Boulnois (Paris: Aubier 1994).

Index